THE RIGHT WAY ON

W.H.T. OLIVE

TIMBERHOLME BOOKS
Langley, British Columbia, Canada

○ ○

THE RIGHT WAY ON

Adventures in the Klondyke of 1898

Memoirs of W.H.T. OLIVE

○ ○

THE RIGHT WAY ON

Canadian Cataloguing in Publication Data

Author: Olive, W.H.T. (William Henry Trewolla), 1865-1940
          The Right Way On

ISBN   1-894254-04-X

1.   Olive, W.H.T. (William Henry Trewolla), 1865-1940.
2.   Klondike River Valley (Yukon)—Gold discoveries.
3.   Yukon Territory—History—1895-1918   I. Title

FC4022.3.O54 1999   971.9´102   C98-920092-2
F1095.K5 O54 1999

First edition

Editors: Tim Lawson and Chris Churney
Designer: Bev Leech
Typesetting: Karen Lea Denis

With thanks to:
Sonia Alix, Debbie Barr, Vivian and Rob Becker, Theresa Best, British Columbia Archives, Wendy Craig, John Hart, Scott Miller, Morriss Printing, Pacific Archives Northwest, Richard and Carrie Sera, Brenda and Neil West, David Young

TIMBERHOLME BOOKS
Langley, British Columbia, Canada
www.timberholme.com

Printed in Canada by Transcontinental Printing

Contents

Publisher's Foreword

W.H.T. Olive's remarkable diary came to my attention at Christmas-time in 1996. I eagerly devoured the stories and submerged myself in the Klondyke atmosphere of 1898.

The astonishing real-life adventures and hardships endured by so many are colourful, amazing examples of human ingenuity and endurance: "The Chilcoot may have the name of testing a man's fitness to survive the difficulties of the trail, but if ever there was a nerve-breaking, back-breaking trail, it was the Teslin. I've seen men lie down and die. Yes, and I've buried them just where they lay." Every time I closed the covers of the book, I felt a real appreciation for all the small comforts in modern life that we take for granted.

Olive's work survived over the years because of his family members, who produced a copy of the manuscript, later deposited at the British Columbia archives. In return, the archives presented the family with seven bound copies. A copy belonged to the wife of my hockey coach, Bill Johnson. Evelyn Johnson, who had been raised by her grandparents, Mr. and Mrs. William Henry Trewolla Olive, had always wished for the opportunity to publish her grandfather's work.

The manuscript was published as *The Olive Diary* and released in the summer of 1998, to no fanfare. I decided to improve the original version and re-release it as *The Right Way On*. In editing this manuscript we have attempted to remain faithful to Olive's style, and have made only minor changes where necessary for continuity, spelling and grammar. The spelling of a number of places, as Olive knew them, has been retained. The names include *Klondyke, Chilcoot, Hootalinka* and *Lindemann*.

It is my privilege to present this memoir, a work that might have remained obscure but has become public in timely fashion, 101 years after the period it describes. I hope you enjoy it and are as touched by this incredible collection of stories as I have been.

Tim Lawson, AUGUST, 1999

The Right Way On

"All aboard," "Let 'em go"
Leaving shore, "Yukon ho!"
Answering the call, "gold for one and all."

What is the right way on—?
The high road, or the low?
We mustn't tarry long—
We're half for there, and half for home.

Steam her north, let it blow,
Together now, in a lonely row.
Up the Chilkoot Trail, beyond the hill, the vale . . .

Now what is the right way on—?
To follow along and not stop?
Arms and legs like stone—
Half will make it, half will not.

What am I doing here—?
It seems so far from anything even human.
What if I disappear—?
No one will know, say it isn't so . . .

It got so cold, many froze,
The biting snow, tired eyes close,
Give me one more day, one more breath, I pray.

What is the right way on—?
The Klondyke won't tell a soul;
And if there's a right way on—
Half the half that started are the only ones to know.

Song lyrics by Tim Lawson © 1997
from the 1999 CD *The Right Way On*

Remembering My Grandfather

W.H.T., as he was affectionately called by his friends and peers, was born in 1865 in Truro, Cornwall. He grew up there and served his apprenticeship in woodwork and architecture.

He was a restless young man and decided to emigrate to Victoria, British Columbia. There was a boom in construction and his skills soon became in demand. W.H.T. worked on the Parliament Buildings in Victoria, installing stairwells and other design features.

Before he came to Canada, W.H.T. courted my grandmother in England. After some time had elapsed, he wrote to Sarah asking if she would marry him. She said, "Yes." He built her a home in Victoria before returning to England. They were married and W.H.T. brought his new bride to British Columbia.

You realize, in those days, you had to come by ship around the "Horn." Grandpa was fearful Sarah may become seasick. Gran came through with flying colours, but Grandpa spent most of the journey hanging over the rail.

While living in Victoria they had four children. In the late 1890s, Grandfather's employer, Francis Rattenbury, decided to send him to the Yukon to build boats. Rattenbury was forming the Bennett Lake & Klondyke Navigation Company. When the lure of adventure called, W.H.T. travelled to Lake Bennett and began the construction of three steamboats, the *Ora*, the *Nora*, and the *Flora*. (The latter was named for Rattenbury's wife). My grandmother followed and they had their fifth child there.

My grandparents lived in Atlin, British Columbia, until 1904, then moved to Carbon, Alberta and homesteaded. W.H.T. built the first school in the area. After many years they moved into the town of Carbon itself and he opened up a garage. For many years W.H.T. served as justice of the peace.

The word "gentleman" fit W.H.T. to a T. He was a modest man and very fond of children. It seemed there was always someone whose problems he was helping with. He took a great interest in politics and enjoyed a good discussion. Friends were always dropping by for coffee around the pot-bellied stove in the garage.

Now this is where I come into the picture. My parents died within a year of each another. Luckily for me, my grandparents decided they would raise their daughter's child.

I had a special rapport with Grandpa. He took me on my first sleigh ride, my first ice skating venture and for long walks. He had a fine voice. In the evenings in winter we sang hymns and songs. We had a Morris chair with compartments on each arm. Grandpa would sit in the chair, myself on one arm, and as soon as we started to sing, our cat Winkie would jump up on the other side to join us.

I remember a dust storm that happened when I was about six. After school, Grandpa was standing there with a blanket. He wrapped me up and carried me home.

If I had reports to do for school there was no need to go to a library. It seemed to me he knew all the answers. Grandpa would pace the floor, talking, and I would write down the information.

One time my social studies teacher asked us to do a report. I don't remember the subject. As usual, Grandpa gave me more than enough material. Upon my return to school, my teacher asked, "Where did you get this information?" My reply: "From my grandfather." "Where did he get the information?" "Out of his head," I replied. "My goodness," she responded, "he must be a very intelligent man." I was so proud.

W.H.T. was a great family man who enjoyed conversation and had many interests. Card games such as bridge and crib were an enjoyment for him. He never missed *Hockey Night in Canada*. His favourite team was the Toronto Maple Leafs. When I was twelve years old we moved to Calgary. Grandfather lived there until he died in July, 1940.

During the thirties my grandfather put pen to paper and recorded his adventures in the Klondyke. Although W.H.T. made preliminary inquiries about publication, his work was never published in his own lifetime. His manuscript has remained in our family these many years.

Evelyn Johnson

Author's Preface

In writing my memoirs, the object has been to present to the reader the picture that it was not all glamour or pleasure going to the Klondyke goldfields. After 1898 the trip was, for many, comparatively easy. The White Pass Railway was being constructed, which made the difficult packing to the pass much easier. Those sourdoughs of the fall of 1897 and the whole of 1898 endured misery and suffering. A very few could look back and call it a pleasure trip. Thousands from the continent of North America saw in the Klondyke gold strike what they thought would be a way out of the hard times then prevailing. Some sacrificed all, hoping to make a new start in life. Home and property were mortgaged to the limit. Remembering that at the time of the gold strike there was a world depression that had begun in 1893, it was little wonder that people from all climes struck out for the Far North. Canadians, Americans, Australians, South Africans, Chinese, Japanese, and Europeans were to be found in the great trek. Like ants they crawled up the Chilcoot and White Passes, some with packs on their backs, some with hand-drawn sleds, some with dogs to aid them; here and there one would find the narrow sled drawn by the ox, whose weight often marred the narrow trail, puncturing its surface.

The finest bunch of men ever gathered together met on the trails leading to the goldfields. Those of less honest intentions remained in Skagway or Dyea. Some looked at the climb ahead—and turned back.

Noble deeds were done on the tortuous back-breaking trails. The seemingly impossible was carried out by fine specimens of humanity. The experiences of many of the intrepid argonauts will live with them till they depart for that last long trek.

I firmly believe, in the not-distant future, a highway will be constructed that will be the pride of all Canadians, leading to and opening up a highly mineralized country. Streams that would not pay to work for gold will then be highly remunerative. The Dominion will then have an outlet, where millions of people can be absorbed and alluvial fields exploited. A western man, as Minister of the Interior, must see the advisability of this rewarding undertaking.

W.H.T. Olive, CALGARY, 1939

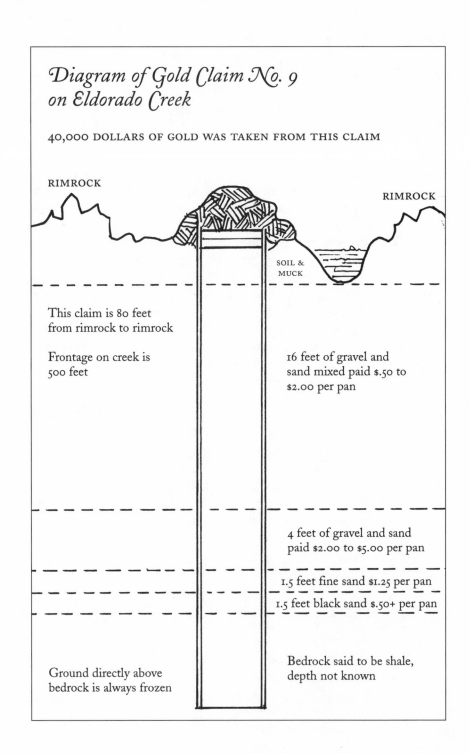

Diagram of Gold Claim No. 9 on Eldorado Creek

40,000 DOLLARS OF GOLD WAS TAKEN FROM THIS CLAIM

RIMROCK

RIMROCK

SOIL & MUCK

This claim is 80 feet from rimrock to rimrock

Frontage on creek is 500 feet

16 feet of gravel and sand mixed paid $.50 to $2.00 per pan

4 feet of gravel and sand paid $2.00 to $5.00 per pan

1.5 feet fine sand $1.25 per pan

1.5 feet black sand $.50+ per pan

Ground directly above bedrock is always frozen

Bedrock said to be shale, depth not known

Gold! Gold! Gold!

Gold! Is there another word in the English language that has such an influence on the minds of humanity as the one formed by these four letters? Gold—the most valuable of the precious metals, the most ductile and malleable, termed "money," representing wealth and riches, its colour thereof pleasing, splendid, a synonym of purity.

In mythology it was the Golden Fleece, in quest of which Jason undertook his argonomic expedition. From earliest history gold has played an important part in the progress and downfall of nations. It has been the demoralizing influence of many, the uplifting of a few who are scrupulous and philanthropic. There are few who haven't read the biblical stories of gold—of the Golden Calf set up by Aaron to be worshipped by the Children of Israel—few who have not read the Greek stories and legends of gold, the Roman and others—the fearful slaughter of the Inca and Aztec by the Spanish for their treasures of gold, the freebooters and pirates who looted the Spanish galleons loaded with bullion on their homeward journey. The magic word *gold* goaded Raleigh, Drake, Hawkins, Morgan, Kidd, and many others to acts of piracy on the high seas, often to fill the coffers of their kings and queens.

The discovery of gold in 1849 in California created a rush from England, Canada, and other places. Men and women braved the lonely trails of the prairies, desert, and mountains to partake in the finding of the precious metal. One will never know the numbers slain by Indians of the plains, the murders committed by bandits, the stage robberies, the laying in wait for those returning from the goldfields. Gold, the cause of most of our crime. The great Cariboo stampede was coloured by atrocious murders after the discovery of gold in the 1850s, and the dangers braved colossal. Judge Begbie, of the British Columbia court, was sent by the Governor Sir James Douglas, of the then British colony, to put a stop to the crime in the Cariboo. He hung without mercy those found guilty. The name Begbie put fear into many a would-be killer.

One wonders that men like Billy Barker (after whom Barkerville was named), having undergone hardship and suffering, trailing, rafting, bucking the swift waters of the Fraser River, starving, at last amassing thousands of dollars worth of gold, would wantonly carouse and dissipate a fortune. One of his favourite acts, when half-drunk, was to take a handful of gold coins and throw them at the mirrors behind the saloon bar. The coins when picked up by the barkeepers would handsomely pay for the mirrors. It seems that the more miners suffered, the greater privations they endured, the more squandering they became when they found the precious metal. It was generally the way of those not accustomed to riches. Could they be blamed? One has to have the experience of exposure to the elements, of travelling over mountains, streams, and forests, of depending often on the gun and fishing in their lonely treks to appreciate, when in a position to do so, abandoning one's self to all pleasures procurable. Making up for lost time of the pleasures denied, but often dreamed of in loneliness. Sometimes, in despair, men became reckless, neglecting their health and succumbing to the dreaded disease of scurvy.

The next notable stampede after the Cariboo, was the Klondyke, from 1896 to 1898. It is surprising that the great deposit of gold in the Klondyke region was not discovered earlier. The country had been traversed many times by prospectors, in particular by George Carmack and his Indian relatives-by-marriage, who depended on the Klondyke River (a favourite spawning place for the salmon), for their supply of fish. Carmack was a citizen of the United States and was termed a "squaw man," taking life easily amongst those who did his bidding.

Carmack and his Tagish relatives, Skookum Jim and Dawson Charlie, were looked upon by many as the discoverers of gold in the Klondyke, but others believed the honour should have gone to Robert Henderson. In 1894, Bob had decided to prospect the Yukon. He packed his outfit over the Chilcoot Pass, and whipsawed the lumber for his boat on the shores of Lake Lindemann. When built, he ran his boat through the Lindemann rapids into Lake Bennett, into Lake Nares (as it was called), into Tagish Lake, and down the Yukon River: through the section north of Tagish (called the Six Mile), into Marsh Lake, through the section north of Marsh, into Lake Laberge, and finally, through the Lewes River section (called the Thirtymile)—prospecting the whole way. Bob panned and rocked Cassiar Bar, as others before him had done, to get a grubstake for the winter. Previously, gold had been taken from the Stewart and Pelly Rivers, but not enough to cause commotion or excitement. Bob made several trips to the post at Sixtymile (near Dawson City) for grub. Setting out often from this point, to prospect in the neighbourhoods of the Indian and Klondyke Rivers and in the different creeks and tributaries, he found good pans, that ran from ten cents to fifty-five cents a pan. He was tireless in his quest to find the good gold deposit that he believed existed in the region. He met with accidents, one after another, often injuring limb and body. Never discouraged, he put several men onto good ground that he had prospected, notably Quartz Creek, which he worked on himself for a grubstake. He held Rabbit Creek in reserve. He recommended the location of Gold Run to others. Henderson was obsessed with the idea that he would find a huge thing if he stayed with it.

In 1896, on his way out for provisions, at the mouth of the Klondyke River, he came across Carmack and his Indian friends and informed them of a find at Gold Run, inviting them over to stake some claims, which they did. On their way back to the Sixtymile post, Henderson asked them to prospect Rabbit Creek, as he believed it to be good. They came to an understanding that if Rabbit Creek was good, Carmack would send over an Indian to let Henderson know, a service Henderson agreed to pay for. Carmack did not fulfill his promise. Henderson, on his way out, met a bunch of jubilant miners. They told him of a great strike on "Bonanza Creek." Henderson had named all the creeks himself and, asking for a description of the creek, said, "Why, that's Rabbit

Creek. I told Carmack to prospect it and send me word." The miners told him, "You're too late now, the creek is staked from mouth to source." One can imagine Henderson's chagrin after he had put Carmack wise. Many thought Carmack had done a mean thing by not getting in touch with Henderson, who had opened up and prospected the Klondyke district, undergoing hardships under which an ordinary man would succumb.

Bob Henderson is the man we should take off our hats to as the discoverer of the Klondyke as a gold region. Only those who have prospected in the Yukon can understand the privation, hunger, weariness, accidents, and so forth that Henderson endured in uncovering the riches of the North. One of the great producing creeks in the region was Henderson's Gold Run, which was afterwards known as Hunker Creek. Here again Henderson had the worst of it. He had worked the creek and found pay dirt. A man named Hunker came along and found Henderson on the stream, saying he had named it Gold Run. Hunker said, "I've named it Hunker." They decided to flip a coin to decide what the name should be. Hunker won, and Henderson was done out of the claim by Hunker rushing off and recording it for himself. As a rule, where gold is concerned, magnanimity is out of the question. It's "me first" and often the one who deserves the most is the one who gets the least. Such was the case with Henderson. However, the government of the Dominion of Canada, knowing what Henderson had done for the district, decided to allow him two hundred dollars per month and 2,000 feet of any placer ground he might find in later prospecting trips. Henderson died in Vancouver in 1934.

Prospecting in the 1890s was hazardous. Today it is comparatively easy. What took twelve months in 1898 can be accomplished today, by aeroplane, in twenty-four hours. Years ago, Horace Greely's advice was, "Go West, young man, go West!" Today, my advice would be, "Young man, go North!" There, one will find work and can earn a competency, if one is willing to suffer inconvenience (which there will be), but it will be nothing in comparison to what the old sourdoughs experienced. In the North one will be taught to think quickly when suddenly faced with danger. This often brings forth qualities in an individual that lie dormant until brought up against propositions that must be conquered.

News of the discovery of gold in the Klondyke travelled fast in 1896. A few got word through the channels of the North-West Mounted Police (NWMP) and letters sent out by lucky stakers of claims to friends outside. In the fall of 1896 and the spring of 1897, quite a few were outfitting for the Far North and the Yukon.

St. Michael, near the mouth of the Yukon River, was becoming a great place. American steamboats were run from this point for hundreds of miles up the river. A lucrative business was carried on in furs and other merchandise to sell to miners, trappers and Indians. Miners gradually drifted in, many believing they were in Alaska when actually they were in Canadian territory. Great quantities of fur were taken out of this wonderful land and many a nice stake of gold was taken from the different streams in the Yukon, hence the necessity for police, to see that Canadian territory (and its riches) was protected. Inspector Constantine and Captain Strickland, with a force of men, were sent into this great hinterland to gather information as to the extent of what was claimed to be Canadian territory. Sending the NWMP into the Yukon was a wise move on the part of the dominion government. They represented the law in every respect, acting as justices of the peace, doctors, commissioners, mining recorders, and coroners—as everything that was conducive to the well-being and orderly conduct of the comparative few who were scattered over the vast, wonderful and enchanting land.

William Ogilvie, the first commissioner of the Yukon, worked for the Department of the Interior and was the head of a survey party that was appointed by the Dominion government to run the International Boundary Line some time before the discovery of the Klondyke, and thus to define the boundary between Alaska and the Yukon. On his way to the coast at the time of the great gold find, he arrived in Victoria in 1897. His lecture there, "Gold in the Klondyke," along with a little booklet, added great impetus to the rush of 1897 and 1898. Before then some people had been dubious; he verified the rich auriferous deposits. Ogilvie's lecture soon flashed around the globe. Men and women came to Vancouver and Victoria from all parts of the world to join in the rush. Mining engineers, miners, lawyers, preachers, gamblers, thugs, merchants, and men from every walk of life were bent on getting their share of wealth. Duke's son and Cook's son, generals, colonels (every other man was a colonel), bishops—all joined the ranks and mingled together with one destination: Dawson. Enterprising individuals planned and formed companies. Money that had been tied up for years was let loose to finance some sound investments. Other investments were as crazy as the men who planned them. Everyone seemed to be afflicted with the gold fever. When the steamboat *Portland* arrived in Seattle from the North with a ton or more of gold from a partial 'cleanup' (a term used after cleaning up the sluice boxes), the news spread like wildfire all along the coast. Men became excited, giving up good jobs and leaving their wives and children, often mortgaging all they possessed to get enough to buy outfits. For what? For many, disillusion, hardship, poverty, blasted hopes, death.

San Francisco, Portland, Seattle, Vancouver and Victoria were busy places. Merchants amassed fortunes by outfitting companies and individuals for their long trip. For years before this, all along the coast (in fact, throughout the United States and Canada), business was at a low ebb. Banks had been put out of business and money was scarce. The period from 1893 to the time of news of gold in the Klondyke was looked upon as one of the worst depressions the West had ever experienced. At last the tide had turned. Money became less scarce and a great optimism took place, which invariably happens after discoveries of gold. San Francisco, Portland, and Seattle were alive to the early opening of their stores to satisfy all those who wished to be off at the first opportunity for a berth on a steamboat, which would often be packed to over capacity. Vancouver, and especially Victoria stores, however, were not in the least disturbed about early opening for the eager and excited argonauts. Merchants sauntered along leisurely, opening their stores at nine and ten o'clock in the morning, causing many to swear and curse at their tardiness. Canadian ports lost considerable business through these conservative methods. Later on, when much gold was coming out of the Yukon, further business was lost to Seattle and Portland, which paid twenty dollars an ounce for gold, whilst Vancouver and Victoria gave only the assayed value.

CHAPTER ONE

Departure from Victoria

It was extremely interesting to watch the loading of steamboats in Victoria. Some outfits consisted of mules, horses, burros, dogs, lumber, picks, shovels, buckets, hay, oats, flour, bacon, beans, rice, Peterborough canoes, boats knocked down ready for assembling, and all kinds of other merchandise. My berth was on the upper deck, giving me a good position to watch the different methods of handling freight. First came the livestock, horses and burros, with a canvas sling under them, hoisted by block and then lowered to the hold. The gangway was used for some. At times the animals would be obstinate, which kept the onlookers interested and laughing. The passengers on this trip were Jews, toughs from everywhere, ladies, some questionable characters, and miners—a few old forty-niners from California, with flowing grey beards, once more travelling in the quest for gold.

"Ah, yes! Those were the days, boys. Our claim was a piece of ground on Williams Creek, marked off by a circle, made with a long-handled shovel and the length of our arms. It's good to be in a rush once more." An old man, straight and upstanding, seemed in his element. Although looking comparatively young, he was over seventy years of age. On the lower deck, card games were in evidence, being played by rough-looking customers who had evidently shipped in from United States ports. They were the dregs of society. I wondered where all the different piles of freight would be stowed on board the steamboat. There were piles of knocked-down sluice boxes, goldpans, ship-saws, boilers and engines for boats, dogs by the hundred of every breed, and things some had never seen before and would not be likely to see again. At times the din was unbearable. Now and again a fight would take place over some trivial matter, started by some bully who thought he was kingpin of the crowd. At times knives would be in evidence as threats. Onto the deck would come the mate of the ship, or the boatswain, threatening to brain them if there were any more rows. This was no idle talk, the officers knew how to handle men.

Hullo! What's this? My attention was drawn to a fine young lady with two dogs in leash, coming up the gangway, a picture of health and strength, dressed in becoming trail garb.

"Hi, there! Deckhand!" said the mate. "Take the lady's dogs."

"Yes, Sir! I'll take them, lady. What's their names, lady?"

"Yukon and Alaska."

"Did you say 'Asker'? What's your name, doggie? She don't answer, ma'am."

"Call him Alaska, not Asker."

"Oh! Beg pardon, lady! Come on, doggies."

The deckhand took the unwilling dogs, who turned expressive eyes to their mistress, who in turn bade them go on whilst she wended her way to her berth. The dogs were beautiful animals, part malamute and wolfhound.

Gradually things began to straighten out. Pandemonium was quieting down, stand-up fights were lessening. The huge pile of freight on the wharf had disappeared and the longshoremen rested after their strenuous labour of loading the boat. At last came the welcome shout, "All aboard! Cast off the bowline!" The boat moved. "Cast off the stern line!" Good-byes were shouted. Handkerchiefs waved. We were off. Some had said good-bye forever. Victoria was at last hidden from our view. Before us was the wreck of the *San Pedro*, a coal freighter from the Dunsmuir mines at Nanaimo, her bow high on Brotchie's Ledge. A smooth sea ran in the Strait of Juan de Fuca and the steamboat got into her stride. On the lower deck, hammocks were strung up for sleeping and everything was at last shipshape. Innumerable card games went on. Improvised tables were made by levelling off sacks and merchandise. The long table on which meals were served was most frequently used.

Suddenly the boat started to shiver from bow to stern. All the passengers rushed to the sides to see what was up. We had struck Plumper's Pass (a shortcut to Vancouver and the east coast of Vancouver Island), when it was none too favourable to go through. It was indeed a wonderful sight. The boat strained and creaked, as if there was an army of men in her hold trying to burst her with hydraulic jacks. We passed through miniature waterfalls and whirlpools. Toward the shore were several large logs that had broken away from booms on their way to sawmills and were circling around in large whirlpools. The constant whirling had polished the surface of the logs. It was doubtful that they would ever emerge from their prison. We were not long in this amazing pass. It gripped us and we were fascinated watching the waters in turmoil, realizing that we were but a toy compared to Nature's work in these wonderful waters. When all was tranquil again, the passengers settled down once more. Here and there groups talked earnestly of their proposed ways and methods of reaching Dawson after they had arrived at Skagway or Dyea. Some were going no farther than Wrangell, en route to the Teslin Trail. Some were going no farther than Skagway, to start businesses, believing that more money would be made by selling merchandise than by wearing themselves out on a six-hundred-mile journey on foot.

Our first stop was Nanaimo, the coal city. Someone in the crowd could give an interesting history of each place we stopped. It seemed that an old-timer from Victoria had taken up the land whereon Nanaimo was situated as a coal base. The coal had been discovered in a creek, with water passing over the exposed seams. On this was laid the foundation for the huge Dunsmuir fortune. Robert Dunsmuir (the founder), was a miner, and his son, who later became Sir James, worked in the mines with him, along with another son, Alex.

We cut through a school of herring coming into the harbour, and in the light of the moon it made a glorious sight as the herring jumped and splashed, reflecting silvery flashes. The lower deck passengers dipped up pails full with fish, which were delivered to the cooks for meals. Here again, a number came aboard to try their luck at Dawson.

Nanaimo was to be the last port of call for some time. We settled down once more to steamboat life and gradually became acquainted. I was entertained by visiting different parts of the boat and noticing the different characters, especially on the lower deck. Some were boxing, some quarreling, some moody and sullen, and some were villainous-looking and seemed capable of doing anything criminal. Rambling around Nanaimo I saw houses, one after the other, that had subsided, owing to the cave-in of the mine tunnels. In some instances the chimneys were level with the streets and still, people lived in them.

The welcome shout came from the bridge by the mate: "All Aboard!" We skirted north along the east shore of Vancouver Island, which was fringed by forests running down to the water's edge. The piece of water we were travelling over was as smooth as glass. The land on both sides gradually drew nearer at Seymour Narrows, where it seemed but a stone's throw from the mainland to the island. At this point we were obliged to drop anchor owing to the tide, which was not favourable to pass through. Whilst waiting we witnessed a steam tug towing a boom of logs, trying to make a bay, to wait until the tide was propitious before going through. The tug's crew must have miscalculated the tide, because the boom seemed to be drawn closer and closer to the turbulent waters. Looking through binoculars, I saw a struggle going on. Smoke belched from the tug's stacks, illustrating its frantic efforts to get to safety. The boom of logs was in the grip of the powerful current. Would the tug make it? We saw a man with an axe, ready to snap the towrope. Saving the boom seemed a hopeless task. At last the axe descended. The rope was severed and away went the boom into the swirling waters. We watched with eagerness to see what would take place. The boom swung round and round. At last it reached a mighty whirlpool and was swallowed up and lost in the vortex, as if it were a box of matches. The tug, with difficulty, reached quieter waters. Seymour Narrows is one of the world's largest ocean waterfalls, which are caused by the coming in and going out of the tides. Among the many groups who watched the grand spectacle were engineers, who talked of the prospect of bridging the treacherous waters and connecting the island with the mainland. Later a movement was afoot to bring the railroad across at this point.

The adjacent country seemed full of game. We saw deer, ducks of all kinds, and bear, as we passed very close to several islands. It was a regular sportsman's paradise. One of the passengers said that he had been in all parts of the world and had not seen a better country than Vancouver Island for sport. Wolves abounded, along with black bear, deer, quail, cougar, pheasant, and fish of all kinds.

At last we were through the narrows, entering Queen Charlotte Strait and Sound, where the broad Pacific rolls—and well we knew it, after having enjoyed the peace and quiet of the inland waters. Many, not having experienced the ocean's tempest, suffered much. Card games ended and everyone sought quiet corners. The Pacific Ocean belied its name at this time.

When at last we got into the shelter of Calvert Island and were again in smooth water, several exclaimed, "Thank God! It's over!" Once more white faces began to get their colour back. Hoping that Fitz Hugh Sound would not be as rough as the straits, all regained a spirit of cheerfulness. Burros brayed, horses neighed, dogs barked joyfully. All were glad the rough piece of water had passed. It was indeed beautiful travelling between the islands. The waters were like millponds. We were surrounded by an enchanted land.

Alas! We entered into Millbanke Sound, rudely shaken from the unutterable magnificence, peace, and joy with a nasty blow that had a dressing effect on many. But it was of short duration. We soon got into the placid water of the inside channels and the sight that met our eyes made us forget the rough tossing. We emerged into a grand body of water that was large enough, it seemed, to hold all the navies of the world. We passed small boats, sloops, canoes, and other kinds of craft bound for the Klondyke. How they had been able to cross the straits in such frail craft was a mystery to those who were not used to seafaring, but at this time the coast of British Columbia possessed some of the finest fishermen and sailors to be found anywhere. At last we came to Port Simpson.

～

We had passed the vicinity of Dean's Inlet, where the great explorer Sir Alexander Mackenzie first beheld the magnificent panorama of the Pacific Ocean. I realized what his feelings must have been after he had passed the barrier of the Rockies. This intrepid explorer was the first white man to make the coast from the interior. The words he painted on a rock are still in evidence at Dean's Inlet: ALEXANDER MACKENZIE FROM CANADA BY LAND, 22ND OF JULY, 1793. About this time another great man, Vancouver, was sailing around the island that would be named after him. Previously, Captain Cook had landed at Nootka Sound and passed these same waters, as far as Bering Strait to the north.

CHAPTER TWO

North to Alaska

We were now near Alaska, that strip of country that had been taken by the Russians and more or less settled by them. The names of many islands are Russian. One has to wonder today how the early voyageurs, in their little crafts no larger than fishing schooners, accomplished their feats. Many must have been the shipwrecks that went unrecorded. Through the boldness and courage of men like Captains Cook and Vancouver, uncharted seas were conquered. On land victories belong to such men as Mackenzie, Samuel Hearne, Simon Fraser, David Thompson, and others. We are receiving the benefits today of the trade channels and vast tracts of lands opened up by them.

As we crossed Dixon Entrance, we were again exposed to the swells and seas of the Pacific, until we entered Revillagigedo Channel, formed by the islands of Revillagigedo, Annette and Gravina. We saw an interesting sight as we crossed Dixon Entrance—a fight between a whale and its predator. The whale was thrashing in its death throes. Many on board were thrilled, not knowing such things could happen. They had heard much about whales, but coming upon one in such close quarters was another matter. After half an hour's fighting, the water was again peaceful and we held our way into Alaskan waters. We entered Clarence Strait, with Prince of Wales Island on the west and Etolin and Zerembo Islands on the east, the end of which brought us into the port of Wrangell, the starting point of the Teslin Trail. This trail (which some called the Dewdney Trail), went along the Stikine River to Telegraph Creek, then overland to Teslin Lake, then along the Teslin and Lewes Rivers to the Yukon River and to Dawson. It was to become known as a trail of disaster and misery.

~

On board was a professor from a great university in the United States. Our group (such as it came to be), listened to his remarks, which gradually caught our attention and interest, about the history of the great country we were about to enter. Before its purchase by the United States, it was known, he told us, as Russian America. He traced for us its history, from the earliest Russian adventurers down to the present. He mentioned Baranof, the first Russian official of Alaska, and Bering, who sailed through what became Bering Strait in 1730. Sitka, the capital of Alaska at the time, was founded by Baranof, and the old trading post established by him stands today. The early Russian church there is a work of art, the altar decorated with fine paintings, jewels and gold—well worth visiting. The great Mount St. Elias was named by Bering.

Alaska was a land of great mystery, its interior unknown. Many white men, both Russian- and English-speaking, who ventured to leave the waterways, were murdered, up until the year 1840. Malakoff, a Russian, had travelled about six hundred miles up the Yukon by boat, but had to return, owing to the warlike attitude of the natives of the coast (the upper waters of the Yukon River).

Yet the bold adventurers of the Hudson's Bay Company (HBC) seemed to get on peacefully with some of the natives. One of the company's men, Robert Campbell, the indefatigable pioneer of this vast country, discovered the Pelly River. His clerk, James G. Stewart, discovered the Stewart River and named it after himself. Fort Selkirk, established here by the HBC, was attacked by Chilkat Indians, who burned it to the ground. The Chilkat had been trading partners with the Indians of the interior and were jealous of the encroachment of the HBC onto trade. Campbell and the Indians of the interior had many encounters with these coastal tribes and his movements were watched, evidently for an opportunity to destroy the post. The opportunity came when he was engaged in looking over other territory. The Indians of the coast swooped down on the post and destroyed it. This was most annoying to Campbell, as at this point he was doing a lucrative business. Having to get permission to build again, he started on a memorable trip on snowshoes in the heart of winter, travelling over three thousand miles through uninhabited country to get the necessary authority.

Fort Yukon on the Yukon River was also established by the HBC, crossing the Mackenzie to do so. Until the purchase of Alaska from Russia, this great territory was looked upon as one of ice, mountains, and barriers. We passed pleasant hours listening to our interesting professor.

We said good-bye to a number at Wrangell. Some we would meet again, others never. Some were en route to the Teslin Trail. The story of the untold misery and suffering on this torturous, ill-advised trail is known. Prospectors met impassable bogs and muskeg in the spring of 1898; thousands of tons of merchandise were abandoned that could not be taken in or brought out again. The Indians had grub stakes along the Teslin Trail for many years. Wolves fed well on the ham and bacon that was left. Many did "their all" on this trail—and didn't come back. Some of those who did lose everything returned to Vancouver or Victoria to purchase outfits again and book passage for Skagway and Dyea, the starting points of the more feasible routes. This caused them great delay, and it was late in 1898 before they were able to resume their journey to Dawson. Some still built boats when they arrived at Bennett; others had had a surfeit of rough going and were glad to take passage on the Bennett Lake & Klondyke Navigation (BL&KN) Company's steamboat *Flora*, at that time the only steamboat on Lake Bennett that connected with other boats at White Horse.

Wrangell, an old Russian town, had wharves to accommodate shipping. Large warehouses and saloons did a rush business, but the liquor was vile. A number of *cheechakos* (as the greenhorns were sometimes called) took the opportunity to get a last drink here before starting out on their perilous journey, little thinking of what lay ahead. Wrangell seemed to be the headquarters for a great industry around carcasses of deer. In one large shed hundreds of carcasses hung ready for the San Francisco market. It was a surprise to many who had never dreamed of finding deer in such vast numbers in this northern town. An old hunter was known for bringing in as many as fifty a day from the surrounding

islands and the mainland. Here also suspicious characters lay in wait
for the unwary, ready to draw them into their meshes. Quite a number
fell, and were finally stranded until they were able to work their passage
away from the scene of their undoing. "Doping drinks" was the cause for
what happened to many of the unfortunates. The scum of the world are
always found following gold rushes.

Leaving Wrangell, we once more proceeded to Skagway, our course
leading through Wrangell Strait, bordered on the west by Kupeanof
Island and on the east by Mitkof Island. Here, on the first day of the
year 1898, it was intensely cold and the wind was blowing hard. The salt
sea spray froze as it fell onto the ship, and it was not long before the
ship was white all over. The masts and spars were all covered with ice
and the decks were dangerous to walk on. Everyone hunted for warm
spots. The second-class passengers huddled together for warmth on the
lower decks. Card games still went on in the smoking room day and
night, and sometimes the stakes were heavy. The signs NO GAMBLING
ABOARD were not heeded. A number of those on board were professional
gamblers, on their way to Skagway or Dyea to reap a rich harvest.

Leaving Wrangell Strait, we travelled through Souchi Channel, then
Frederick Sound, then Stephens Passage, stopping at Douglas on Douglas Island. Here was the famous Treadwell Mine that was, by report,
owned and operated by the wealthy Rothschilds. Away from the town
was the famous Glory Hole, where thousands were employed. We saw
the miners as specks on the side of the mountain, working with their
compressed drills, demolishing the mountains of gold-bearing rocks.
It was reported that every day one man lost his life in this vast undertaking. Across from Douglas was Juneau, with its quaint Russian spires
on churches and missions. Juneau, before the Klondyke rush, was the
starting place for intrepid miners prospecting in the range of mountains
and on down from the headwaters of the Yukon.

Once again the professor talked of Alaska. Russia, in the midst of the
Crimean War, had wanted to sell it and was urgent in the matter. Russia
thought that England would capture Alaska and fly the Union Jack over

the Russian posts. The United States offered a ridiculously small amount for it and was refused, but after a time the amount was increased. Finally, a deal was consummated and Alaska became United States territory. England, in not seizing this vast country, lost for Canada a veritable storehouse of treasure. The wealth taken from Alaska during its first few years as American territory more than paid for its purchase. One wonders at the Russians parting with this wonderful country. It was very rich in furs, and up to 1867 they did a most profitable business with the Indians.

When English-speaking people explored the Yukon and found gold in many of its streams, especially on the bars of the Stewart and Pelly Rivers and on the Fortymile River and other rivers, the only excitement created was local. Juneau and Douglas were affected, but only a small number had the courage to face the difficult journey over the Chilcoot Pass (or the Dyea Pass as it was sometimes called) and through other entrances into the vast territory.

As soon as the country was acquired by the Americans, they bought out the interests of Russian steamboat companies and other commercial enterprises and applied vigour to the sealing, fishing, mining and trapping industries. The industry created brought to Alaska men like Jack McQuesten, in the 1870s, as well as Harper, Mayo, and others, and the Alaska Commercial Trading Company. Many prospectors were scattered over the land, from the upper waters of the Yukon to its lower waters, each not knowing of the presence of the others. Prospecting then was a hazardous calling, with many not knowing whether they were in Canadian or American territory.

~

We were all disturbed, while listening to the professor, by the young lady with the two dogs. She had slapped the face of a man, who was about to retaliate, when another man stepped in. The second man pushed the first aside, saying evenly, "This young lady doesn't wish your company." The man who had been annoying the young lady made a charge, and a tussle took place. It was not long in duration, as the lady's champion got the better of the scrap and was watching for his opportunity to get a hold on the fellow, which he did. He would have thrown the fellow overboard had not another man stepped in and prevented him.

The defeated fellow slunk off, saying, "We will meet again."

The skipper, noticing the fray, remarked, "The damn fool deserved it." However, at suppertime the fellow did not show up, perhaps because of his battered face. After this we all kept a watchful eye on our young lady passenger to see that she was not annoyed again. It seemed that the gentleman, as he posed himself, had suggested a life of ease and affluence during the conversation that ended so abruptly.

From Douglas Island, several miners would, at different periods, leave their jobs, attracted by reports of gold found over the mountain range on river bars. Alex McDonald, who became rich in the Klondyke and died poor, had at one time worked in the old Treadwell Mine on Douglas Island.

A man named Millar, years before the 1898 rush, found gold in what is now called Pine Creek, which empties into Lake Atlin. Nothing was known of his discovery at first. That year, his brother Fritz, following Millar's directions, mined the same area. Discovery City, on the banks of Pine Creek, soon sprang into existence. After enduring hardships, Fritz, with broken limbs, reached Juneau, but never had any ambition to return to Discovery. His experience was like a nightmare to him for years.

We left Juneau after climbing several hills, getting an enchanting view of the surrounding islands and waters. We were now in Lynn Canal and the cold became intense. We were on the last leg of our journey. Some were bound for Dyea; the majority were bound for Skagway, the city of tents and a few frame buildings, with others being erected in feverish haste. Bill Moore, who had blazed the White Pass Trail in 1896, had built a wharf by the side of a bluff at deep water, where our steamboat tied up.

CHAPTER THREE

Skagway and Stevedores

After we had tied up to the wharf and the gangplanks were let down, we saw several Japanese men, in readiness to handle the freight. They had no sooner brought the first freight onto the wharf when a volley of shots were fired into the air by white stevedores who had previously been attending to all unloading. It was disturbing to see the workers scamper back on board, evidently knowing what to expect should they attempt to unload and take the place of the longshoremen. A strike by longshoremen was nothing new. Unfortunately, a few Japanese fell into the icy waters and were drowned. What could be done? The boat must be unloaded. At last a bargain was made and the whites won. The Japanese did not appear again. The captain of the steamboat was powerless, the marshals of the town indifferent; they dared not meddle. The rough element ruled the town.

Watching the freight being unloaded was as amusing as watching it being loaded in Victoria at the start of our journey. The dogs were delighted to be on terra firma once more, as were the passengers. Burros and horses made for the bales of hay. Dogfights took place—"man fights," as well—and there was general pandemonium. All were eager to be the first away. With all the excitement and haste,some were destined never to reach their goal; many could not withstand the temptations and allurements of the gambling halls. They gambled away their outfits in a very short time. Even the women received little consideration from greedy, selfish individuals, whose only thought was to get their share of gold. Alas, for dreams—those lofty peaks had to be scaled—the first day on the trail would decide whether a man had intestinal fortitude or was a weakling.

Very obliging and courteous inspectors and deputies, the head of which was a Mr. Sylvester, performed customs inspection. After clearing I proceeded to find a place to make camp. Skagway was not a cheerful sight. It looked dreary, desolate, bleak, and uninviting. The outgoing tide exposed great mudflats. January was a bitterly cold month, yet vessels still came, unloading their seekers of wealth. There were two main streets running at right angles to each other, one going in the direction of the White Pass, the other going north. The river was strewn with boulders that had been washed down by the floods from the mountains when the thaws commenced in the spring. There were several good-sized general stores, and already many secondhand stores, which had naturally come into existence to serve those who could not stand the strain of packing and sledding their outfits up the steep climbs. These prospectors sold their outfits for a mere song and squandered away the proceeds, either at Soapy's (Jefferson Randolph Smith, ringleader of the town's lawless element) or the saloons. Secondhand dealers did a lucrative business from the summer of 1897 until the rush was over. I saw tents everywhere, with caches or piles of merchandise piled around them, and was surprised to see so many people on the streets in all kinds of winter garments. Many said, "So this is Skagway? And a damned cold Skagway at that." It certainly was, with a temperature below zero and a bitter cold wind blowing in from the sea that froze me to the marrow. If the wind came off the land it was just as bad, because it was laden with the icy breath of the mountains. The wind turned some back from their adventure. The cold dampened their romantic feelings. Still the argonauts came, boatload after boatload. What a reception, in the month of January.

The dance and gambling halls were full, as were the saloons, by those seeking shelter from the stormy blasts. Money and liquor flowed freely. High stakes were played for in the gambling dens. Men cursed and swore, wondering when someone would start and break the trail. A blizzard had been raging for days. No one left Skagway or came in from the White Pass. At night the town was alive with rowdiness and carousing. Every day there was news of a dead man lying in some out-of-the-way place—a victim of some gambling dispute or drunken brawl. New-comers were watched narrowly by an element of lawless toughs, bent on luring the unsophisticated into some game or another, intent on extract-ing their money. Every day gangsters from all parts of the world were landing, swelling the numbers of those already in the business of crime.

Snow was heavy on the streets and trails. Cheechakos hauled their outfits from the wharf in an endless procession to their tent camps, a taste of the beginning of their hard experience. Evils and dangers yet to come flashed through their minds.

I saw many incidents concerning dogs at the wharf. Many of the dogs being harnessed had never seen or felt a harness before. Many were wild and vicious, others tame and domesticated. Some men were patient in their task of breaking in the dogs to pull the sleds, but others were brutal, half-killing them, possessing no tact whatsoever. I saw a woman holding a gee pole (fastened onto the right-hand side of a sled at about a 45-degree angle, used to guide the sled right or left) and a man going on ahead, leading the dogs. In this way dogs were broken into the work with little or no trouble. Some sleds had only two dogs, some three; many had six, all hitched in a row.

"Here, you damned fool! Stop clubbing the dogs! Let me have them!"

"What's that? Call me a damned fool! Take that!" A lunge was made at the other fellow, who dodged, then flew at his partner and left him prostrate in the snow. Incidents like this were the deciding factor in breaking up partnerships. The man who had stopped the clubbing took the dogs in hand, patting and coaxing them. Soon he had them pulling their load in real earnest. Some of these dogs, if they had the power to speak, could have told stories of woe and suffering. Sometimes the dogs would not stir to the command to move.

I heard a shout from an outfit: "Gee-haw! Marche—on! Marche—on!" It had been a Frenchman saying "Marche—on," to his dogs who gave to the North the starting command that eventually became "'Mush—on."

Dogs. Many a man's life has been saved in the Far North by his dogs; some have more sense than their master. When a man has no friends, when he is lonely, when he is in a tight pinch, in ill health, hungry, cold, and freezing to death, generally it is the faithful dog (sometimes the abused dog), in the Far North who saves his master's life. Snuggling at his feet when weary at the end of a hard day, compelled to lay out in the open, not able to make camp, throwing his heat into the man's body. Faithful. Yes, often 'til death. These dogs would sacrifice their lives for their master and in many instances, men sacrificed their lives for their dogs, especially in that long tramp to Dawson. More fights took place over dogs on the trail than for any other cause. Those who mushed dogs over the White and Chilcoot Passes will ever remember the faithful brutes. On a stiff climb, with heads down, shoulders into collars, forelegs bent, digging for a foothold, plodding along, some fearful at the crack of the whip, expecting to feel its sharp cut, some looking at the driver with a turn of the head, as if to say, "I am doing my best," with a wag of his tail.

Many, after years have slipped by, and those who have long since left the scenes of the mad scramble for gold, see the picture in their minds of their faithful dogs, who endured torture and weariness and pulled the loads from cache to cache in blinding blizzards and perishing cold. Well can be remembered their delighted bark when the going was good, their scampering away so that the sled would not run onto their heels. How good it was to jump on the sled and take a longed-for rest on a downgrade, after miles of walking, pulling, and running, until the next incline.

Often the narrow trails were wiped out by the big blow in the night. Sleds were upset. Waist-deep in snow, men endeavoured to get their sleds back on the trail, putting on snowshoes to tramp a trail for the dogs to follow. What misery and suffering. For what? Were they not on the trail for Dawson, their goal? Many had turned back, but the fever had held the rest. The lure of the trail was catching. It was "follow the leader" and on they went. No waiting now for someone to break trail. From early morn until late at night it was "Mush-on." Some were jovial, some sad and weary, others swearing and cursing, venting their tempers on the poor dumb brutes, their dogs. It made men of some, devils of others, and some wore themselves and their dogs down to skin and bones. Caught by disaster at times with a broken sled runner between caches, many would have to sidetrack for repairs. Many slept on the cold snow until morning, with dogs curled around for warmth, until help arrived from those who had started very early on the trail before the traffic became continuous.

~

Every day boats came and the population increased. Away in the draws, sheltered by scrub trees, were mules and burros, corralled for packing freight. Oxen and horses were in evidence as well. Those who owned oxen had made their plans. After the hauling to the headwaters, the oxen would be fattened on the bunch grass growing in the ravines, then slaughtered and sold for a dollar a pound. Enthusiasm abounded. Who would be the first to break trail? When would someone start? No one had been in or out of the White Pass, the dividing line between Alaska and the Yukon Territories, where the NWMP were stationed.

The town grew more rowdy, the gamblers bolder, the saloons fuller. Soapy Smith and his gang were in full sway; the marshals being just a name. Money flowed freely; outfits piled up, mountains of them ready for Dawson. I occasionally saw a member of the NWMP interspersed amongst the crowd, a sight that gave those who were law-abiding the hope that soon they would be within police jurisdiction. Once the prospectors had packed their belongings to the White Pass, they would be gone from a place that was run by a pack of gangsters and cutthroats in a lawless town, but a heart-aching task was ahead of them before they reached the international boundary.

Skagway was indeed an active place. Wharves were being constructed to take care of the tremendous amount of passengers and merchandise. Pile-drivers were busy. Men earned big wages. The wharves were long, having to be built out to deep water to take care of the many ocean boats. In 1896 and 1897 the boats came in as far as possible on the mud-flats on high tide and unloaded when the tide went out. The argonauts would haul or employ men to haul their perishables to dry land. If it was not hauled away, the heavy stuff remained until the next tide receded. Imagine the toil. Men sweating, shouting, and cursing. Never had men worked harder than when at the task of hauling their merchandise to safety.

A wagon road as far as possible toward the mountains was already being built and arrangements had been made to build the White Pass & Yukon Railway (WP&YR). Engineers were on hand to survey the land as soon as the snow in the foothills melted. All was hustle and bustle. Doctors were called to attend to the weaklings who had collapsed under the strenuous work entailed in caching their goods.

The BL&KN company was already on the ground at Skagway, with a first consignment of material for the building of three steamboats at Lake Bennett, to run between that point and Dawson. The project's promoters were Frank M. Rattenbury, architect of the British Columbia Parliament Buildings, along with two others from the city of Victoria. Mr. Rattenbury had paid a visit to London, England and raised $250,000 as a starter for the enterprise. He had entered into the proposition on the condition that he could hire a certain man to look after things up in the then-unknown country. I had had much to do with the construction of the aforementioned parliament buildings and was therefore appointed manager of the BL&KN company.

Captain Spencer from the Columbia River was also here. He was related to Captain John Irving, of the Pacific Coast Steamship Company, who was to build another steamboat, the *Willie Irving*. Everyone knew of Captain John, the most popular man on the coastal service. The *Emma Knot* was another boat on the scene, a Victoria enterprise, small, with little power.

One company's advance agent was hunted up and found in the gambling hall. He was supposed to have made arrangements for the men who had been hired to work on his company's project. But in trying to redeem what he had already lost on the tables, he lost all—not an isolated case, by any means. Others had started out in the spring of 1897 but got no farther than Skagway, preferring an easy life compared to that of climbing the barriers before them. Eventually some of these lost everything they possessed. Others made another effort after 12 months of idleness, when they were lucky enough to get in with a good crowd with enough vim and manliness to face the trail.

CHAPTER FOUR

Breaking Trail

When we decided to break the trail, I rounded up my men and got everything ready, allotting to each man a particular part in the journey. Although the White Pass Trail had been blazed by Bill Moore in 1896, thousands still used the Chilcoot Trail. We were headed for the White Pass. Those who had snowshoes were to go ahead and break trail. The hand-drawn sleds followed. These sleds were only lightly loaded with provisions to take them to Bennett. It was slow work, plodding along, and the day closed in. The men were tired and ready to rebel when they saw a tent with smoke curling out of its stovepipe, bearing the sign, REFRESHMENTS, LIQUORS AND TOBACCO. A whoop went out from a few of the gang. "Happy day!" they shouted, and entered. Inside were two men playing cards. They came forward, smiling at the fact that at last the rush had commenced on the trail.

"What's the chance of stopping for the night?" I asked.

"Every chance in the world. How many?"

"Ten. What's the charge?"

"Fifty cents the night. Your own blankets and the ground."

"How about meals?"

"Righto! The larder is low, but we can give you a meal. Nothing fancy, for fifty cents. You'll pay double when you get a little farther on the trail."

One of my men spoke up, "Say, boss! Where's the drink you promised for breaking trail."

"Alright, line up, boys," I said. "What's the price?"

"Twenty-five cents."

"Mine's a beer," ordered one of the men.

"Sorry, gentlemen, beer freezes."

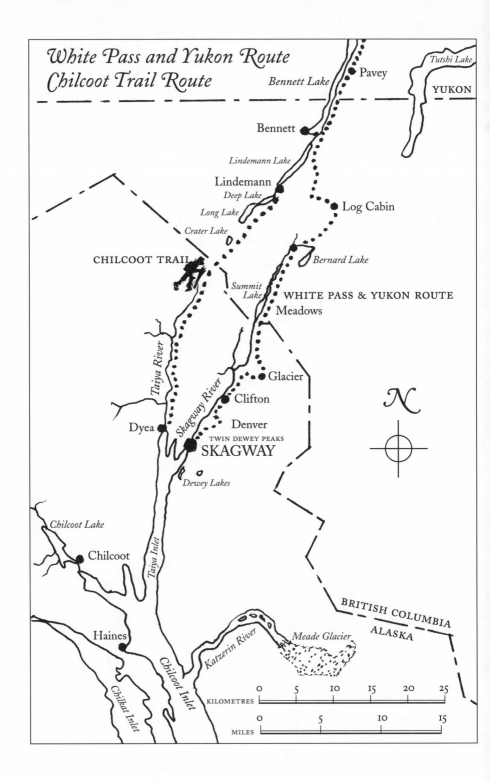

White Pass and Yukon Route
Chilcoot Trail Route

Tutshi Lake

Bennett Lake • Pavey

YUKON

Bennett •

Lindemann Lake

Lindemann •

Deep Lake

Long Lake

Crater Lake

• Log Cabin

CHILCOOT TRAIL

Bernard Lake

Summit Lake

WHITE PASS & YUKON ROUTE

Meadows

Taiya River

Skagway River

• Glacier

Clifton •

Dyea •

Denver

TWIN DEWEY PEAKS
SKAGWAY

Dewey Lakes

N

Chilcoot Lake

• Chilcoot

Taiya Inlet

Haines •

Katzerin River

Meade Glacier

BRITISH COLUMBIA
ALASKA

Chilcoot Inlet

Chilkat Inlet

| 0 | 5 | 10 | 15 | 20 | 25 |
KILOMETRES

| 0 | 5 | 10 | 15 |
MILES

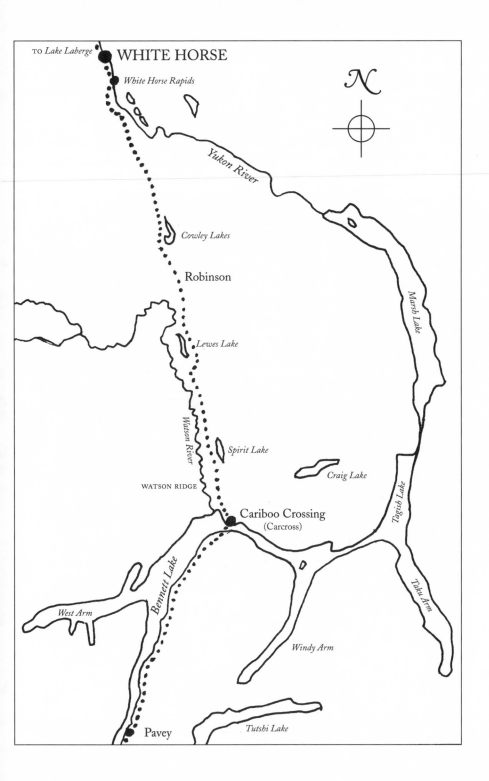

"Give me a whiskey, then."

"House of Lords, eh?"

"Good label, " said another, "but it looks old."

"Ten whiskeys and hurry up, we're freezing," I said. "All ready? Then here's to the *Ora*, *Nora*, and *Flora*." We raised our glasses, swallowed the contents, then spluttered and coughed.

Someone said, "What in hell brand is that?"

"Our special blend—'White Pass special.'"

"Get us the meals!" One man ordered the other, "Jake! Set up meals for ten."

We hugged the pot-bellied heater to get a thorough warming. Jake was gone a long time, but we were warm and our pipes tasted good. After an hour or so our meals were ready and at last we heard the welcome words, "Come and get it, boys! Moose meat for ten."

The boys decided to have an appetizer. "Fill 'em up again, Mister!" The glasses were placed on the bar, which was a rude structure. The glasses were clearly made for profit, their bottom halves being solid glass. After the second drink we all lined up to the rough table, which was a couple of planks set on two barrels, and began our meal. From time to time during the meal the boys glanced at each other; their looks seemed to say, "I don't know what you think, but my moose meat is damned tough." After the meal the proprietor suggested a little game before turning in. Several responded and after the game found they were "minus dollars." We laid our beds around the heater for warmth.

The proprietor said, "Now, boys, if you feel cold in the night, here's plenty of wood." It was a cold, long, bitter night. One man after another, not being able to endure any longer trying to sleep on the ground, got up, stoked up the fire and sat around it, waiting patiently for daybreak.

"Say, Boss," one of the men said, "they tell me we are only six miles from Skagway. At this rate we'll be ten days getting to Bennett." Many wanted to turn back, but after much shaming and persuasion on my part, they decided to stay on.

We started at daybreak on our journey, but had not gone far before we came across the carcass from which our supper was supplied. "The sons of guns," we exclaimed, "dead horse!" The steaks had been chopped out with an axe. We called that place Dead Horse Camp, and it was always alluded to as such.

We next stopped, after passing a lot of difficult places and boulders, at White Pass Hotel. From this point we could see, looking back, a long string of sleds, with men pulling and tugging them; some had dogs. At the very back, single horses were hitched to narrow sleighs to preserve the trail and avoid capsizing. When anyone got into a difficult situation and had to stop, everyone behind had to stop, as the trail was so narrow one could not pass without an upset in the deep snow. Night and day, thousands were continuously on the trail, making caches five or ten miles apart, or shorter, depending on the nature of the going.

The next stopping place was named the Ford, where the higher altitudes began. Above the Ford was a very narrow pass; disaster would overtake the careless here. Once, a horse and sled that had taken the corner too fast were precipitated to the bottom of the gorge below. When the sled slid over, the horse frantically held on, but at last, with a scream almost human, over it went—which was the last of that outfit. So many met disaster at this point that an enterprising party finally secured dynamite and widened the pass, making it comparatively safe. It would be hard to describe the happenings on the trail day after day; the language used shocked even those who were accustomed to swearing and cursing.

After steadily climbing, we passed the timberline and emerged onto a windswept level. We felt the wind keenly after our arduous labour of getting through the Ford. Before we had perspired freely, now we were chilled to the bone. Stakes denoted the packed trail. I kept wondering how the enormous amount of merchandise would ever get up to the White Pass.

Ah! At last we saw a flag appear, as if level with the snow. It was the Union Jack! We turned suddenly into a passage that was cut out of the mountain of snow and were confronted by a Mountie in front of a large tent. We could see only the entrance; the rest was hidden by piled-up snow. This was the customs house and general quarters—what a dreary place. The police did sentry night and day, and any member of Soapy Smith's gang who tried to get into the Interior was speedily turned back, with a boot after him. At this point, with the rush in full swing, the police confiscated quantities of liquor from those who had no permits from the North West Issuer in Regina.

When this post was first established, at the commencement of the winter, they pitched camp, erected tents, and started heaters. After a few days they found, by the sinking of the heaters, that they had camped over a small lake. The late James Wilson, a sergeant in the police force, told a bunch of sourdoughs years later of the tough time they had in shifting the camp to what they knew was firm land. Americans and others of different nationalities felt safe here, and respected the piece of cloth that flew from the masthead, rejoicing in the thought that at last they were at the boundary that led to law and order and had left the side of lawlessness. Much has been written about the Mounties. Enduring the terrific cold and the blizzards while watching this inlet to the Yukon took men of robust constitution, and all for a mere pittance of two dollars per day. Prior to this time the pay had been only one dollar per day. No one could pass these vigilant men without stopping; those essaying to do so found in themselves in bad grace and were put on a blacklist.

After leaving the White Pass we started on that bleak stretch toward Log Cabin. We were all clothed in fur caps, Mackinaws, and parkas. The icy winds were almost unbearable. Some of the men wanted to give up, being thoroughly fatigued, but a helping hand from the more robust men accomplished wonders; otherwise, these men would have collapsed on this part of the trail.

Those who have travelled this trail know of the drop down into the moraine just before Log Cabin. On a later trip, I found this part of the trail covered. During the night, snow had drifted and the drop looked vertical. We were using horses, since the trail had been well beaten. Our lead driver stopped and waited for help, which came from the next driver, who knew the trail. He said we must be on top of the grade. By this time several had arrived. We attached ropes to the sled, to hold it back as a brake. Suddenly, without warning, the horse, driver, and sled settled down in the snow, and away they went, sailing down the incline and then emerging by the side of the moraine. The passage was open once more, with a beautiful arch over it. The rest of our outfit followed without mishap, gradually being introduced to the hardships yet to come.

It was not long before scores of others arrived at Log Cabin, and glad of it. The stopping house was full, with many having come from Lake Bennett. Those from Skagway felt they had had enough for one day and they decided to stop and camp, feed their dogs and horses, and have a good rest. I gave orders to have the tent erected and told two men to get firewood and spruce boughs. There was a thick growth of spruce trees at Log Cabin. Two others found a suitable spot for camping. The snow was very deep, from ten to twelve feet. However, they used snowshoes to tramp it down and when the snow was firm enough, up went the tent. The cook soon had his stove going. We laid spruce boughs a foot deep, laid out our beds, and all lay down to enjoy a good smoke while the cook prepared a supper of flapjacks and bacon. It was twenty degrees below zero outside, but after having been buffeted about on the trail, we felt that being inside a tent, hearing the sizzling of bacon, and seeing the flapjacks being tossed was a boon. We drew cards to see who was to sleep in the centre of the tent. The high card drew the centre, the next-highest card drew the next warmest spot, and so on. I drew the lowest card and had to sleep against the wall.

It was early morn when the cook called breakfast. He had found it easier to sit by the fire all night than to stretch out, especially since the heat of the stove had thawed the snow so that the stove settled several feet below the beds. We all awoke shivering, still tired from the exertions of the previous day. However, after a fill of coffee and tea, flapjacks and bacon, we felt equal to any emergency. To get our blood warm and circulating, even though the thermometer showed thirty degrees of frost, we planned to pull camp and start for Bennett. Already there was a busy stir and many were on the trail. Once more it was pulling and tugging on an up-and-down trail amongst dwarfed spruce trees until encountering a rocky, rugged bit of country with a magnificent view of Lake Linde-mann and Lake Bennett.

One man in the outfit remarked, "Grand!"

"Damn the 'grand,'" chimed in another, "let's get down out of this damned wind to shelter and warmth."

"Come on boys, the last lap to Bennett!"

With renewed energy, we made Bennett.

CHAPTER FIVE

Finding a Mill Site

In Bennett, it did not take us long to locate the Yukon Hotel, a tent structure with roaring heaters, and to enjoy the hospitality (not forgetting their excellent brand of Hudson Bay rum) of Tom Geiger and Turner, the proprietors.

After we had left the Yukon Hotel, we wended our way across the spit into another little bay to a log cabin. The door opened for us. It was Black Sullivan, an old-timer of the Yukon. "Come on in, boys!" And in we filed. This place looked more like solid comfort and we appreciated it. Sullivan beckoned us to the bar and poured each of us a glass of whiskey—in the same make of glass that we had seen at Dead Horse Camp.

"On the house, boys! Drink hearty!" This concoction was an improvement on that which we had experienced on the White Pass Trail, but could still be further improved. I asked if we could stay the night. "Sure, spread out on the floor. Fire will be going all night."

"Alright, boys, bring in the bedding," I said. "How about grub, Sullivan?"

"If you have a cook, go to it, there's the stove."

It was not long before we found boxes and other seats. On this occasion the cook excelled himself. How good, after a wearisome trip, to relax and feel safe, after having been exposed to the severe weather some of us were not used to. One of the gang, who was rather exuberant, sang out, "Come on, boys, my treat." Black Sullivan was on hand and again, the glasses with the solid bottoms were filled, for fifty cents a drink, with very little even at that. We were now beginning to get into country where the price of things was high. We had another round, and yet another, until all had stood treat. We were then in shape to hit the floor. Blankets were unrolled, and soon ten men were oblivious to the world, enjoying a sleep as only men from the trails could enjoy. Many of the men yelled out in the night, however, with cramps in their legs that been brought on by hauling, pushing, pulling, and breaking trails for several days. They awoke after sleeping the round of the clock. A card game had been going on all night and was about to finish. This was our introduction to Bennett.

I had been given a letter of introduction to Captain Rant, formerly of the Lancers, now the British Columbia agent in Bennett, from Captain Livingstone of the Lancers. Captain Rant was to give me a permit and timber site for the BL&KN company. The day before, I had gone in search of Rant; today I inquired again for the captain and learned that I had not far to go, since this redoubtable person was in our midst. The letter was duly given and, after a little consideration, in his inimitable way, he said, "There is no timber around here. My jurisdiction extends only a few miles down the lake; go down and find a location yourself, and if anyone comes across you and interferes, send them to me. You've got a job on your hands. The idea of building three steamboats up here.—Say, Black, give these men a drink." Away went the men, on my orders, to find a suitable camping ground and make things as comfortable as possible.

I was introduced to Mike King, who had located on the only timber worthwhile. He appeared on the scene and was told what I had come up for. His remark was, "By the lovely Dove! I thought *we* were crazy—now I know there are some more crazy fellows. Fill 'em up, Black, and mind it's the special." The special bottle was brought forth, the best yet produced. King proceeded to tell us all about his winter logging and his getting ready for the 1898 business. "By the lovely Dove! I think she'll be a humdinger. The boys will not whip-saw their lumber for boats if they can get it from me."

Quite a few were stranded here, not having finished their boats in the fall of 1897, before freeze-up. Throughout January of 1898 the cold was intense, but nevertheless, a steady stream of trekkers were coming into Lindemann and Bennett, rapidly taking up every available spot and erecting tents. The NWMP police building was a very crude structure. Already the police had a couple of prisoners, who were kept constantly bucking wood to keep the place warm.

I spent a few days making arrangements for further freight from Skagway. Our tents were erected. In the meantime I, with one other, went to cruise for a timber lease and a mill site in which to manufacture the material for the steamboats.

I believed finding a site would only take a short time. We skirted northwards, along the shores of the lake. Stopping midway, we came across a solitary tent with one occupant. We received a very welcoming reception. He soon had pork and beans, and ptarmigan ready with hot coffee. It was a meal we thoroughly enjoyed after our fourteen-mile tramp with a sled and tent. Our host was tickled to death, he said, to have someone to talk to. We stayed the night and next morning hit across to the west arm of the lake, gradually working around to the Wheaton and Watson Rivers. At Wheaton we found the best site and posted notice of the lease being taken by the BL&KN company. We camped at this place all night, erecting our little six-by-eight tent amidst downfalls, so as to have a good fire in front, and talked of the timber, which was rather small, figuring the amount of plank required. The night soon passed and morning came. Striking camp we crossed the bay to Cariboo Crossing and entered Lake Nares (the strip of water that connected Lake Bennett with Windy Arm and the north Taku arm of Tagish Lake). Along the right-hand shore, in a sheltered spot, we came within sight of a cabin that was occupied by a Mountie and several others who were held up until the ice was safe for travelling.

Questions were plied: "How long was since we had left the city? What was the latest news? Were there many on the trail?" And so on. After they had heard about the thousands who were on the trail, those who had stopped at the cabin decided to start for Bennett and get the balance of their outfits. We decided to leave at once, as it was getting dark, and believed we could make Bennett by midnight—a distance of thirty miles. There was not an hour to waste if we were to build three steamboats in time to catch the first movement of the ice going out, and we knew it would be a Herculean task.

We bid the Mountie and the rest good-bye, and with a last swig out of our flask (leaving just enough of Black Sullivan's special in case of emergency), we started off. We heard a rustling in the trees overhead, but paid it little attention. When we turned at Cariboo Crossing to enter Lake Bennett, the wind was fairly strong and we talked of turning back. However, deciding time was too precious, we pushed on, thinking we should try to make the island.

At last, a mighty wind that had blown all snow from the ice overtook us. There was no choice but to make for the trees for shelter. Time after time we tried to mount the barricade of drifted snow, and finally were rewarded for our efforts. Hauling our sled up was the difficult part, but when this was done we erected our tent; luckily, there was a lot of fallen timber for firewood. About midnight we became very hungry, but the only thing to eat was one ship's biscuit, and to drink, about two tablespoons of whiskey. There were only two of us; one slept while the other kept the fire going, and the night passed. In the morning we went to the edge of the woods and found the wind blowing harder than ever. The lake was a sheet of beautiful green ice, with not a vestige of snow. Night came again. The biscuit and whiskey were now divided, and we both hoped the blow would soon be over. The next morning broke fine and calm. After packing up, we were soon on the lake.

The ice was like glass, and the going hard and cold. As we were half-famished, our progress was slow, but at last we spied a spiral of smoke across the lake and made for it. This party here had made camp just before the blow in a sheltered spot. The dogs barked; the tents opened: "Come in! God! You fellows are travelling early. Just in time for breakfast. Help yourself. I'll make some more flapjacks." We drank down hot coffee and then answered the questions that were put to us: "Are you from Dawson?"

"No, we are from Lake Nares—just been on a cruise from Bennett, staking a timber claim."

After giving the man all our information we proceeded on our way. We made good time, considering we had been held up for two days. We met scores of people who were packing part of their outfits by dog team to the next cache. It was unbelievable to see, in a short space of time, the steady stream of dog teams making their way down the lake. Finally, getting to Bennett, we saw a multitude coming from Lindemann and from the Skagway Trail, pouring into the rendezvous of Bennett, the start of the waters for Dawson. Good samaritans looked after those who were sick or had frozen hands and feet. Some women who were travelling with their husbands had their hands full, ministering to the unfortunates. Men related the sufferings that had been caused by mishaps and cursed the day they had started out on their quest for gold.

~

By about the middle of January we had cleared the site of the mill and shipyards of the BL&KN company at the mouth of the Wheaton River. No one believed it was possible to have the boats running in time for that year's traffic. Even the men hired to work on the project rebelled at having to expose themselves to the rigorous weather. I threatened them, saying, "No work, no pay."

I coaxed and appealed to their sense of honour, to which some responded. Others said, "Hell, we all know it's impossible."

"Boys, be reasonable," I said. "Try it for a month. Get down to business. Your wages will be raised. You have plenty of tobacco and grub and the company will see that every week you get rum rations. Hands up those who are willing." All hands went up—what magic there is in the word "rum."

Thus, the work started. Cabins were built, logging commenced, lumber was manufactured, stacked, and dried. Because we lacked coal for blacksmith work, we made charcoal. Things began to hum in this lonely spot away from the beaten track. Getting the boilers and machinery over the mountains to this spot had been no easy task. It was incessant toil, and only those who have similarly handled cumbersome material in the same way know to what we resorted to overcome some of the obstacles.

Money! It flowed like water. The work meant that three men had to go over the trail to Skagway and back, night and day, unceasingly, to round up and check on the freight. Along the way they would find caches after a snowstorm, combat blizzards, help unfortunates unversed in the art of trailing. Owing to the continuous procession, nighttime was best for backtracking and getting to Skagway; it caused less commotion, swearing, and cursing than travelling in the daytime. Large pack trains were now on the job—Bartlett Bros., Hinckley & O'Brien, Pells & Feers, Joe Brooks, and many other smaller outfits—packing night and day.

Sometimes a mule or horse would drop, never to rise again. Methinks I see them now, taking a last, appealing look, knowing the end has come. The merciful blow or shot was given, the carcass was pulled to one side, a spare mule was brought on and loaded, and it was "away again." This was a frequent occurrence. What did it matter? Mules and horses arrived every day from Oregon. The wild cayuse was rounded up, by the thousand, for the job. One trip over the pass to Bennett tamed the wildest of them. With a few hundred pounds tied onto its back (with the famous diamond hitch), the animal was (if not physically), in heart, broken. The jostle and motion of the rough trail made the animals grunt and squeal. Somewhere along the old trail is a bronze tablet erected as a reminder of the horses and mules that perished as a result of the punishing burdens they carried to enable the argonauts to get to Bennett. The men who drove the pack trains were as hard as nails, and only men of extraordinary physique and constitution could stand the peril of blizzard and cold to get their different caches.

It is now nearly forty years since the stampede. Often in quiet hours I look back on the scene and see the long procession of horses and burros grunting and groaning whilst trying to make a difficult crossing—men and women doing the same. I can see still—men on a cold morning, having made a particularly hard climb, doing their own packing, raising their fur caps to cool their heads, the perspiration striking the cold air and looking like steam coming from a locomotive stack. Strong men were in the procession, relaying their outfits without dogs, pulling and straining at their sleds with a rope over their shoulders and a gee pole to steer, cursing and swearing. It was indeed a gruelling task. "Hi! There! Step out if you can't get a move on," and other lurid and unmentionable language was heard. The weary individual, rather than reply with words, would step out for a good long rest, and wait for an opportunity to find space to enter the mad scramble.

CHAPTER SIX

Tales of Lindemann

Bennett is connected to Lindemann by a few miles of river, with rapids at the halfway point. In January, Lake Lindemann was already a busy place, with tents everywhere along its shore.

Trees were being felled, and saw pits were being created to cut the logs into planks for the building of boats. They were called pits, but were really platforms made of four uprights, with well-braced sills placed longitudinally on two sides and crosspieces on the sills. The log that was to be cut was made stationary by bracing, sometimes with a "dog"—a piece of iron whose ends had been sharpened and bent to right angles, one end driven into the log and the other into the sill.

Sawing the logs was a task that required one man on top and one below. The twang and zip of the saw made music when handled by experienced hands. Alas for those not used to the saws, especially greenhorns. They had some trying times in getting the saws to start. Perspiring, one man would blame the fellow on top; the top man would blame the one below. Then they would change places, which did not mend matters. It was difficult to keep the saw in line with the chalk markings. Some planks would vary in thickness from one quarter of an inch to one and a half inches, rendering them useless for the building and planking of boats. Finally, the greenhorns would give up in despair and run to Bennett to buy planking from the Lovely Dove, Mike King's sawmill.

Several people at Lindemann had left Victoria in the spring and summer of 1897, and had many tales to tell about why they were not in Dawson with the others. I listened to one fellow's stories: "Call it damn luck. We were on the Skagway trail when Grant took sick and died. We had to look after him and send his body out. Jack here was laid up with spinal meningitis. He had to be nursed. Another party travelling along broke his leg on the damned glacial rocks. Bruce took pneumonia and here we are, alive and kicking, waiting for the ice to go out.

"We have our boats and believe it's better to wait than to pull our hearts out like a lot of the others, losing our packhorses and burros in a damned muskeg and then having to buy more. These didn't last us to Bennett. We crossed a muskeg in one place on the top of dead animals. When once down it took all our time to save the freight and often got bogged ourselves. That was the finish of the animal; a hit on the head or a slug from a gun and it was all over. Eventually we crossed on a bridge of dead animals. The stench on the trail was unbearable—some took fever and died. Gad! It was tough.

"Still, we're going to Dawson. We've been working here all the winter, making good money. Some are fine fellows with plenty of money, but without the faintest idea of doing anything. They couldn't build a boat or build anything. That outfit over there is from Chicago; they paid one dollar and fifty cents per pound to get their outfit over the Chilcoot to here. They are good sports and seem to be out for the fun there is in it. Anyway, we are getting a good slice of their pocket money. Perhaps this will be as good a gold mine as we'll strike in the Klondyke.

"Across the way is a poor fellow suffering from meningitis. A woman from the next camp is nursing him. I believe she'll pull him through. Up the shore a bit is a fellow suffering from scurvy. We clubbed together and sent for fresh meat and vegetables for him. He's in pretty bad shape from letting himself get run down; his only rations were pork and beans. Damn the pork and beans! My guts rebel at the sight of them. Take the oatmeal, for instance. Most of it on hand here is mildewed and we feed it to the dogs, boiled up with tallow. They thrive on it. Most of the bacon is green and bad. No wonder so many of the boys got sick on the trail. If we ever get out, the firm that outfitted us will wish they were in Timbuktu. Fancy packing that rotten stuff from cache to cache until it became a part of us, then to find it not fit for human consumption. Anyway, we had to have dog feed.

"Say, some of the women here are trumps. God bless them! They bring us something tasty once in awhile. Sometimes we go off for a day and bring home spruce grouse, ptarmigan, and sometimes a moose—hey, boys! Did the women enjoy it?—On these days we have a regular beano. We pay the woman up yonder to cook us some hot buns. We hope she won't go, but her husband, now that the ice is firm, is thinking of pulling down to White Horse before the breakup. Here's hoping she'll stop, as many a poor bloke will die if that woman pulls out. Here's wishing them luck. The man is a go-getter . . . Say! Got a flask on your hip?"

Luckily I had one, and produced it. It was appreciated, and left behind for a poor fellow who was suffering from a chill, across the way. It was an understood thing amongst most of the men on the trail to never touch "the bottle" in below-zero weather or to pack it on the trail, as it had been many a man's undoing. These men, soft when they started from Victoria, were now as hard as nails.

"Yes, Macauley got to White Horse. He's got a snap. Made a stopping place there and is building a tram to take merchandise below White Horse, so as to miss Miles Canyon and the Squaw Rapids. He has a bonanza with that and his saloon. I made a trip down to see him after the freeze-up, but felt I had to come back and look after the patients. Well, here's hoping the worst is over."

Bidding the boys "So long," I was eager to catch up with a party that had come from Dawson with his dogs. He was loaded down with *mazuma*, as he called it. He hoped that Soapy would not get wind that he had gold with him, but he and his boys said they were ready to meet Soapy and his murdering cutthroats if they did attempt anything. He told me that one poor devil had been held up a few days before, his dust taken away, and that the people in Skagway and Dyea were so incensed by Soapy that they were thinking of forming a vigilante society to protect the miners coming out and to wipe out the lawless element—a huge task indeed.

This trip was made with a team of good dogs and they knew their work. Compared with the White Pass Trail, the Chilcoot Trail was better and shorter, although still bad enough until one got past the canyon.

It seemed no time passed before we reached the summit, where the good old Union Jack flew and the Mounties guarded the pass. We halted and had a good chat with them. After unhitching the dogs we got to the bottom of the Scales, as the Chilcoot base was called, and watched the busy scene. Here again we saw a never-ending procession—old men, middle-aged men, young men, and once in a while a woman; some were loaded heavily, some lightly, puffing and blowing, veins bulging from their heads. Some of the loads looked like they were liable to break the backs that were bent under them. The resting places that had been cut into the snow by the side of the ascent were so steep one could stand upright and rest his load in them.

CHAPTER SEVEN

Sunday in Skagway

The Chilcoot Trail was the one that had been taken by the early pioneers (Bob Henderson, Bill McGee, George Carmack, and a host of others) in order to get to the interior long before the great rush started. We left this scene of bustle and hardship and proceeded south, to Sheep Creek, Canyon City, and finally, Dyea. A gasoline boat plied its way between Dyea and Skagway. This we took, and arrived at Skagway in the course of an hour. What a change had taken place! Tents everywhere, the town growing every day in size and population; Soapy holding sway; dance halls patronized more than ever; gambling joints at their climax; cut-throats in evidence; pea and shell game men—at this time under cover, as it was still raw and cold—the customers were many.

A young fellow sat in one game, deluded into believing he could play poker. In came a man—tall, lithe, and magnetic. "Drop the game, Phil," he said to the young fellow, "I'm waiting!" The gang playing cards went for their guns, but before their hands had moved very far they were covered by two 45's. "Drop your guns, damn you, or look out!" Silence pervaded the room. Soapy was there, but was told to keep quiet. "Remember what happened at Leadville and don't try anything tough. Come on, Phil." And Phil went, covered by his partner, backing out of the den of iniquity.

"Alright, boys, we'll attend to him later," said Soapy.

That was a mere incident in this hell of infamy. Lives counted for nothing when big money was at stake, but respectable, serious-minded citizens were quietly organizing in order to curtail the powers of the gang and destroy its leader's influence. Soapy was a vain gunslinger and murderer. He had attained his position by ruthlessness and held his followers in place by fear. Many were the men who had lost their lives when they dared to question the squareness of the games.

The love of excitement seems to lie dormant in many people, and when an opportunity opens up for lawlessness, the old daring, the primitive urge, arises to the surface in full swing. And no one, not even the marshal in Skagway, dares stop it. Men let go of themselves with an abandon not known in well-regulated cities. It is easy to play and drink, to fall in line with an element where danger lurks. "All men think men mortal but themselves" until their lives are gone like the snuffing of a candle. Many went this way.

Still on the seekers after wealth came, and in the offing could be seen vessels coming and going, their human freight wondering whether there would be any ground left to stake, to work, to dig, or to delve into, for that which all were bent on getting. Miners coming out would hearten those going in by saying, "Hell, boys, the ground isn't scratched yet. There are thousands of miles in the Yukon that are anyone's to prospect."

"Listen, Bill!" someone said to me, "It must be Sunday. They are singing." I had been wondering what day of the week it was. We didn't know Monday from Wednesday or Saturday—no track was kept of time. Men loaded their sleighs, dogs barked, and outfits marched toward the trail. It mattered not whether it was the Sabbath or any other day. Every day it was business as usual. "Hold the Fort," was sung lustily in a large tent. We went in to rest awhile after our journey, and the Reverend Sinclair passed us a book of hymns. I looked toward the platform—lo and behold, our old friend, the professor of the steamboat, was just beginning an oration.

"My hearers. It is indeed a pleasure to be amongst you this afternoon by the kind invitation of the reverend gentleman. I am indeed glad to see so many of you have found time to rest awhile from your arduous labours. This relaxation will do you good. You will, I know, when you are once again on the trail, meet difficulties and trials you little dream of now. You are on the threshold of a wonderful country—Alaska and the Yukon—as large as the States. The country you are about to traverse has been laying dormant for ages. Yes, eons. The mind cannot comprehend the length of time this vast territory was a long, vast field of ice. Along your path you will see the wonders and beauties of nature—the grand mountains, the paths of enormous glaciers that formed the great ravines and gorges, grinding down mountains, pulverizing rocks by a constant drip, drip, drip as the climate became warmer; the glaciers gradually became streams, then creeks, then rivers; the glaciers' enormous weight ground off everything thoroughly, polishing by its water actions, the smooth, massive rocks you will meet on the White Pass Trail. In the Klondyke region the glacier ground rocks into small fragments—gravel and sand. The heavy metals contained therein sank to the bottom and settled on bedrock. Glaciers are still in this vicinity, moving slowly and imperceptibly toward the point of least resistance. We see it at Taku Inlet and Cook's Inlet, where great icebergs drop into the sea. You, my friends, will be digging and delving into creekbeds and rivers, hunting for the precious metal. You will come across old channels at different depths, across strata of rock and slate and other formations that will show you that at one time this was a tropical climate. You will find prints of tropical vegetation in the rocks and probably the impress of animals found as a rule in warm climates.

"My friends, you will find it no easy task to get to your goal. You will see wonderful sights in this wonderful land. My advice to you all is to always follow the example of pioneers you may be lucky enough to fall in with on the trail. They dearly paid for their experience. The trail is beset with many dangers, on land as well as on the water. Don't be afraid to ask of others more experienced than yourselves as you journey along, and don't forget to admire Nature's works. Dwell on the wonders surrounding you and be in tune with the poet who exclaimed, "Sermons in stones, books in the running brooks, and good in everything." When the blizzards rage on the mountaintops and wipe everything from your view, don't lose your head. Always keep the direction of the wind in mind, and if possible, throw up some kind of shelter, until the clouds and darkness that hide the wide and unbounded prospect from your view dissipate. You will be disheartened. You will feel like turning back. Unexpectedly the skies will clear. The grand beauty is all around you, and you will realize that a great intellect orders these things in perfect harmony."

The professor continued, and time passed with wonderful rapidity. Many took fresh heart at the thought of going forward, even as the ordeals yet to come went through their minds. We were thoroughly rested ere the professor had finished his talk and departed, none the worse after hearing the discourse. I silently wished that unobtrusive, unassuming man, who was trying to hearten weary voyagers, good luck and good-bye, believing him to be doing far greater work than many who advertised their calling and commercialized their profession.

The Reverend Sinclair was bent on erecting a church and someone suggested that he ask Soapy for a contribution. Soapy was appealed to; he was elated to think that even the church knew he was a powerful figure, such was his vanity. He produced one hundred dollars as a subscription. But before the reverend gentleman had reached the street, the one hundred dollars disappeared. When Soapy heard of this he was mad, and gave the party who filched it a certain amount of time to restore it to the Rev. Sinclair. In due time the contribution was returned. Soapy, it was said, was liberal with the Salvation Army, and when the evangelists arrived he would often throw a five dollar bill on the drum at their meeting on the street.

CHAPTER EIGHT

In Pursuit of Gentleman Harry

I had enjoyed my bit of rest at the service, but there was no time to renew my acquaintance with the professor. Business had to be transacted and the trail taken again. I accidentally overheard the following conversation. "You damn fool, why did you let her get out of your sight? I tell you, she's worth a fortune if we can get her with us. I have sent Gentleman Harry to catch up with her on the Dyea Trail. If anyone can persuade her, it will be him, but the Lord help him if he runs afoul of the two dogs Alaska and Yukon." I waited no longer to hear more from these dregs of humanity. I knew well what the conversation meant and who Gentleman Harry would overtake. I hit the trail back to Dyea immediately, hoping to be in time to stop any undue influence on the young lady or to prevent her from being ensnared in immorality and vice.

I hurried along the Dyea Trail, to protect the young lady whom Gentleman Harry was seeking. I had taken the boat to Dyea, travelling light, with my snowshoes slung over my back. It had been snowing and would likely continue. From Dyea I pushed on to Canyon City, and from there, to Sheep Camp and then on to the Scales of Chilcoot. The imminent storm had halted traffic. Up the Scales I went. As I arrived at the summit the police sentinel challenge rang out, "Who goes there?"

"Friend," I called back.

"This way. Oh, it's you. You're making a quick return."

"Yes, I've got to overtake a person who's had a good start."

"You can't go on in this storm that's brewing. Inspector Lindsay would like you to stop."

"Thanks, but I must push on."

"Be careful or you'll meet the same fate as Williams, who was taking out the news to Juneau of a gold strike on the Fortymile. Better stay the night."

"Thanks, but I'm after the safety of a young woman."

"Oh! Oh! Miss Smith? Bless my soul! You're the second one who's looking out for the safety of that young woman. I'm afraid the storm will overtake her unless she is trail-wise and makes shelter in time."

"Do you know the party inquiring about her before me?"

"No."

"He's one of Soapy's gang, by the name of Gentleman Harry."

"By Gad! I would go along but we are short-handed. To think I gave him a pass! He said he had a letter to deliver to her."

"Well, here's off before the storm gets too bad," I said, shuffling into my snowshoes.

I was off, with a shout from the policeman: "Good luck!" No sooner had I got into my stride however, than—from nowhere it seemed—came a terrific wind, engulfing me. The storm had burst. It became bitterly cold and I considered retracing my steps. I essayed to do so, but reflected that going forward would bring me to a camp; I decided press on.

The storm increased. It seemed as if a million voices were shrieking and laughing at my predicament. The snow became deeper and the going more difficult. I kept plodding on, afraid of making any false steps. Knowing the wind, icy and penetrating, was from the north—my only guide—I kept on, not daring to stop. It was hard to see ahead and after some time I became weary and tired. Coming to a hummock of snow I took what shelter it offered for a rest, which chilled me through. "My God!" I exclaimed, "I'm in a pickle. Well, here goes. If I stay here I'll be covered shortly."

Thoughts fearful and ominous flashed through my mind. I had heard of snowstorms but never dreamed of one like this. I shouted, thinking I might be near a camp. I might as well have held my breath; my shouting was in vain. Every step was torture as I plodded along. An hour passed. It was impossible to give up. There was nothing to do but push ahead. "I'm too young and virile to be snuffed out. God!" I breathed a prayer.

"I never thought I'd be in this plight." It carried me back to the years when I was a child, at my mother's knees. My life flitted before me. I tried to balance the good I had done against the bad. Yet I was no coward and trudged on, ever hopeful, the thought of the young lady—who I now knew as Miss Smith—giving me fresh impetus. I trusted she was out of danger and in good shelter.

Leg-weary, owing to the deepening snow that drifted like ocean waves, and asking myself how much longer I could endure, I kept plunging on. All landmarks were obliterated. Not letting despairing thoughts take possession of me, I held my course and desperately shook off the weary and sleepy feelings by trying to think of the pleasant things in life, but the unpleasant things kept recurring, keeping my mind alert. Fearful at every step of plunging into some crevice, I promised myself that if I emerged from this I would be more weather-wise in the future. It was hard to believe that I would come through, yet how much longer could I stay with it? The icy wind cut like a knife. Oh, for a cup of coffee and a cosy fire. "I must reach some place soon. I can't allow myself to despair." I shook off a kind of stupor that was coming on. In spite of my courage, I was tempted to dig in and get out of the cutting blasts that I thought I could no longer endure, but digging in might bring my last sleep. The sound of dogs barking close at hand aroused me, and with a few more steps I stumbled on a mound of snow. Underneath it, dogs snarled and a feminine voice strove to quiet them.

"Who's there?" came a voice, which I knew was that of the young lady. "Be quiet, Yukon! Down, Alaska!"

"Thank God!" I said, "I'm your steamboat table partner and nearly all in."

"Speak louder!" she said. I had to shout. Miss Smith untied the flaps of the tent and with great difficulty the snow was shoveled away. The dogs were ready for any emergency, but at a command from their mistress they quieted.

I slid inside and sank prostrate on the floor. "Your face is frozen, let me rub it out," she said. And forthwith, she thawed out the frozen parts by rubbing snow over them. The dogs knew me at once. She quickly prepared a cup of coffee over her little spirit stove. Never had anything tasted so good. Miss Smith stood wondering what had brought me to her tent. As warmth crept into my system I started to explain my mission, but first I upbraided the young lady for taking the trip on her own. She said, "Oh, I'm perfectly capable and take no chances. Not far from here is a camp; before the worst of the storm they came to see if I was alright."

"I'm jolly glad to hear that," I said, and told her of the gang's plan, which was to have her join their ranks for a cleanup in the dance halls at Dawson, after the boom had quieted down at Skagway. "You know the man who caused such a disturbance by insulting you on the boat and thrusting his company on you at every opportunity? He's bent on kidnapping you."

"What an idea! What do they take me for?" was her response.

"I happened to overhear his plan and hence this trip."

After my exposure to the fierce storm I felt drowsy. I asked if I might have a sleep. "Be sure and call me if you hear anything, or if the dogs make any sign," I said. Making myself as comfortable as I could, I passed into a well-earned sleep.

Morning broke and with it, clear skies. I awoke and the growling and barking of the dogs resumed. Looking out of the tent, I saw approaching a man whom I recognized as Gentleman Harry. I stood in front of the tent, and was accosted by, "Oh, it's her on a proposition."

"What you have to say, you can say here to me."

"So that's it. I guess you have had a pleasant time through the storm."

"Cut out your insinuations and vamoose!"

"I'm seeing the young lady."

"I say you're not."

"Oh! Oh! My bold ladies' hero!"

Miss Smith was having a hard time holding the dogs in check; they knew that danger lurked and wanted to be outside. Gentleman Harry's hand slowly went to his buttoned coat. He had unbuttoned his mackinaw by the time I realized what his intention was. I flashed my gun on him and said, "No you don't!" With my gun in Harry's ribs, I removed the other man's gun from his shouldered holster and threw it away in the deep snow. "Now, will you vamoose before I set the dogs on you?"

Gentleman Harry was in a dilemma; it was not often that he was the one to have the worst of it. He had at first planned a grand coup. The dogs—what mattered they? He would shoot them and take the young lady. But then he wondered how could he get through the Chilcoot Pass sentry if the young lady proved to be obstinate? He would rather not kill the dogs. He planned instead to tell her a story about an urgent message that was waiting for her Skagway; his manner and bearing would dispel her doubts. He saw himself victorious with the gang once more, his pride intact. He asked himself now what the gang would say when they learned of his unsuccessful experience and how this damn Bill had put it over him.

He said, "Well, I'll be seeing you. Watch your step in Dyea or Skagway."

"Hi, there, you don't go that way." I had slipped on my snowshoes, made Harry halt in his tracks and pointed him in the direction of the Chilcoot. "If you can pass Lindsay of the police, okay—we don't wish any scum on this side of the line. I shall be watching you and may follow. Now, right about, and get, before I turn the dogs loose. If I do, the Lord help you. If you had your desserts, you should be down beneath the snow, like many others will be—your victims—dead to the world, for keeps."

"I'll have you for this!" said Harry.

"Get, or I'll have you—and keep heading west," I replied. I watched Harry until he was out of sight, then turned back toward the tent, finding the woman white and saddened. She had heard all that had taken place and realized that had it not been for my presence something tragic might have happened.

Trying to cheer her up, I said, "Forget it, sister, I've admired your grit and fearlessness. I see by your ring you are evidently going in to meet your husband. Here's hoping you will get there." Miss Smith looked at her hand, but passed no remark. She got me a cup of steaming hot tea and we proceeded to take the tent down. Shovelling off the snow was a fairly easy task, followed by packing, loading, and hitching the two dogs to the sled. When everything was ready I told Miss Smith to jump aboard. She objected to my upsetting my plans for her, but I tucked her in on top of the tent and headed the dogs. After a few miles, we were out of the track of the last night's storm and on to a good trail. I took the handles and away we went, to Lindemann, where I introduced Miss Smith to another woman, asking the woman to help make her comfortable. I left quietly as the two women talked.

CHAPTER NINE

Back to Bennett

In Skagway, my partner went to work, boosting the freight that was to be packed from cache to cache. Some of the freight had been lost and had to be traced, which entailed endless and wearisome going to and fro. Some of it had slid into the Skagway River. A great deal had to be ordered from Vancouver or Victoria. Hurried trips were made to Juneau to replace articles known to be damaged beyond repair. Sometimes a heavy snowfall would obliterate caches. Many valuable hours were lost finding and uncovering freight.

Many of the adventurers had weary expressions on their faces. Those who had started out full of hope and vim looked worn, thin, and depressed. Some, nothing seemed to disturb. One man was heard to say, "I'm going to Skagway and sleep for a week." How sweet was sleep to the trail-worn man and woman, the lack of which was the cause of so much sickness. Some would not exert themselves to cook proper food before retiring or to bed down properly. Often they would jump into their sleeping bags with their tent under them, too weary to set it up, too far away from a stopping place, too exhausted to walk farther. Chill through sleeping in damp sleeping bags was generally the start of meningitis.

The sun at the end of January, higher in the heavens, made the valleys warm and pleasant. People would shed heavy clothes as they pulled and tugged at their sleighs. Once they got to the higher altitudes, where the cold wind struck, they would keep plodding, believing they could make their cache before it was necessary to clad themselves warmer. This was another cause of sickness, often pneumonia. The warmer clothes were generally left at the last cache. Oh, that last stretch when suddenly exposed to the cold, chilly blasts before getting to the Mounties' quarters. It was a trying ordeal.

People seemed to quarrel during the my whole trip back to Bennett. Some days, everyone wanted to help each other, and you would meet some of the finest fellows in the world; other days, you would meet the most cantankerous.

At one point, an old fellow with a team of dogs got tangled up and his sled overturned on the narrow trail. Consequently, traffic was held up as the old gentleman tried to rebuild his load. A tall Missourian with a pack train could not pass without detouring into very deep snow. He swore and raved, calling the old gentleman an old fossil, wanting to know what he was doing on the trail, saying men his age should be thinking about turning up their toes—generally using unprintable language. He thought he was impressing those around him by acting the tough. The old gentleman went on quietly building his load, tying his dogs to the sleigh and starting to take off his coat. The Missourian called him a son of a bitch. The old fellow stepped into the middle of the trail and said, "I've met your kind before. Now we'll see what you mean. I don't allow anyone to call me what you said. Let's see if you are as good as you say. Show the gents in your train." The tall fellow made a lunge at the old man, who was as agile as a kitten, not there to be grabbed. He tripped the fellow nicely and sent him sprawling headlong into the snow, amidst the cheers of the trailers. Bellowing with rage, the Missourian got up with his arms outspread, about to close in on the old chap. Adroitly side-stepping Mr. Missourian, the old chap landed a fierce blow on him—surprising, from one so slim and so old-looking—and down went the Missourian again. The old gent now carried the fight to close quarters, punishing the man until he cried "enough," much to the chagrin and derision of his partners and to the delight of those on the trail. Skirmishes like this occurred frequently and we got accustomed to them.

"Clear the trail!" was heard as we proceeded, "Man dying!" We all edged as near as possible to the outside to let them pass. Sometimes it would be a broken leg, more often a run-down constitution.

Bennett again, and what a crowd. As I walked through lines of merchandise I came across a keel being laid for the *Willie Irving*, the steamboat that Captain John Irving was building, and two other small steamboats. The sound of hammer and saw was incessant. Men boasted of their dog teams. Bets were made over which team could haul the biggest load in the quickest time over a given route, and if one man's six-dog team could out-pull another man's. Sleds would be loaded down with flour sacks and piled on, until the best team won, the winner making a fifty-dollar bill. They even bet on dogfights.

At this time a regular procession was going down Lake Bennett. One could scarcely tell how many people were in Bennett or how many had passed down the lake. Here was a steam tractor being put together; another was already travelling down the lake. These unwieldy things had been knocked down and brought in over the trails. Close by, large scows and boats of all descriptions were being built, from those that were shaped like coffins, to well-designed craft.

Still on the crowd came, full of excitement, eager to get to the gold-fields. The shores of the mouth of the Lindemann River were lined with tents and warehouses that belonged to the BL&KN company. The hotels Yukon and Victoria, and Black Sullivan's, did a lucrative business in meals, drinks, and tobacco, while the ever-present game of poker went on. Police and their dog teams rounded up transgressors of the law. Considering the cosmopolitan population of Bennett and on the trails, which increased every day, it was indeed surprising that so few were incarcerated for misdeeds. Those who were held by the police, were kept busy bucking wood to keep the fires burning.

The argonauts made numerous complaints as they settled down, waiting for the ice to go out. In checking the invoices for their provisions and in carefully examining their packages, they had found, in many cases, that the bacon was rotten and that other foodstuffs were green and rancid. It was fortunate indeed that the merchants who had outfitted these boys were not present. After the trailers put their life's blood into packing this stuff over the passes, several of them had to go back to Skagway or Dyea to replace their rotting stores, enduring once again the agony and misery of the trail. Years later, several provisions firms received tongue-lashings—and even thrashings—for their dishonesty in shipping food that was unfit for anyone but dogs. I can still hear the horrible, murderous talk of these firms' victims. Some had no money with which to buy fresh provisions and had to work to get a fresh supply.

CHAPTER TEN

The Chilcoot Snow Slide

On April 3, 1898, unconscious of impending disaster, men and women relayed their outfits as usual from place to place. Every day a constant stream left Dyea, with ox teams, horses, and even goats. The trailers trudged along, keeping up their spirits with jocular remarks. Some passed slower ones, giving advice or crowing over some of the unlucky ones. A good trail had been made. No one foresaw, or dreamed, that tomorrow's sunbeams would shine on their shrouds. Yet many had wondered, as they passed the Irene Glacier, "What if the overhanging mass were to break off? Our trail would certainly be spoiled." Once in a while chunks of ice did break off, the echoes reverberating for miles. Still, on came the trailers, in single file. The Indians and the pioneers had given Sheep Camp, past Canyon City, a bad reputation, telling those who travelled through this wide-open space that it was dangerous, that snow slides had occurred in the vicinity. Often, just a shot fired at a mountain goat would loosen vast, overhanging mountains of snow.

Sheep Camp was occupied on this day by a number of greenhorns. For a few days, it had been snowing and storming on the summit, but they were oblivious to any actual menace—it looked so far away. Unaccustomed to mountainous regions, they rejoiced in the fact that one more relay would see them at the summit, with the hardest part of the journey over. Nearly everyone exclaimed, "Thank God." With the feat accomplished, they looked down and wished the toiling multitude behind them good luck, sympathizing with their straining efforts.

The storm did not deter the hardier ones from packing from the bottom to the top of the last climb, even though it was difficult to see ahead. In January, enterprising individuals had driven stakes into the deep snow from the bottom to the top, at intervals. To these stakes a rope was fastened as a guide. Steps had been cut into the snow. The rope and the steps helped everyone gain the summit, where hundreds of caches were piled.

A constant stream of sleds was coming and going. Suddenly, there was a mighty roar. Down came an avalanche of snow from the mountaintop, engulfing about one hundred people who were in its line of movement. It was a horrible experience. A survivor who narrowly escaped death in the snow slide described the experience this way.

"Along with a group of others we were trudging along. It was blizzarding and at times it was hard to see even those a few feet ahead. The stinging particles of snow, like fine sand, affected our eyes and cheeks, as if fired from a shotgun. Still, on we trudged, bending and turning our heads away from the cruel blasts of the north wind that penetrated to the very marrow. I thought, 'What a fool I am to go through all this.' I asked myself, 'What am I doing this for when I could be comfortably working on the job I left in a southern city?'

"I heard a sudden ominous sound, as of a hissing fiend. With the sound came a fast-flowing river of fine, frozen snow that made it difficult to raise our feet. The snow came up to my knees. I tried to get on top of this rising flood of snow, but could find nothing firm to hold me up. Just ahead of me was a man who had fallen; I fell on top of him. All this happened in the twinkling of an eye. Frantically I got on top of the now-lifeless form—how fine it was to feel some support underfoot. Yet the river of snow kept rising, and I felt myself caught in the rising flood of snow.

"Feverishly I tried to extricate myself. A pole swept toward me. I clung to it, and with great exertion, managed to raise myself up from the engulfing mass. Perspiration oozed from me. I raised myself erect and stood on the pole, which was fast becoming submerged. It was only a matter of a split second before the avalanche was up to my waist again. 'Great God! Was I to be swallowed up at last?' The body of another man was swept up to me, also lifeless, it seemed, and was stopped by my position. Another frantic struggle, and I was on top of him, glorying in maniacal glee that I had once more a firm base to rest my feet on.

"I was beginning to tire and wondered when this rising river of snow would stop. It overwhelmed me again; I was in the grip once more of the sandlike snow that was packed hard and tight all around me. Would this ever-rolling snow ever cease? I was about to give up in despair—in fact I did—resigning myself in helplessness to the orgies of this monster. Only my breast was above the snow. At last I realized that the hissing, rolling movement had ceased. Knowing that underneath me lay a few whose bodies had provided me with firm footing, I worked a hole around myself by swaying my body in a circle. Thus extricated and able to move my limbs, my sanity was restored.

"All was quiet. I thought of those underneath, and clawed away the snow beneath me, thinking that perhaps life had not wholly departed from them—ah, here was the one I had stepped on. Raising his head, I found him still breathing. Then an army of help arrived and began to uncover a few others who were also near extinction. Their shovels worked with lightning speed. Some who were dug out were lifeless. These were laid out side by side—a gruesome sight. I sought my tent, which luckily was not touched, lay down exhausted, and slept—goodness knows for how long."

When word of the snow slide reached Dyea, Skagway, Bennett, and Lindemann, many volunteers rushed to the rescue, hoping their partners on the trail were safe. Miss Smith, with her dogs Alaska and Yukon, rushed to the scene to be of service. The trail was good and it did not take long to get there. It was exhilarating, with a good team of dogs, to race to keep out of the way of teams that followed. The dogs reveled, as the men did, in travelling when the trails were good, as they were on this day, when they were hurrying to the scene of the disaster.

At least 70 people died in the Chilcoot slide. One of the men, working strenuously to extricate both the living and the dead, finally said to his partner, "Come on, pal, we can do no more here." They had been trying to rescue a chance acquaintance.

His partner replied, "Perhaps it's best. He was a good scout. Fancy not knowing his name." The enormous exertion had made this strong man weak and nerveless. "We'll get to the tent or we'll be next. It's no good staying here." Off they went, in sadness, scarcely believing that some-one they had met, who so full of life just a short while before on the trail, was now numbered with the dead, leaving no name and no clue to his identity.

It will never be known exactly how many died on the Alaskan side or the Canadian side. Mothers watched year after year for sons, sisters for brothers, wives for husbands—for those who had been swallowed up by the elements of snow, wind, and water. Familiar faces—their names to many of us unknown—were blotted out of existence in an instant, finding their last resting place on the road and river to Dawson.

It was a long time before any identification at all of the unfortunate victims could be made. On the Alaska side of the summit, a guard was placed over the bodies until they could be looked after officially. Two men had been seen rifling through the bodies in the dark. Shots were fired by the guards. The men ran, and no doubt kept on running. Many thought the men were part of Soapy's gang, which comprised some of the lowest scoundrels on earth. Quite a few of the bodies were sent south for burial; others were given burial at Dyea, their resting place a monument to the hazards that are met in the quest for gold. Women—the angels of mercy—were on hand to administer relief to the suffering. Women were generally on the spot in times of distress and illness— especially during a catastrophe like this—even though the number of women was few and far between. A gloom hung over this place for a long time. Many turned their backs on the trail and departed for home and safety. Some who had narrowly escaped burial alive required a few days in which to recuperate.

After the snow slide, the weary procession continued. Constantly passing over the trails I noticed again the absence of fear or danger. The days got longer, the trails rottener. There was a scramble to get to Bennett before the trails became impassable.

An old Cariboo miner had this to say. "Hell, boys, it's tough, the poor fellows wiped out by the snow slide. It's the same every strike I've been in. If the old Fraser could speak, what a tale it would be! In sixty-two, sixty-three, sixty-four, talk about suffering. People perished by the wayside, going in and coming out. Cameron and Stevenson—the lucky devils—struck it good. Barker and others were in good ground.

"I remember 'old what's his name' sinking a shaft. One day they struck yellow strata that was all gold. Two of them were at the bottom of the shaft. One of the partners signalled to another to pull one of them up—the old man's partner. They strapped him to the bucket, but when they got him to the surface he was as crazy as a loon—completely nuts. We took him out to Westminster, where he died. The sight of so much gold had finished him. Believe me, boys, the Klondyke has to go some to beat Cariboo, and mark me, Cariboo will fool 'em yet, if they go deep enough. Sickness? Why the trail was strewn with smallpox victims. I'll give the Klondyke the once-over and it's then back to my first love, old Cariboo.

"Those were the days, boys—flour two hundred dollars a sack, candles two dollars each, nails four dollars per pound, and everything in proportion. We tramped out in the fall since there wasn't enough grub for us to remain. Now, boys, take my tip. If you have any money to invest, take in what you think the miners will want. You'll make more selling merchandise than you will by digging for gold. But we're not there yet, and it's a long way to go. Be seein' you in Dawson. Here goes. But it's a hell of a climb, boys, up that grade."

Around the time of the slide orders were given to the NWMP to let no one enter the Canadian side unless they had a ton—about a year's worth—of provisions. The authorities did not want a repetition of what happened in 1896 and 1897 in Dawson, when there was a shortage of provisions. The police themselves experienced rationing. But most of those who were turned back returned before long to present their manifests again and enter the portals of Canadian territory.

CHAPTER ELEVEN

Springtime in Bennett

Every day smoke curled out of numberless tents and hundreds packed their sleds to start a new relay cache down the lake, perhaps to Cariboo Crossing. The trail was well worn all the way down. On this windy day, an enterprising individual, evidently having had enough of pulling sleds, put a pole upright in the front of his sled and braced it well. Then he created a square sail by tacking a tarpaulin onto a crosspiece. When ready and the wind was fair, he gave the sled a push, jumped aboard, and off it went. He kept the sled on course by poling on one side or the other, depending on the direction he wished to guide it. It was not long before hundreds were using the same method, cheered on by crowds. Many would delay their departure in the hope of a favourable wind, thus saving themselves physical exertion. By this mode of travel, it did not take long to reach Cariboo Crossing, a distance of about twenty-eight miles.

About halfway down Lake Bennett was a spot known as the Island. The Island was a narrow piece of land formed by a spit running out from the turning used to get to the West Arm of Lake Bennett. This spit also formed a bay on the upper part of the lake. Here, a trail branched off toward the Wheaton River, where *Ora*, *Nora*, and *Flora* were being built. The BL&KN company managed, through strenuous effort, to land freight here in a very short time, although accomplishing this required work during the night as well as the day. When the engineers complained that they didn't have bricks to line the fireboxes, which they needed to hold steam and fire in, I hired two Frenchmen to dig for clay that I believed would be found near the river. After digging down a distance of twenty feet, they struck blue clay. We took the cook's salt and mixed it with the clay to the proper consistency, made moulds, and started a kiln. A beautiful brick was produced. We lined the fireboxes with the bricks, laid in a clay mortar that had been mixed with salt, and lit a fire to test the boilers for steam. The inside of the firebox achieved a wonderful glaze and lining, as if it were one piece, which would later aid the performance of the boats in bucking swift waters. Many of the other boat builders, on the lower reaches, bought bricks from our outfit at a dollar each. Some bricks were shipped to Dawson for the same price, plus freight.

As the spring wore on, the sun got higher in the heavens; at midday the glare on snow and ice was hard on the eyes. Many poor fellows who had no goggles to protect their eyes suffered from snow blindness. They overcame their difficulties by burning a stock and rubbing the charred part of it underneath their eyes each morning, forming a black patch that alleviated the irritation. It was queer to see blackened eyes on every other person, as if they had just emerged from a rough-and-tumble. This soon became the fashion.

Everything at the shipyard went on rapidly. We were all eager to have the *Ora*, the *Nora*, and the *Flora* finished and ready in time for the breaking of the ice. Picture in mind, if possible, men being brought in from the coast and over the rails, heavy machinery being packed, and everything being done that was necessary for the construction of three boats—all in a few short months. Trees were felled and logged, sawmills erected, lumber manufactured, and houses built. Hardship— and hard work—was suffered in order to have steamboats ply the Yukon River and the upper lakes, and all was accomplished at the headwaters of the great river.

Tents and caches were in place at every nook and draw on the shores of Lake Bennett. Sleds would veer off the main trail to these relay points, where you could hear the sound of the axe and the twang of the saw in a pit. One would see miniature flags of all nationalities, often the British and American together. Farther on you could see a crude sign: COFFEE LIKE YOUR MOTHER MAKES. How good it was to drop in and get refreshed. You could generally tell where women were camped. God bless them. They cheered us up and their sympathy and encouragement helped us on our way. On fine days when the sun was shining, little rivulets of water would run down the side of the mountain. You could see men with gold pans test the gravel and earth until the frost came at night and sealed everything up. They would repeat their test the next day, as soon as the sun's welcome rays had melted the frost of the night.

The town of Bennett was still growing. Every day engineers and mining men would arrive from places such as the Rand (South Africa), Ballarat (Australia), New Zealand, Peru, Bolivia, the headwaters of the Amazon, or elsewhere. In the evenings, surprising encounters took place. Men who had lost track of each other for years would meet each other again, drawn here by the news of gold, and talk in groups of their experiences on the trail.

Although several representatives of different banking institutions were at Bennett waiting for the opportune time to get to Dawson, no bank had been established there. Cheques were offered in payment of debts contracted but usually no one would take them. Who could trust such a heterogeneous crowd? One enterprising individual did take a chance and, after having seen letters of credit from Vancouver, Victoria, Seattle, Portland, or other such places, cashed cheques—at a twenty-five percent discount—and sent the cheques immediately by messenger to their various destinations. Every cheque was honoured.

The BL&KN company had two men constantly on the trail, one the son of a baronet, the other the son of a judge. They each made two trips a week, on foot, since the trails in April were such that using horses or dogs would be too slow. In this modern day of the automobile, people would scarcely believe it possible to walk 160 miles (sometimes, over 200 miles), over difficult trails, on foot, in seven days.

Still, on the people came, pitching tents around Lindemann and Bennett. The scene was a busy one. Those who had braved the cold trails and blizzards earlier in the year were far better off than those who now, in April, tried to get over slush and mud and potholes. Many sorry-looking sights were seen, as men came in, wet from head to foot like drowned rats. Freshets ran during the day and, partially sealed by frost, at night.

The Skagway and Dyea Rivers were raging torrents. One would have to make a plunge to get across and strike the trail.

A few miles of road were being built. Those using the road gladly paid a toll to miss much of the rough going. The WP&YR made rapid strides, wanting to handle some of the enormous business. No obstacles seemed to dampen the spirits of those anxious to get to Dawson. The names of men at the head of the WP&YR were Hawkins, Whiting, Heney, Haslitt, as well as others and myself. The blasting that went on through the draws and mountain valleys, for miles, at times held up pedestrian traffic.

One particular blast was let off and the usual warning given for men to find shelter. Thirteen men sought the shelter of a huge mass of rock that looked as if it was part of the mountainside. One young fellow left this place, hurrying off to be with other companions. He had no sooner arrived at his new shelter than the blast went off. What had seemed to be the safest shelter—the place where the twelve men huddled—started to roll. Before the men could get out of the way, the huge mass rolled down the mountainside, taking them with it and forming a tombstone for them. Not one of them survived. Was it by chance the young fellow escaped? One year after this happened, Haslitt, while in Chicago looking after the WP&YR interests, was run down and killed by a locomotive while crossing the railroad tracks, after missing death by inches more than once when surveying for the WP&YR. Haslitt was missed by all who knew him for he was a fine fellow.

~

One of the men with an outfit on the Skagway-Bennett Trail told this story:

"One morning as I was preparing the usual morning flapjacks, Sam Trewolla put his head through the tent flap and imparted the startling information that some of his goods were missing. Forcing the flapjack job on Sam I rushed to count my cache. Then along came Black Douglas, roaring that some of his supplies were missing. Ray Philpots began raving that a man who would steal grub on the trail should be shot. Black suggested that Ray stay in camp next day and do the shooting. Sam said, 'We can't afford to lose our precious stuff after packing, swearing, cussing, and wearing ourselves out to a frazzle. It seems to be part of our very souls. We have rescued it from ocean tides, rivers, and floods.'

"Sam drew the lucky straw that elected him watchman that night. A game of seven up decided who should wash the dishes and then we turned in. In the darkest part of the night, Sam sneaked into the tent and aroused me out of a shivery sleep. Softly he whispered, 'It's that damned lanky cuss with the red toque about two hundred yards down the trail. We'll get him in the morning.'

"The next day Sam explained that he had heard a dog growl and had seen a shadowy figure approach Ray's cache, take out a package of bacon, and then go to Black's cache, gently lift the tarp, and quietly sneak back down the trail. Sam had followed silently and had seen him enter his tent. 'There was a light burning,' said Sam, 'I could see that damn red toque—the only one in and around camp.'

"After considerable argument we decided to capture Red at gunpoint and make him restore the stolen goods. Red was duly captured, but denied all knowledge of the stolen goods. A hurried search gave the lie to his words, however, and he began to beg for mercy. Sam, who knew the man, was in favour of turning him over to the police, but time was a factor to be considered, so we planned instead to scare the liver out of him. We summoned the entire camp for a powwow. Ray acted as spokesman, and the unlucky Red was placed on a box with a rope around his neck. The other end of the rope was thrown over a pole lashed between two trees.

"'Gentlemen,' began Ray, 'on the other side of the line, we put up with much that was similar to what Red has done. We've caught him red-handed, stealing our goods. Who can place a value on our supplies? Boys, you've gotten this far on your journey and it's useless for me to enlarge on the misery that we endured packing our precious freight. I ask again—who can place a value on our goods? No one! On this side of the line, where the scarlet tunic puts fear into the hearts of criminals, who would have expected this to happen? I think you'll agree with me, gentlemen, that we do not want any fellows of this breed in the Yukon. Our lives depend on our grubstakes. If this man had asked for help we would have gladly given it, but he came like a thief in the night and robbed us. You, gentlemen, are the jury in this case. What is your verdict?' A majority shouted, 'String him up!'

"Sam was given orders to get things ready and climbed onto the box with the thief. As he worked he softly whispered to Red, 'When I cut these ropes, run like hell. They'll probably get after me but I'm remembering the help you gave me at the Ford.' When the order was given to kick the box from under him, the culprit, with a mighty bound hit the trail running. A volley of shots fired in the air lent wings to his flight. Red's cache was found to comprise packages bearing the marks of different owners, who lost no time claiming what was their own."

Spring saw the staffs of different banks start to come in, amongst them Robert W. Service, who would later capture the spirit of the argonauts. In his inimitable way he portrayed the feelings of both the cheechakos and seasoned pioneers. Reading his verses again takes one over the trails, sailing the lakes and rivers. They never exaggerate, but are true to life in the Far North. Very few have dwelt on the misery and suffering experienced, especially by the cheechakos, on the trail in 1898. If not for the many brave, strong men who aided the weak ones on the trail and down the treacherous waters, more disasters would have taken place.

～

Brutal and tragic incidents continued to take place in the gambling and dance halls. There was no let-up. I was compelled to go there to find parties with whom I had to transact business and often witnessed poor, gullible fools losing their all. In Skagway, there was talk of asking for martial law. This would come later on—a blessing for the unsophisticated that gave people a feeling of safety while preparing for the trail.

Who can forget the scenes of heroism on the trail? One scene was of Dick Sterling picking up a youth who had fallen by the wayside, packing him in his arms for miles, and placing him in the safe keeping of another good Samaritan. When this young fellow met Dick subsequently in Dawson, he threw his arms around his saviour and kissed him. A few days after, when Dick was taking the side of a weaker party, he was struck on the head with a bottle wielded by a tough, the bottle breaking and leaving a fearful gash on his brow.

Another scene took place on a bitterly cold day, when a man by the name of Ham arrived at the pass and went into the tent restaurant. At the entrance he spied a purse and found it crammed full of currency. A constable was in the vicinity, so he passed it to him saying, "You may get some inquiries for this." At that moment a youth showed up, looking wretched and despondent.

Ham said, "What's the matter, kid?"

"Oh, I've lost everything I have in my world."

"And what is that?"

"My purse."

The constable passed the purse behind his back to Ham, saying, "Can you describe your purse, kid?"

"I certainly can." When he was done, and had described the exact amount the purse contained, Ham produced the purse and handed it over to its owner. The kid threw his arms around Ham and gave him a hearty kiss, saying, "Oh you good man. What's your name?"

"Oh, just Ham," he replied.

The kid bade both the constable and Ham goodbye, and waving with both hands ran to catch up with his party for Dawson.

Ham, who was bound for Dawson, eventually made it there and struck out for the creeks to stake a claim. After an absence of some months he returned to Dawson for a rest and to relax. Meeting some of the boys from the banks, whom he had known on the trail, he decided to take in the dance hall with them. The boys had talked about "the finest lady there" and were bent on having a dance with her.

Everything was in full swing when they arrived. Ham sat down in his trail clothes and took everything in. When a dance was over, the men would take their partners for a drink "on the percentage plan," the ladies deriving a nice little sum from the transaction. The bank boys were alert for a dance with the greatest lady in the hall but she refused them, walking straight up to Ham. "Your turn next, Ham."

"My dear lady, you must be mistaken," Ham said, and thinking they must know each other said, "Have we met before? Perhaps in Montreal?"

She replied, "Never mind, Ham, come along."

The bank boys were amazed and remarked, "Pretty foxy—she must be an old flame." During the dance, Ham was unable to get information as to where they might have previously met. When the dance was over they went, as was customary, for drinks. She winked to the bartender and Ham was not allowed to pay. Ham said again, "Now, madam, where have we met before?"

She said, "Don't spoil your evening, Ham, and don't worry." The bank boys hastened to ask for the next dance, but she said, "Sorry, boys, but the next is also Ham's." This was beyond all understanding and the boys wanted Ham to let them in on the secret.

He answered them with, "All I can say, boys, is I'm as much in the dark as you."

"Cut it out, Ham, you old rascal," they said, but away went Ham, letting himself float to the tune of a nice dreamy waltz and saying to the lady, "This compensates for the rough trails and waters; it's worthwhile to come to Dawson for this."

He made a promise to the lady that he would be on hand again the next night. The boys roasted him, "Come on, Ham, out with it. Where did you meet her?"

"Honest, boys, it's got me guessing. I'm bewildered. Rack my brains as much as I will, there is no solution."

"Bah! Say that to the Marines, not to old soldiers."

The next night Ham and the boys were again in the hall. Immediately, at the sight of Ham, the lady went over to him. "You next, Ham." Again the bank boys were puzzled; in spite of Ham's rough clothes, the lady apparently preferred him to them. Finally, Ham refused to dance again unless she enlightened him and made her identity known.

"Alright," said she, "after one dance with one of the bank boys we'll rest and have a chat."

When the dance was over, she at last came and sat down. "Ham, I will tell you a story. There was a time in my life I shall never forget. Do you remember finding a purse that belonged to a boy one day?"

"Yes," said Ham, "but what has that got to do with this?"

"I'll tell you—I'm that boy."

"For heaven's sake! I cannot credit it."

"Don't be surprised Ham—how I like the name! When you said, 'Just call me Ham,' you sounded so genuine. I knew you were one of the world's gentlemen. To get into the country I had to pose as I did. I do want you to think well of me. My young brother was at university. Our parents had died and I did not know how to keep him there. We were financially embarrassed and worried and everyone was talking of the rich goldfields. A thought came to my mind. If it was possible to get here, I would. Loving dancing made me more determined, and here I am. Ham, don't think hard of me. I have kept myself straight. No one can accuse me of being otherwise. I am respected. Young men talk over their troubles with me and give me their trust. There is no one who dares take liberties with me. The boys would not stand for it. My drinks, by arrangement, have always been cold tea. Am I a gold digger? Certainly not! As soon as the season is over I am going out and believe me, my young brother will carry on his studies. You will be drifting and soon it will be home sweet home for me, with enough to keep me comfortable for some time."

Ham could not find words to express himself. "You are a brave woman. I will certainly get the boys to keep their eyes open and protect you."

"Don't, Ham! You are the only one I have spoken to about this. You say you are going up the Stewart River. Let us say goodbye."

Outside, Ham muttered to himself, "I'll be goldarned if this isn't a queer place. What a girl will do for a brother. Good luck, girl! May you and your like be protected from harm." His fears for her were allayed somewhat by recollecting her words.

Ham neither saw nor heard any more of her. There are a lot of fine fellows I know, rough outside, but gentlemen in their behaviour with women.

CHAPTER TWELVE

Liquor: Cases for Raising Spirits

The shores of Lake Nares were lined with tents and camps. The shores of the "Little Winds" and "Big Winds" (on the north Taku arm) of Tagish Lake were shunned, as the wind seemed to be always blowing in this locality. Camps could also be seen here and there on the Six Mile, in sheltered places. There were camps scattered on the shores of Marsh (or Mud) Lake and on down the Six Mile to the now-busy settlement called Macauley's, the starting place of the swift waters, Miles Canyon, the Squaw Rapids, and the White Horse Rapids.

Several parties who had travelled over the ice from Dawson and arrived at Bennett had heard of Soapy's gang in Skagway and travelled in numbers. They exclaimed, "God help the bandits if any attempts are made to rob us." These men were grim, equal to any emergency, and well armed with Winchesters. They arrived in Skagway with their wealth, as no attempt was made to molest them, and they marched straight to the steamboat, ready to go south and to civilization.

Major Walsh of the NWMP came out on the ice via Dyea. When he heard of the idea of steamboats plying their way between Bennett and Dawson, he laughed at it. It was rumoured that the Minister of the Interior, the Honourable Clifford Sifton, was with him on this trip, looking into the possibility of big business in the area, but this rumour I did not believe. I would have known if it was correct. The rumour was also that he had an interest in a steamboat named the *Domville* at St. Michael, waiting for the ice to clear out, left in the charge of someone who was said to be related to the minister). Senator Domville (the man) was rumoured also to have "an interest" in the cargo, which consisted of five thousand gallons of spirits—rum, whiskey, brandy, et cetera.

Several shipments of liquor had arrived (and continued to arrive) at

Skagway, Dyea, and Bennett. These had to be conveyed over the passes by American customs deputies. One shipment (of two thousand gallons) was brought over the Chilcoot Pass. When the kegs were unloaded from the pack train, one keg in particular attracted the attention of many. It had innumerable white marks were all over it, caused by the pegs that had been driven into it to fill the holes made by gimlets. The convoys had inserted straws into the kegs and drunk the liquor whenever they had gotten thirsty—they were drunk as lords when they landed in Bennett.

This is a copy of an invoice for one shipment of spirits. The prices shown are what the purchaser paid in Victoria.

Victoria Phoenix Beer

25 cases, quarts @ $24 per case

25 cases, pints @ $26 per case

Pither & Leiser

87 cases Due de Sarmont Champagne, pints @ $80 per case

87 cases Epernay Champagne, pints @ $80 per case

24 cases Kupferberg Champagne, pints @ $33 per case

25 cases Gold Medal Bourbon @ $32 per case

25 cases Cyrus Nobel Bourbon @ $33 per case

50 cases Lapoire Triple Cross Brandy @ $80 per case

Turner, Beeton & Co.

100 cases Four Crown Scotch Whiskey @ $32 per case

5 cases Coat Ila Whiskey @ $32 per case

10 cases Red Gin @ $30 per case

30 cases Mathers Whiskey @ $32 per case

15 cases Crawford Whiskey @ $30 per case

12 cases Hennessey Brandy @ $36 per case

16 cases Single Cross Hennessey Brandy @ $33 per case

14 cases Triple Cross C.V. Brandy @ $34 per case

11 cases C.V. Brandy, flasks @ $33 per case

13 cases C.V. Brandy, ½ flasks @ $34 per case

10 cases Schedam Gin @ $28 per case

10 cases Plymouth Gin @ $27 per case

5 cases Old Tom Gin @ $26 per case

17 cases Kellogs Bourbon Whiskey @ $34 per case

19 cases (cut in two=38 cases) of Stout, pints @ $39 per case

10 cases of Stout, quarts @ $39 per case

10 cases Ale, pints @ $50 per case

7 cases Carte Blanche Champagne, quarts @ $64 per case

12 cases Dry Monopole Champagne, pints @ $82 per case

2 cases Le Beau Champagne, pints @ $74 per case

25 cases Pommeray Champagne, pints @ $84 per case

5 cases Champagne, pints @ $62 per case

2 cases Bretonnet Sonne Champagne, pints @ $78 per case

4 cases Dry Imperial Champagne, pints @ $82 per case

5 cases Mumm Champagne, pints @ $82 per case

9 cases Carte Blanche Champagne, quarts @ $62 per case

4 cases 1887 Vintage Epernay Champagne, quarts @ $74 per case

8 cases Mausard Champagne, quarts @ $66 per case

4 cases 1880 Vintage Epernay Champagne, quarts @ $82 per case

22 cases Pommeray Champagne, quarts @ $82 per case

1 case Mumm Champagne, quarts @ $80 per case

12 cases Perinet Champagne, quarts @ $80 per case

8 cases Clicquot Champagne, quarts @ $80 per case

This shipment had come via Skagway. The cost for freight to Bennett was a little fortune; to get the same to Dawson an unbelievable sum was paid. One can readily understand the reason for charging exorbitant figures for a thimbleful of "the clear McKie," as they called it in Dawson. Black Sullivan paid for his shipment of five thousand gallons with thousand-dollar bills from the old Bank of British Columbia, up in the 'teens. Bill McRae also paid a big amount for his consignment to Dawson. Some liquor was bought for as high as two hundred dollars per gallon. It was claimed that Domville and his associates cleared a fortune after they had disposed of their consignment of liquor. The BL&KN company had a permit for two thousand gallons and made a lot of money out of its sale. What Black Sullivan made is hard to conjecture.

Much of these shipments was doctored at Dawson before the consumer drank it; one can therefore realize that fabulous money was made in this business. Champagne sold for twenty dollars to twenty-five dollars per bottle. The higher the price, the more the demand. Several fellows, after an all night's carousal, would recklessly buy bottles of whiskey (at outrageous prices) to take along to the creeks, spending most of their cleanup, believing there was no end to the gold in their claims.

Above: (PLATE 1) Family portrait, Cornwall, England. W.H.T. extreme right, back row.
Below: (PLATE 2) W.H.T., and Sarah Olive with Trewolla R., and William H., 1895.

Above: (PLATE 3) Justice of the Peace Olive,
centre, with two police officers, Carbon,
Alberta, 1918.
Right: (PLATE 4) Francis Mawson Rattenbury,
noted architect and promoter of the Bennett
Lake & Klondyke Navigation Company.

ove: (PLATE 5) *Stampeders posing in Nanaimo before departing by ship for the Klondyke, 1898.*

low: (PLATE 6) *Members of the Victorian Order of Nurses onboard ship, 1898.*

*Above: (*PLATE 7*) Stampeders hauling their goods over the Chilcoot Pass, 1898.*
*Below: (*PLATE 8*) The summit of the Chilcoot Pass, 1898.*

Above: (PLATE 9) *The Boundary Line on Chilcoot Pass, 1898.*
Below: (PLATE 10) *Men among their caches at the Chilcoot Pass Summit, 1898.*

Above: (PLATE 11) *On the Summit of Chilcoot Pass after the snow slide, April 3, 1898.*
Centre: (PLATE 12) *Exhumation of the bodies of the Tramway men buried in the snow slide.*
Below: (PLATE 13) *Stampeder with short haired sled dogs, Chilcoot Pass, 1898.*

Above: (PLATE 14) *Dogs resting on the trail, near Atlin, B.C., 1898.*
Below: (PLATE 15) *Dog team in front of the Victoria Hotel at Log Cabin, 1898.*

Above: (PLATE 16) *B. Williams & Co., supplier of goods for prospectors and adventurers, 1898.*
Below: (PLATE 17) *Jefferson Randolph 'Soapy' Smith, the notorious Skagway gangster, 1898.*

CHAPTER THIRTEEN

The Teslin Trail

Victims of the Teslin Trail would arrive at Skagway. These men had seen very tough times. Some had with them parts of outfits, others had none, having left "their all" on the trail. Their looks were sad and wistful but they were still bent on getting to the goldfields. Having put their hands to the plow they intended to press on. They painted vivid pictures verbally—of quagmires, of muskeg, of dead and dying horses. Yes, and mules and dogs, and men who had given up in despair—boats wrecked, the incessant toil of towing up the Stikine River, the treacherous Teslin Lake. Stories were told of corduroying muskegs and wreckage of merchandise unloaded on seemingly good solid ground that was actually morass, so that the whole cache sank and disappeared. All along the Stikine were signs that read OUTFITS FOR SALE—CHEAP. Who was there to buy as the exodus took place? Even the gamblers had left, knowing full well that only a few would get through, and those who started a little late on their journey were doomed.

The crowd in Skagway would unfold story after story of the Teslin Trail. A professor (another one—every trail had its professors and colonels) recalled the trail. "My God! What a crime! To boost such a route to the Klondyke as the Dewdney Trail ("the old Teslin Route"). I've seen more broken-hearted men, and men dying off with scurvy, frozen hands, frozen feet and legs, giving up and wanting to be left alone to die, than I want to see again. I've seen that big-hearted John Pringle help many a poor man out of his difficulties and pack his load for him." (Reverend John Pringle represented the Presbyterians.)

"Those of us who started a little late had to turn back and here we are. We were too late to catch the frozen ground and muskeg. We have had our little hell."

"Say, professor, what do you expect on the White Pass?" someone asked him.

"Well, from what we've heard, it's paradise compared to what we met on the Stikine."

"It all depends," said a White Pass trailer. "There are a lot that don't think so. You have the railroad for a few miles, but watch your step for showers of rock that have maimed many on the trail, and look out for Soapy and his gang."

The professor laughed, saying, "Gad, boys, we've met them. Maybe not Soapy's gang, but I guess just as smart. The gamblers acted like rats on the Stikine. They knew when the ship was sinking and cleared out. Bet you most are in Skagway or Dyea now." The professor introduced an elderly man by the name of Dr. Wann. In '96 he had taken the Edmonton trail via Chicago and Calgary. He was deaf so the Professor gave the Doctor's experience. "Leaving Edmonton, the poor doctor, in company with others, got tangled up in the Peace River district and lost mules, dogs and his whole outfit. He finally got to Vancouver, where the Dewdney Trail was recommended. And gentlemen, here he is—two years on the trail, and just making another start. Here's hoping he'll get there. Come on, boys. The drinks are on me. Doc and myself haven't quite drowned out the memories. Did I hear someone say, 'fill 'em up'? Ah, yes. Well, here goes."

At Skagway, outfitting for Dawson was no trouble. The faint of heart, those who were not willing to face the hardships of packing over the passes, sold their outfits—for ridiculously low prices—to secondhand stores, and—for greatly enhanced prices—to those without outfits. There was no dearth of outfits. Victims of the Stikine lost no time buying outfits and were soon on the trail for Bennett.

⟲

Many accidents could be attributed to liquor, as well as most quarrels and drownings. Liquor, more than anything else, was the undoing of men. When rundown, wet, miserable, and weary on the trails, many found comfort in it, especially in the month of May, when the going was slow and there were hidden perils on the way. The early morning travel was not bad, but at noon, when the sun had unsealed the night's frost, a man could sink into a pothole of icy cold water and be unfortunate enough to take cold or pneumonia. The beasts of burden, also, once down, seldom rose again. Thousands of dollars' worth of merchandise was lost when the thaws set in.

Outfits would stop along the lakes at treed places, where they could get logs to build a scow, raft, or boat. One outfit went to find a clump of trees they could fell and build boats and make camp with, up Taku Arm. (The Taku Arms of Tagish Lake are exceedingly long pieces of water that run south into British Columbia).

In May, at noon, the sun was unbearably hot, the glare on the ice most trying to the eyes. The freshets ran and water laid all around the shores of Lake Lindemann and Lake Bennett. The ice that remained was honeycombed and exceedingly dangerous to travel on. Still, it held, day after day, and people wondered if it would ever go out. Some nights the ice would freeze harder than others, and many risked travelling over it.

The trail from the Chilcoot was rotten, with water often running in places under the trail. The trail from Canyon City to Lindemann was under an arch of snow, badly worn, with a glacial stream running underneath. Of the hundreds who used this trail, those who made it safely did so by skillful handling of their sleds. The trail dropped steeply from top to bottom, with a raging torrent running on one side. The precious freight of one man who got near this side of the trail toppled over. In went the man after it, to save what to him, was more precious than gold. The icy glacial waters came up to his waist. He was rescued, and part of his outfit saved. The other part of it was carried underneath the arch of snow and down the stream, to Lindemann. After he was taken into Lindemann, he developed a severe chill, after being in a fever of perspiration. In Lindemann, Miss Smith, the young lady on whom Gentleman Harry had designs, had beckoned to the rescue party and told them to take the man to "the old ladies."

These women immediately took charge of the man, now in the first stages of spinal meningitis, which had by that time become prevalent. No one will ever know the part, in its fullest, played by the women on the trail of '98, who sacrificed time and money to attend to the poor unfortunates struck down by this dread disease. When suffering from this complaint, the victim's head was drawn back and mouth pulled wide open. If the patient did not recover within three or four days, death would usually result. Several men who were fortunate enough to have these good, noble-hearted women attend to them were nursed back to health. Much has been written about women devoting themselves and their lives to suffering humanity and their names have been handed down to posterity, but unsung and nameless are those women of the North who laboured in a work of love for those stricken by pneumonia and other diseases caused by overexertion, improper food and inattention to cleanliness. It has been thought that only rugged men were in the march on the trail of '98. But often those who seemed frail stood the trail far better than those who looked sturdy and strong, who were often brought to death's door by the hardships they endured.

CHAPTER FOURTEEN

Showdown with Soapy's Gang

As the manager of the BL&KN company, I received in Skagway a draft from the Bank of Montreal for a considerable amount of money to pay for freight, wages, and incidentals. No one knew of this but myself and the First Bank of Skagway, who would naturally have advice of the same. I did not tell anyone about it, not even my agent. But from the time I arrived in Skagway from Bennett, I was shadowed. At first I did not notice it, yet something seemed strange and tense. In an indefinable way I sensed that everything was not as it should be. And a number of Soapy's gang were very much in evidence.

I went to the bank, produced the draft, and it was okayed. There were several men lounging about, amongst whom were some of Soapy's men. The teller was unusually loud in speaking, and said, "You will have to take half in gold, since notes are scarce."

I was a well-known figure, familiar to many. I answered the teller, "You can keep your gold. I want payment in notes." I had suddenly seen through the loud talk of the teller and knew why Soapy's gang was present. The information had leaked out. Continuing my conversation with the teller, I said that I was packing no gold coin over the trails.

"Scared, mister?" taunted a bystander, evidently listening to the conversation.

"Mind your own damn business! Say, teller, I'll be seeing you again when your audience is smaller. Where's your manager?"

The teller replied, "Inside. Walk in."

"Howdy do, Moody," I said to the manager of the bank.

"How do."

"About the draft from the Bank of Montreal. I'm not taking gold on the trail."

"Alright, Bill, call in between three and four o'clock and we will try and get bills enough to pay the draft, at any rate, within a little." This was also said loud enough, and in a tone meant for other ears than mine.

When I left the bank, I saw two men leave with me, leers on their faces, nudging each other in perfect understanding. I walked down the street with the two men following. "Well, I'll be damned!" I thought, ignoring the two followers, whom I now recognized as having figured in several brawls. It was lunchtime. Knowing where my agent dined, I proceeded to the place, and found him. I lost no time in telling what happened at the bank.

"Holy smoke!" exclaimed Jack, my agent. And then, "There they are, sitting across the way. I know them, Cap." (Cap was the name I was often called.) "Soapy's lookout? For God's sake be careful. They're known as the Weasel and the Panther. Don't run any risk, when packing the money to Bennett. They'll get you as sure as the Lord made little apples."

I said, "If I don't pack it they'll still get me, to get the money. They'll believe I'm carrying it, whatever I do. But I've promised the boys at Bennett to pay them tomorrow and, by all that's great, my word will be kept—Soapy or no Soapy." I opened the door and called to the marshal, "Take a seat, Marshal. Cigar?"

"Ah, yes, thanks, Cap."

"Who are those two men, Marshal?"

"Oh, just a couple of good fellows."

"Look here, Marshal, those two fellows have been following and shadowing me ever since I came in. They were at the bank this morning when I was talking over money matters, and now they're just outside the café. Isn't there any business done in this burg without Soapy knowing about it? He must have his spies everywhere, in everyone's business. What rake-off does he get from the bank? Or has he pledged himself to leave the bank alone for consideration of information? It looks fishy."

"It's a damned good job I know you, Cap, or you couldn't talk to me like that about the bank. You're imagining things."

"Oh no, I'm not. Watch your step, Marshal."

"Do you mean to insinuate, Cap, that . . ."

"I mean that the public are in no mood to stand for anymore of Soapy's or his gang's slippery and cunning work. After last week's robbery they're worked up to such a pitch that something is going to happen."

"You're nervous, Cap."

"Never cooler, Marshal."

"Well, I must be going. Duty, you know."

"Alright, Marshal, but don't say you weren't warned. Good-day."

Outside, one of the gang members followed the marshal, stopped and held an earnest conversation with him. Jack and I transacted our business and planned our mode of action, to throw the two toughs off their calculations and outwit them. We said our plan loud enough for the two gangsters to hear us.

Jack and I called in at the bank at the time agreed. Some plain talking ensued between the teller and myself, and the staff just laughed at my insinuation that Soapy in some way knew the bank's business. I said, "Look out the window. Can you see those two men? They've beenfollowing me all day. They were here this morning when I presented the draft for payment."

"Hell," replied the banker, "that was only a coincidence."

"Rot! They have been following me all day!" I said. "I have made arrangements that if anything happens, investigations will be made and the bank will be included."

I received payment in bills, and one thousand dollars in gold eagles. We left, leaving the banker in a quandary. The two toughs were still outside waiting, keeping strict vigil.

Suppertime came. Jack and I were greeted by our acquaintances at the hotel, the gangsters still hovering closely around. Quietly, I said to Jack, "Now's our time, with the boys present. I'll let everyone hear that I'm going to get a little shut-eye and meet you at 2 a.m. Then, when everything is quiet, I'll slip off and catch the Dyea boat. You be sure to be on hand at two. All set?"

"Righto."

Then, in a louder voice, I said, "Here's off for a sleep, Jack. Wake me at 2 a.m. and we'll be off on the White Pass Trail. Goodnight!"

Having made my plans public, I went up to my room, locked the door, threw myself on the bed, and listened. I heard stealthy footsteps outside my door. They halted. Feigning sleep, I snored, and heard a whisper, "All right." They went stealthily away. After allowing plenty of time for things to quieten down, I noiselessly changed my clothes, eyed myself in the glass and saw that the change was good. I stowed away the currency on my person and left my room with boldness fitting the occasion.

Entering the bar, which was occupied by a few customers, I ordered a drink for a stranger, who was by my side, and myself. Leisurely, I raised my glass and cast my eyes around the bar. Assuming an air of carelessness, I saw the two toughs playing a game of cards, whiling away the time. Yes—the ruse had worked. Lighting my pipe, taking my time, I slipped through the batwing doors. Stopping around the corner, I waited a few minutes to see if the gangsters had noticed. With an air of relief, I hastily made for the Dyea boat.

Luckily, I was able to slip aboard just as they cast off. I went down into the little cabin congratulating myself, but saw a man sitting in a corner, huddled up, a soft felt hat pulled down over his eyes, apparently asleep. I wondered who the fellow could be—he looked suspicious.

Dyea at last. The seemingly sleepy man was suddenly very much alive as the boat sheared to the wharf. He was the first to leave the boat, and disappeared. I wasted no time stopping at Dyea. Instead, I took a straight shoot up the river, coming at last to the place where the bridge (two trees that had fallen across the stream) should be. The freshets had evidently washed it away. Since the other side of the river was better going, I decided to cross. I was up to my knees in water, about halfway to the other side, when, *bang!* I whirled and returned the shot, firing at the dying flash and smoke. A moan was heard, and then all was quiet.

Meanwhile, at Skagway, Jack did what had been agreed upon. He saw the two gangsters waiting patiently for me to emerge from my bedroom at 2 a.m. Recognition between Jack and the two toughs was mutual. He went upstairs, knowing full well that I would be gone. Coming back down, he exclaimed to them, "Damn you! Where's the captain?"

The gangsters immediately came to life, turning their guns on Jack. "Come on, mister man," said one. "What does this mean?—Tim, take a look. He didn't pass this way, he knew the window was guarded.— You've double-crossed us." Tim came back, verifying that I was gone. "You think you're smart, mister agent. Now open your mouth and explain, or by the living God, I'll force you to."

"I explain nothing," Jack declared.

"Alright, come along with us, we'll soon get an explanation. The captain has escaped us here but both the Chilcoot and White Pass Trails are well guarded." Jack was forced to the street door, with a rod pushed at his back.

The door opened from the outside, however, and an officer of the U.S.A. infantry and a Mountie confronted them. "Hullo! What's this? A hold up?" Seeing the gun in the gangster's hand, the officer, with one swift move of his cane, struck the gun from the gangster. Before the other gangster could draw his weapon, the Mountie tackled him. "Now, then, suppose we have a little explanation of what's been going on."

"Oh," said one of the toughs, "it was only a bit of fun."

"Fun, be damned!" said Jack.

"Here, you fellows!" said the Mountie to the toughs. "Don't try to slink off. Stay put or I'll treat you rough. Sergeant, I'm covering these fellows. Take any arms they have from them. Jack, get on with the story."

Jack explained my bluff, and said, "The Captain is more than likely at Bennett, or close to it, by this time."

The gangster chuckled, "You'll see."

Jack said, "You were just in time for me, Constable, they would have given me the works." The officer questioned the gangsters. He threatened to arrest them, but knew the time was not yet ripe. He had recently arrived at Skagway and was still sizing up the situation. He knew that Soapy would protect his followers. They slunk off, as the officer warned them that law and order would be here in short time. The constable asked Jack when I had started. Jack could not say exactly, but thought I must be all right, considering the behaviour of the gangsters.

The constable added, "Trust Bill—he's a good shot, well able to take care of himself."

Back at the river, after my encounter, I made straight for Molly's camp. Molly stood at the tent opening. "Hullo, Cap. What was all the shooting about?"

"Ask the other fellow, Molly. Is it too late for a cup of coffee?"

"Oh, no—I'm waiting up for Dad."

"You're foolish, Molly. I'm afraid he's too deep in the gambling game to throw it up."

"He's promised to do so, so often," she replied. Molly was another poor victim of the Rush, who along with her father had made my acquaintance on a passenger boat. Molly had made many friends there, and was glad to number me amongst them; I was someone to whom she could unburden herself. She had done well at this camp, serving coffee and cake to trail-worn men and women. I sat down for a cup of coffee and gave Molly all the latest news. I rubbed my leg with my hand unconsciously, and when I brought it back up to the table, Molly saw that it was covered with blood. "Why, Captain!" cried Molly, "You're hurt." Molly, who had been a nurse, was soon on her knees. She rolled up my breeches and exposed a not-serious flesh wound.

"Just a scratch, Molly."

"How about the other fellow, Captain?"

"Oh, I guess he got what was coming to him. More than likely he was one of Soapy's gang. Well, Molly, thanks a lot!" I slipped a five-spot on my plate, which Molly refused. "I must be getting along." Off I started. Molly shouted to me to wait for my change, but I took no heed, waving my hand and saying, "Au revoir! Get your dad out of the country, Molly."

Refreshed, I soliloquized, "Good old Molly. What a crime to bring a girl to surroundings like these—the father gambling away her hard-earned money." Appreciating Molly's first aid, I recalled some lines of poetry: "O Women! In our hours of ease, / Uncertain, coy, and hard to please, / When pain and anguish wring the brow, / A ministering angel thou!"

On I went. At Canyon City, drinks were still being served to a few late customers who had been relaying their caches. Not stopping, I was soon at the top of the short climb to the trail. Trudging along, I suddenly saw a figure at the bend of the trail slip behind one of the big cottonwood trees. "Well, here goes," I thought, "Soapy's gang or not." Out came my gun and I advanced, pointing it toward the tree. But was I deceived? I swore I had seen a man dive behind this tree. As I commenced to walk backward up the trail, my gun still pointing toward the tree, my foot caught on one of the many surface roots that were on the trail. Down I went, my gun going off. I found myself in a sitting position and saw a man running off in the opposite direction. I knew that each of us had been as scared as the other, and indulged in a good laugh.

At last, Sheep Camp. Here, a game of poker was in progress—no doubt, an all-night affair. I passed by and climbed the Scales. (An aerial tram was being built here to handle the freight over the pass, but before it was completed the bulk of the argonauts' freight had been packed over this difficult section of the trail.) I saw roseate hues in the east, signals of the approaching dawn. One has to be in the higher altitudes to witness this glorious scene, the sight of which brought new hope and life to many a worn and weary traveller. Even this early in the day, many were preparing for another arduous trip. Lone travellers who had to travel at night always appreciated the smell of wood fires—smoke curling out of the little Klondyke chimney pipes—and of coffee. Roused from my reverie, I saw a man with his dogs and sleds approach, bound for Dyea. It was Harry, a man who had worked for me.

"Well, well, Cap! I've waited long enough for that account you owe me. This is a good time to settle it. Off with your coat and I'll take it out of your hide."

"Hold on, Harry," I said. "It's not that I wouldn't like a scrap, but I've got money to pay all the boys."

"My God! What a wad!" said Harry, when he saw all the bills in my hand.

"Oh, no you don't, Harry!" A gun appeared in my hand.

"Never had a thought of that, Cap!"

"I didn't think you did, Harry, but I'm taking no chances." Harry was paid the three hundred dollars he was owed, and long after this incident, I employed him again, and he proved to be one of my trusted men.

Lindemann once again. Here, things were a little quieter than usual, since the trails were now mud and slush, which stopped much of the traffic. Yet, because these were the headwaters of the Yukon River, many built boats for their trip down the river from here.

Bennett at last. "My God! Is it you, Cap?" was the greeting I received when I appeared at my tent. "Word just came in you were shot at the White Pass."

"Didn't come that way, Cockney."

"We all thought it was you, Cap. Word came they were out to get you."

"Get me a shakedown and a cup of coffee. I can do with some shut-eye."

Another employee came in. "Great Scott! We all thought it was you who was shot. Some other poor devil must have been taken for you. His belt was found thrown across the trail. He resembled you but papers showed he was from Portland."

"Tell the boys that wages will be paid at noon. Now, vamoose!" Before falling asleep, I thought about the unfortunate man who had evidently been mistaken for me, and had consequently suffered in my stead.

CHAPTER FIFTEEN

Lake Travel

Bennett once more. What a change in a few days! The ice on the lake was getting rotten and honeycombed. During the heat of the day it was not safe to travel, but at night everything sealed up again. Many were anxious to get their caches to safe places before the ice went out. Scores took advantage of small, flat-bottomed boats built for the purposes of sled and lifeboat all in one. Runners, shod with flat iron strips, were attached to the bottom, and lifelines that were used to pull the sled acted as safety lines; should one go through the ice, he could pull himself out. It took several days to cross the lake with this method of travel.

One party of two men, making a trip from the West Arm point to the place on the Wheaton River where the *Ora*, *Nora*, and *Flora* were being built, met with slush ice. Their combination sled and boat settled down, but the two men were lucky enough to fall onto the deck of the craft. It was a case of staying there all night or somehow making the three miles between them and shore. They had only a chocolate bar between them. They fastened a rope around a heavy sledgehammer, tying one end to the thwart so the rope would be safe. Whirling the sledgehammer around until the momentum was right, they let it go, and the hammer pierced the ice. Then, with the aid of a pole, they pulled themselves to the anchor made by the sledgehammer. It took all day to make shore—they became experts at throwing the hammer.

Another party, also of two men, on a trip from Bennett to the Wheaton River, experienced several duckings as they hauled their combination craft loaded with freight. Finally, they decided to stop at the West Arm point and wait for the nightly freeze-up. Lighting a fire and drying out as much as possible, they made a billy of tea. While they were warming themselves, two other men, who had come out of the woods, approached them. These men had been travelling the shores of Bennett to get this far—a gruelling task. They asked the men with the sled-boat to take them across the lake once the frost had done its work of sealing up the soft spots, offering to pay for the accommodation. At this point in the year, the ice froze hard during the little time the sun was hidden by the mountains, for there was practically no darkness.

One man was well able to look after himself, but the other was emaciated. He had taken ill, with spinal meningitis, and his former partner had neglected him, taking everything in the way of grub and other useful things—even his pocketbook—and struck out for Dawson. The sick man was found by his present companion, who nursed him back to convalescence. He had been conscious when his pocketbook was taken, but could not speak. When he was able to inform the police, they were not able to travel in pursuit, owing to the condition of the ice. The police promised to track the thief as soon as conditions were fit, but the man, thinking he would be able to make it over the ice, had tried to overtake the low rascal himself. He found it practically impossible, however, hence his appearance at the camp.

During the night, the ice froze hard and, with the sick man in the sled-boat, the four made the trip in good time. Not once did any of them fall through the ice. The sick man and his companion had their breakfast at the camp, after which they were in a hurry to be off, before the sun thawed out the frost again. They were sure the ice was strong enough to make a shortcut across the bay to Cariboo Crossing. They were warned not to try it, to which they paid no heed. Those who were still onshore watched them, and all seemed well until one of the watchers, who had a pair of binoculars, shouted, "My God! One of them is down and the other is trying to get him up! . . . Hell! They are both through!" Immediately, the sled-boat was brought out and willing hands went to the rescue. When the rescuers arrived at the spot, all they could see, at the place the two men had been struggling before they finally disappeared, was open water.

Although around the Island and shores the ice had melted, away from the shores it was still solid. If the ice was strong enough, people with teams of horses teams would travel over the ice on the lake. Teams would still go through the ice, however, and it was amusing (although serious for the owner) to see the rapidity with which the teamster would race to the horses' heads. The owner would put a noose (made by the reins) around the neck of a horse and draw the noose tight, choking off the horse's wind and raising its body. Generally, a crowd would be about, and run to the rescue. Some would hold the horse's head, others its tail, and, with a united pull, draw the horse on to firm ice and firm footing. Not every attempt was successful, as many teams went to the bottom. Some of them could be seen, after the ice had gone out, still resting in the position, into which they had fallen, in the shallow water. It was customary for those traveling on the lakes during the thaws to carry a pole. If someone fell through a patch of the bluish, honeycombed ice, the pole, generally, would be long enough for the unfortunate to rest on, and to raise himself up, using the firm white patches. Scores travelled in this manner.

Who can say the number of men who lost their lives in the treacherous waters of the lakes, especially when the ice had become rotten? Men took chances that in ordinary circumstances they would not risk, but the magic word "gold" lured them on, to brave both danger and destruction.

～

About the time the two men were drowned, the steamer *Ora* was nearing completion, waiting for a few missing parts that were being rushed along the trail with all possible haste. These parts were coming by special carrier.

It was early morning and the ice was fairly firm. The carrier had been warned not to take any chances, but at the same time, to get the package to the *Ora*, "never mind the cost." He made some tempting offers to anyone who would cross the lake. An eye-witness tells the carrier's story:

"'Twas the first week of June. The ice was still on the lake, though honeycombed and rotten. The freshets were on and there was from twenty to fifty feet of water along the shore before one could reach the ice. The winter of 1897–98 was very severe and it was still freezing at nights. Men were packing supplies from cache to cache. It was light nearly all the twenty-four hours. We were in the land of the midnight sun.

"Just below the Island, halfway down Lake Bennett, were camped several outfits waiting for the ice to go. On this memorable morning a man with an urgent desire to cross the lake arrived. He had a small piece of machinery, needed to complete the engine of a new steamer waiting to be launched on the opposite side of the lake, and after failing in several attempts to reach the thick ice, he made an offer of one hundred dollars to anyone who would deliver the needed piece. A young fellow immediately accepted the offer, saying he wished it had been an hour earlier, as the sun was getting warm.

"He ran across to a tent and called someone inside. 'Miss Kate! Ho! Miss Kate! Are you awake?' Receiving an affirmative reply, he said, 'Keep my belt. My money is there, also correspondence from my mother. I am going across the lake. There is a chunk of money for the job.'

"'Don't do it, kid,' came the response from inside, 'I'll be out in a minute.' But the kid pushed his belt inside the tent and was off, picking up a two-by-four tent pole as he went.

"Strapping on the light pack, he gave instructions to the man to hand over the one hundred dollars to Miss Kate, then ran to where the thin shore ice looked strongest. Here he lay down with the tent pole under him, at right angles with his body, and slid along until he was on thick ice. Cautiously, he gained his feet and pursuing a zigzag course, he made his way through to the white ice, avoiding the blue honeycombed.

"By this time quite a crowd had congregated, most of whom believed he could not make it. A startled cry arose. 'He's gone!' The man who had hired him shouted, 'Come back! Come back!' Then came the shout, 'He's out! He's out!' And there was the kid crawling to firmer ice. The arrival of Miss Kate, in a towering rage, brought a feeling of personal guilt to those who heard her tirade.

"'You miserable curs—to let him go out there on an errand like that! He'll never cross safely, and you know it. You have your opinion of me, damn you—you think I'm a polluted wretch. But have you seen anything wrong with me on this trail? That boy is worth more than all you put together. He is pure gold. Were I a man, I would put you all to shame. I would go out and force him to return.'

"A few men tried to launch a sled on the ice but broke through repeatedly. The kid was still going when Miss Kate sobbed, 'My God! He's through again. You dirty cowards—to let him go!'

"Someone shouted, 'Five to one he makes it—half to go to the kid when he gets back.' 'Ten to one he don't—half to go to Kate for him,' said another. The man who had hired the kid shouted, 'Fifty to one he makes it.' 'Taken,' cried another. 'Let's appoint a stake holder.—Here, Kate. Will you handle the money?'

"'Sure I will,' replied Kate.

"Meantime the kid had progressed so far he was but a speck, and several binoculars were brought from caches. Again the cry arose, 'He's through again!'

"'Give me those glasses,' commanded the frenzied Kate. 'God, but he's plucky. He's out again!—'Boys, he's the greatest gentleman I've met. When I was slumped on the Chilcoot it was he, with a pack on his back, who fastened a rope around his waist and gave me the end. He told me I looked like his mother. Shall I ever forget the bulging veins in his neck and forehead? At one time I could stand it no longer and let go of the rope. He stopped, tied the rope around my waist and forced me to keep it there. Then up we climbed until we reached the top. Great God! It made me feel like another woman.'

"A shout went up, 'What's the matter with Kate?' and a hearty chorus answered, 'She's alright!'

"The betting continued, with, 'Come on boys, who's next? Fifteen to one he makes it.—Here Kate, take the money.—Half to go to the kid's mother, half to Kate. There he is, gone again, this time for sure. No, there he is, out again. Any more bets?'

"Keen eyes watched the kid's progress through glasses, as the hours slipped by unheeded. Near the opposite shore, the kid went down again, and though the glasses were focused on the spot he did not reappear. The crowd looked dejected and after a time someone asked about the bets. Someone else suggested that they wait until a messenger be sent around by shore to Cariboo Crossing. In desperation Miss Kate offered to bet one hundred dollars that the kid was safe. She thought inwardly that he couldn't have drowned. Surely the good Lord wouldn't let a boy so noble die. The bet was taken up—half to go to the kid or his mother.

"Then the crowd dispersed, each to his own tent, their hearts filled with sadness. Kate, worried, went to her tent, closed the flaps and sat on her blankets and thought of the past, of the man who had deserted her for another, and what life had once meant to her. This boy had saved her from despondency. Yes, she had taken this trip to try and forget. At times she felt unequal to the hardships she endured. The boy had aroused her motherly instincts, buoyed her up, and lovingly she dwelt on the words he had said, 'You look like my mother.' 'Good Lord, in Thy mercy save him,' she prayed.

"Rousing from her reverie, she started to do what she thought the kid would have requested. She took the money from his belt, tied it in a bundle, and then read the letters. Her motherly heart was breaking. The tears could not be kept back. To the package of money she added that which belonged to the boy—the winnings from the wagers. Then she wrote a letter to his mother. Weary with grief, she lay down and fell into a troubled, dreamy sleep.

"The sun rose in rare splendour. The frost had been a heavy one during the short hours of the night. Across the frozen lake, a figure with a pole was picking his cautious way. Near the shore of his destination he lay down flat and crawled across the thin shore ice, once again on terra firma. With a profound sigh he said, 'Thank God for that!' Approaching the tent, he called in a husky voice, 'Miss Kate! Miss Kate! Are you awake?'

"Startled from her troubled sleep she demanded, 'Who's there?' Then she recognized the kid's voice, and jumping up, opened the tent flaps and took him into her arms, giving him a motherly embrace. In a few moments the kid was inside. 'Sit down, boy, and tell me all about it.' Tears of joy flowed as the kid proceeded to give his experience.

"'I was confident that I could do it. I lost count of the number of times I went through. When I reached the other side it was open water. Well, it was impossible to get any wetter, so I jumped in. A few strokes brought me to the mill site. The trail led straight to the cook's kitchen. The boys were at breakfast. What a surprise for them. They treated me handsomely, digging up clothes to change into until mine were dry. They shouted, 'Hooray! Now we'll have the boat in the water.' Miss Kate, it was hard to believe. There are three beautiful boats on the way, ready to launch. Don't you think we had better wait until they run and book passage?'

"'Bless your soul, my boy,' she replied, 'We will."

"'That's fine,' he said. 'All our worries will be over. The boys at the camp wanted me to stay until the ice went out. However, I saw it would freeze so I sneaked out early, and here I am.' During his explanation she had started the stove and prepared a meal.

"'Sit up, boy,' said Miss Kate, 'It's all ready. Say, kid! You had me worried. I wrote a letter to your mother and had this package all ready to send out. Open the package, but give me the letter.'

"'Where in the world did you get all this money?' asked the astonished kid."

CHAPTER SIXTEEN

The *Ora*'s First Trip

On May 29, 1898, the day the ice finally went out, there were many campers on the shores of the Island watching the ice crash upon the shores by the force of the mighty chinook wind. All were surprised to see the number of craft following the receding ice. Some craft cleared the narrow passage, chased along by the strong blow. Whitecaps and curlers raced after them, as if they did not intend to be cheated of their prey. Some craft collided with larger ones.

Many people were unable to manage their vessels, and were naturally driven into the bay, which was exposed to the full blast of the gale. The inexperienced came broadside into the bay, and were lifted—and crashed down—by the heavy seas onto the shingle beach. It was not long before the ends and sides of some of the scows were knocked out. One scow, with silks and satins and other fancy merchandise aboard, came into the bay end-on. The craft was too unwieldy to handle. The ends were knocked out, and water flowed in, destroying everything. The two men on the craft—evidently partners—jumped into the raging waters and tried to rescue the articles. It was useless toil. The breakers seemed to laugh at their endeavours, the wind blowing stronger than ever. Frantic over the disaster, and having managed to save their demijohn of whiskey, they gave way to drinking the liquor, and were soon howling and cursing the day they had decided to go down the waters in a scow.

One can imagine their feelings—to be dealt such a blow, after having toiled and struggled over mountain passes for months, eventually arriving at Bennett, battered and bruised, with their precious freight. Many thought the battle was won when they settled at Bennett, but undefined evils were yet to be met before they completed the six hundred mile trip to Dawson.

Several incidents like the one above were experienced on Windy Arm, the strip of water connecting the north Taku arm of Tagish Lake with Lake Nares and Lake Bennett. The smaller craft fared better than the larger. When small craft were blown upon the shore, men would jump over the side of the craft and haul them up to shore. With the help of wind and breakers they pulled the craft to comparative safety, out of the reach of the fury of the elements. After the wind had abated, the different craft coming down the lake were more easily handled. Some travelled along with a certain majesty, decked out with square sails, made of drawing-room or sitting-room carpets. Their variegated colours were a great contrast to their unpainted hulls and their black-pitched seams. Some were rigged with leg-of-mutton sails that were made out of tarpaulin, others with lugsails, jibs—every kind of sail. Certainly the Yukon had never beheld such strange craft. What a sight! Never before was seen such an armada, but many were destined never to reach port.

Lake Nares was very a shallow piece of water and at Cariboo Crossing the water was low. Some craft that required deeper draft than others met with great difficulty passing through it in the early part of the season. Later, the water got deeper, as the snows melted from the mountains and the freshets found their way into the rivers and lakes. (In the fall of the year the lakes lose much of their water, draining themselves into the mighty river Yukon.) The steamer *Goddard* was able to make its way into Tagish Lake through Lake Nares, and some larger-draft scows were towed by men along the banks. The steamers *Ora*, *Nora* and *Flora* were equipped with what were called grasshopper legs, thus enabling them to be lifted over the bars.

~

As soon as the ice cleared from Lake Bennett, the *Ora* left the ways. The workmen were elated when she was christened in the old fashioned style, and the drinks were thoroughly enjoyed by all having a share in her completion. In Bennett, the days were now crammed with hustle and bustle. Steamers were running on schedule and passengers, weary after the nauseating trail, patiently waiting to get on a boat for Dawson. Merchants, professional men, and newspaper reporters—including a lady representing the *London Illustrated News*—were eager to be on board to be out of the way and to take shelter from the mosquitoes. All tried their best to avoid the bugs by dodging in and out of tents, and smudges were going at full blast. The mosquitoes were so thick that one could almost believe they were the cause of the haze that shut off the full blaze of the sun's rays.

Bill Braid, of the famous Braid's Tea and Coffee, was a passenger, as were more professors, from different parts of the world, taking note of the wonderful stampede. The professor who had been on our steamboat from Victoria was astonished to find himself now going on a trip of six hundred miles in a boat that had been built in such a short space of time. He remembered that the material for this new boat had been on the Victoria boat and now, to the other passengers, described what an enormous task transporting the material had been—what it meant to engineer the boilers and machinery over the passes and trails and to manufacture the material for their construction in this northern latitude.

There was great rejoicing when the *Ora* arrived in Bennett. Those who could afford it sold the boats they had purchased or built, saying, "We've had hell enough to get this far." Others sold outfits for a mere song and took advantage of the steamboat's first trip to Dawson, buying tickets with a sigh of relief. Crowds came to view and examine the steamer, which was now ready for freight and passengers.

The boat's appearance seemed almost miraculous to some, who concluded, "She must have come up around St. Michael."

Someone enlightened them by saying, "A few months ago the trees were standing at Wheaton. They were felled and logs were hauled to the mill site. Sawmills were erected and logs were sawed into planks and manufactured into siding and material for the framework. What you see now was, a short time ago, lying on the wharves at Skagway and Dyea. What it means to see those engines working with beautiful rhythm, the smoke belching from her smokestacks, can only be fully understood by those who helped in her construction. They alone know the heartaches and the incessant worry—hunting up freight reported lost, strikes by men for higher wages, the loss of valour in men who disappeared through the night, lured away by reports of great gold discoveries, the hunt for men to take their places, and other things incidental to the successful production you see before you."

The BL&KN Company moored the *Ora* at the wharf at the mouth of the Lindemann River, around which it had acquired property. The company had built warehouses and filled them with merchandise, ready for transport to Dawson.

However, there was still a great anxiety in the air. Many said it would be impossible to for the steamer to negotiate the bad waters of Miles Canyon and the Squaw and White Horse Rapids. I had carefully looked over these waters with a man by the name of Dixon, a constable who was also an outstanding boat pilot. I wished to put Dixon in complete charge of piloting the *Ora* through to the quieter water below the Six Mile.

❧

At Macauley's Landing, the argonauts could get advice about the dangers that faced them in the swift waters, and pilots would be onsite offering to help the inexperienced safely through. Constable Dixon was one of these pilots. But the help of the pilots was sometimes refused. One man, travelling with his wife and daughter, decided to go through with a scow alone, perhaps because he (mistakenly) believed that the pilots would insist on charging a fee. (The NWMP wanted to encourage prospectors to use the services of the pilots; in fact, Dixon had been given the power to waive the five-dollar pilot's fee if a prospector could not afford it.)

The man made preparations to cast off. At this landing stage the water was fairly swift. Away went the crowd, scampering to the Miles Canyon cliff to see if the scow would make it. "He's off, boys!" yelled someone. On came the scow, the mother and girl sitting on top of the flour that was piled, crisscross, amidships. The scow neared the narrow entrance to the canyon; the water became swifter here, as all the water from the vast watershed of the lake district passed through this narrow portal. "Here he comes!" someone shouted. "He's a greenhorn! My God, he can't straighten her! Yes, he's making it. Gad! His woman and kid are aboard. Ah! He's a little too late." The scow swung. She struck the dangerous projecting ledge. The end went out. Frantically, the man left his steering sweep to save his wife and daughter, still sitting on the stack of flour, which was now floating out into the boiling caldron of the lake. The man disappeared, evidently struck by some floating timber, to never be seen again.

But, miracle of miracles! On floated the stack of flour. The water in some way had congealed the mass. Willing hands ran down to the shallows formed by the wide expanse of water above the Squaw Rapids, and rescued the woman and girl. Once more, Miss Smith, the young owner of the dogs Yukon and Alaska, was in evidence. Heartfelt sympathy welled from the hearts of the rescuers. Miss Smith tried to console the heartsick wife, who raced up and down, waiting to see if her beloved would appear, but another life had paid the forfeit. Miss Smith also provided a temporary home for the mother and child in their distress. Who was this philanthropic young lady?

"Great Scott! If he hadn't the money, why didn't he say so? I would have portaged his freight to White Horse and the pilots would have taken his scow down. Poor devil! The trouble is, they will not state their position. And others have the money but are too damned mean to pay the portage fee or to hire pilots, and they have come to the same end— we have picked up their bodies in the eddies, with their belts crammed full of mazuma." Norman Macauley, the owner of the horsedrawn tram portage that went around the White Horse Rapids, had helped many out of their difficulties. His rate for packing freight from the landing was certainly low.

"Well, boys, come on! Who's paying for the drinks?" said someone after this incident. It seemed anyone who refused a drink was looked upon as a peculiar individual in those days.

"See Superintendent Steele if you want me to put the steamboat through the rapids," said Constable Dixon, in response to my request for him to pilot the *Ora*. "Then, if anything happens the onus is on him. Not that anything will happen but I must have absolute command. She's a willful cuss. Sometimes she behaves herself but her mood changes every few hours, owing to the volume of water increasing daily, and she has to be humoured. Anyway, I think I have her tamed to my ways now. I'll get her through when you get the order from the colonel."

"Good," I replied. "He's already been interviewed and has given permission, on condition—not to pay Constable Dixon a dime." (Superintendent Sam Steele, often called "the colonel," was the Officer Commanding of the NWMP, which had a detachment in Canyon City, at the head of the tramway.) Constable Dixon suggested that a frame be erected, high enough for a sweep to rest on. The sweep had to be long enough to clear the stern wheel and have power enough in the water to throw the stern, either to port or starboard as occasion required. A platform was built, the width of the stern, for six men to handle the sweep. A drift bolt was driven down on the frame and a large hole bored in the sweep, so the sweep could swivel either way. Two drift bolts on each side of the sweep acted as rowing locks. This sweep would be a powerful factor in keeping the boat from striking the projecting ledge of Miles Canyon. In addition, two sweeps were fixed, in a similar manner, on each side of the bow.

CHAPTER SEVENTEEN

Speeches and Toasts

All aboard for Dawson. Captain Richie at the *Ora*'s wheel. He was an old Mississippi River captain. (The law required that two captains be on each boat, one having his Canadian certificate. It was the "swift water captain" who usually handled the boat.) Those who had their boats ready to sail down the lakes and rivers envied the passengers. A few short days and they would be in Dawson. It was great to be aboard after the buffeting they had received going over the rough trails from Skagway to Bennett. Some were ready to leave in their boats, others were on their way sailing down the lake. On the *Ora*, everyone felt comfortable as they settled down in seats, glad to be on the move, enjoying the breeze that swept away the mosquitoes that were so unbearable onshore.

Inside, there was a little cubby hold (as it was termed), just big enough for the steward (or purser, as he was sometimes called) to stand upright. A shutter was taken down and presto, a small bar was seen. Immediately a number were attracted to it. One of the numerous professors suggested that, after combating the "terror that flieth by day" and the filthy nauseating trails, it would be fitting to drink to the success of the boat and the captain, and also to the staff. "It's my treat, gentlemen," he said. "Here's how! Drink hearty!" The drinks flowed freely until the steward was called away on urgent business and the bar closed.

"As I was about to say, gentlemen," continued the professor, "when at Harvard I had a vision of such wonderful land, enchanted, yes, as this certainly is. We have passed from pain and torture onto this beautiful lake, the water reflecting like a mirror the grand mountains on each side of us. What a wonderful peaceful country now that we have left the busy scene and noise made by the people hammering nails, necessary for the completion of those 'apologies' for sailboats and rowboats, in which many, no doubt, will never reach Dawson. Still, I wish them luck."

Ah, here comes the steward, who again takes down his little shutter: "Who says another?" Speech after speech was made.

"Well here's to the few ladies aboard. Their profession—journalism —is a great one. May they give a faithful portrayal of this far northern land and a true picture of this great trek, also of this trip just started. I know the countries they represent are anxiously waiting for their reports."

$\sim$

The bar was shut again as we neared Cariboo Crossing. All hands would be required to help the boat over the shallow bar, owing to the low water. We entered Lake Nares and some of the cheechakos, seeing a huge animal on the opposite shore, fired a few shots. Then they stopped, and ran for shelter, as the fusillade was returned, by the owners whose dog had been mistaken for a bear. The steamboat entered Tagish Lake and encountered a stiff blow. At this part of the lake, rightly called "Big Windy," it always seemed to be blowing. After passing through the Six Mile, we made a stop at Fort Tagish, where the NWMP had their headquarters and customs house.

The water at the port here was shallow. The *Ora* was moored to the end of a very narrow pier, constructed by stakes that had been driven down, with a crosspiece nailed to them. A narrow plank had been laid on top. This pier extended about one hundred feet from the shore. The *Ora* blew her whistle. At the first blast, the few Indians who where squatting on the shore ran away to hide in the bush. Down came two stalwart constables, in full dress, to honour the advent of a steamboat service to Dawson. Gingerly, they walked over the springy pier—that had been constructed by them—came aboard, and asked the question: "Any liquor aboard?"

"Yes, Sir," was the reply.

"Where is the permit?" The permit was produced, along with the ship's manifests. Everything was examined and passed inspection. "Say, Steward, what's the chance for a snort?" one them asked.

"Certainly," said the steward. He opened the shutter of the cubby hold, produced the nearly-solid-glass glasses, and filled them to the brim with Hudson Bay rum, which all called "the clear McKie."

"Ah, that's great!" There was a fumbling in pockets to pay for the drinks.

"This," said the steward, "is on the steamer, gentlemen."

"We'll have another, on ourselves. Gad, this is great stuff!"

"You'll have to go slow, boys. The stuff is forty overproof."

"We'll watch that part of it," the boys remarked.

The professors came along, and introduced themselves, saying they were pleased to meet the representatives of the law. "Gentlemen, the liquor on board is fine. It will give us a great pleasure if you will join us in a social glass before resuming our trip." The steward, seeing the constables were getting nervy, said, "I must close the bar and attend to some important business."

One professor replied, "Have a heart, Steward. Just one more with these fine fellows. Just one, the last." However, it was not the last. Suddenly the legs of the constables gave way and they found themselves in a sitting posture on the deck and laughing like hyenas, incapable, but not actually drunk. Hudson Bay rum overproof had this effect on many.

The steward closed the cubby hold. The passengers were enjoying the spectacle, helping the constables to their feet, when the steward espied the Officer Commanding (OC), coming down the flimsy pier. "My God!" he said to the constables. "Here comes the OC, boys, for goodness' sake pull yourselves together"—but it was useless.

The OC stepped aboard and took in the situation. Wearing his monocle, his look was awe-inspiring. He gave a shrill whistle and his man came down on the run. "Call the guard and see that these two men are put in the guardroom!" The guard arrived—two strapping, fine fellows —and, placing their hands under the constables' arms, they raised and steadied them. The OC ordered the steward to serve no more drinks to anyone and to keep the bar closed.

Meanwhile, the guard advanced with their burdens to the first plank of the pier. All went well until the second man stepped on the plank.

His weight caused it to sag and spring under the strain. All at once, the guards lost their equilibrium and the four were precipitated into the water. The OC, standing at the corner of the boiler house, watched. The passengers, laughing boisterously, enjoyed the constables' predicament. Even the OC was obliged to turn his head in an effort to suppress a laugh at the sight of his men, struggling in their efforts to get up. The steward offered his apologies for what had happened, but the OC was in no mood to hear explanations, and walked away. The steward received a severe tongue-lashing from the captain, who wanted to know, "How in hell are we to get the information we require—and only half our business done?"

The constables, regaining the use of their legs through the sudden contact with the water, speedily came to life, and raced ahead of their guards to the guardroom, amid another burst of laughter from the passengers. "Shut up, you damn fools! Do you want to make it harder for us to complete our business?" Immediately, all was quiet. After a half-hour's cogitation, with no one appearing from the fort, I called a deck-hand and said, "Go to the steward, give him this order, and bring what he gives you to me."

When the deckhand returned with his load, I said, "All right, follow me." We went along the pier and stopped at a door that had this sign on it: OFFICER COMMANDING. Then I said, "Get back to the boat and tell the mate to get everything in readiness to leave. Put the cases down and get!"

I knocked at the door, and heard the command, "Come in!"

The OC and another officer were together. I said, "I'm captain of the *Ora*, and have come to apologize for the fool conduct of my steward."

"Forget it, Captain."

"It is nice to hear you say that, gentlemen."

"Say, Captain," said the OC, "the major and I have been talking it over. You know, we couldn't very well be too hard on the constables, since they've been cooped up here since last fall, away from the bottle. They did not realize the strength of the liquor."

"Thank you, gentlemen. Excuse me, just a moment." I opened the door and brought inside the two cases. "If you will kindly accept this little present from me, it will make me feel a lot easier."

"Now, Captain, you should not do this. However, we thank you very much."

"It's thanks to you, gentlemen, and I wish you good night."

"Just a moment, Captain, you can't go without joining us in sampling the contents of your present," whereupon hammer and chisel were produced in quick order, as well as a bottle and three glasses. The pop of the cork sounded, then the gurgling of the liquor in the glasses. "Well, Captain, here's to a lucky trip down to Dawson." They all drank.

"Gad! Andrew Usher's Old Vatted, and is it good!" they exclaimed.

I then said, "If you will kindly say that everything is in order, it would expedite matters, as we wish to make all time possible."

Everything was approved, with a hope from the officers that the boat would safely pass the rapids. "Get Constable Dixon to give you all help possible," the OC said. "Sergeant Joyce will see to it. Take him this note. Good night!"

"Good night!" And away went the captain, relieved and cheerful, thanking God that the NWMP had men in the force who understood human nature and the failings inherent in them. He would tell those damned professors to be more careful when they stopped off at police quarters along the river. The passengers, when they saw the captain come aboard smiling, knew that everything had been smoothed over.

The order was given: "Cast off!" The crowd aboard all voiced the opinion that the police stationed at Tagish were fine fellows and gentlemen. A professor shouted as the boat was leaving, "Three cheers for the Mounties! Hip, hip, hooray!" This was heartily joined in by everyone. The professor then began to explain to the crowd how to tell when a man was drunk. The constables, he said, were sober, but he could not understand how they had lost the use of their legs. One of two men, evidently doctors, gave a satisfactory explanation, quoting the effect alcohol had on a certain nerve centre. Our popular professor summed up the case: "He is not drunk, who on the floor doth lie and rise to drink some more. He is drunk, who on the floor doth lie and cannot rise to drink some more." All pondered over these lines. A few said the constables were drunk, while others said they had behaved in a gentlemanlike manner all through, especially in the water.

As the boat left Tagish it was hailed by a man coming alongside, with great speed, in a canoe. He climbed aboard with amazing dexterity, tied the painter securely, then shouted, "Where is the blankety-blank son-of-a-gun who shot my dog?—the best damned dog that ever hit the trail!" The steward said he had heard some shooting on Lake Nares, and that was all he knew about it.

Our professor, ever ready in all emergencies, came to the rescue, saying, "My dear sir! Are you the fellow who fired the shots at the steamboat and made us all run for shelter? We saw a black bear on the opposite shore—or rather I should say the sporting passengers did—and after a few shots, with no apparent damage done, we were deluged with rifle bullets, presumably from you. We are not far from the fort and I suggest that the captain turn back and lay a charge against you for firing a rifle with intent to do bodily harm."

Many of the passengers felt less shaky after the professor had spoken, but again the man shouted, "I want the man who shot my dog! I'll go to the fort! The police? Say, they're gents, and'll laugh at your damned information. They know what a man's dog is to him. You poor simps. Don't you know a dog from a bear?"

"My dear man," said the professor, "you must take into consideration that these men are—what do they call them?—ah, yes, cheechakos. They have 'deer fever'—I mean 'bear fever.'"

"Damn the fever! How about my dog?"

At this answer, and seeing the man was in earnest, the professor pulled out a five-dollar bill, saying, "I'm sorry for this fellow five dollars. How much are you fellows sorry?" The hat was passed around, a respectable collection was made, which appeased the man, and he departed in his canoe.

Sometime later, when the man was telling the story of his dog (which had not been shot at all), to a body of ready listeners camping on the lower reaches of the Yukon, he wound up by saying, "It was the easiest money I ever made. The bluff worked!"

After the dog episode, I called the passengers together, and addressed them. "Everyone! When you see anything moving again, as you did at the Lake Nares, call me before you use your rifles. Don't take a rabbit for a dog, or a dog for a moose. I know how things can be magnified when you have a shooting craze. We want to reach Dawson, so act rationally, and for goodness' sake, keep your nerve when we enter Miles Canyon, the Squaw Rapids, and the White Horse Rapids. All those who wish to can go over the portage."

By this time, the *Ora* was well on her way down the Six Mile, which emptied into Marsh Lake. Everyone was interested in the beautiful stream, with its sandy and gravelly bottom. The professor's attention was drawn to a school of fish following the boat. There were lake trout, not in dozens, but in hundreds, keeping up with the boat—and this is not a "fishy" story. One could see monsters, three to four feet long, and now and then one would open its mouth and swallow a fish half its size. "Fish! Great heavens!" said the professor, "I have never heard of trout this size. I must take note of this for future reference."

When we were almost at the entrance to Marsh Lake, we were hailed by campers. It happened to be a police fish camp. The boys wanted to trade fish for whiskey, which was done. Who had the better of the bargain? It was hard to say. The whiskey was ten dollars per bottle. The boat did not get such an amazing quantity of fish but, nevertheless, it was fresh and no one aboard had seen such fine specimens. The cook was an old sailor. At mealtime everyone wanted fish. What a change, after pork and beans, even though they had been cooked and dished up in every way imaginable. The price of each meal on the boat was two dollars and fifty cents. This was cheap, when the prices that were paid for packing over the passes to Bennett were considered.

One of our passengers knew the man in charge of the police fish camp. "Why, hullo there, Leader!" he shouted, "Where in the Sam Hill did you come from? The last time we met was at Fort Qu'Appelle! You old dog-musher!"

"Well, so help me, if it isn't Bill!" shouted the man. "Say, I'm broke, Bill! Get me a bottle!" Bill went away to get the bottle. The *Ora* blew her whistle and was off. Leader jumped in his canoe and raced after her.

Bill reappeared, with the bottle. "Be seeing you again, old-timer," he called, after he had thrown him the bottle. "Au revoir!"

Leader had one last comment: "Say, Bill, this is a hell of a life! They've given me the job of looking after the dogs. See the fish drying for next winter?" The fish were hung on lines, well out of the reach of the dogs. The dogs themselves—mostly malamutes—were around the bend, on a kind of island. As the boat passed, we saw their fangs bared. They looked like a pack of wolves. One would pity the fellow who got in amongst them.

The *Ora* entered Marsh Lake, whose waters were generally muddy and very shallow in places. On the far side, the M'Clintock River emptied into the lake. (This river being named after a surveyor who was sent into this country by the government years before to map out the land.) Leaving Marsh Lake, we entered the Six Mile, which flows into Lake Laberge. In some parts of the upper Six Mile the current ran swiftly, and the captain had his work cut out for him, dodging uprooted trees and snags that had been brought down by the freshets the melting snows caused.

We saw a number of otters, some diving and coming up with fish in their mouths. Earlier in this area's history, an enormous number of otter skins were paid, as a royalty, to the Russians for the privilege of trapping in this great fur-bearing country. We were amazed by the number of ducks, there were literally thousands of them, and when they were disturbed, the air would be thick with them. Ducklings would scamper away under the banks. Here was the breeding place of the world's finest: the canvasback, the mallard, the little teal, and nearly every other variety.

CHAPTER EIGHTEEN

Shooting the White Horse

The *Ora* turned a bend in the river and came in view of Macauley's Landing. A shout went up from the passengers and from those onshore: "Hooray!" In the distance, we could see the yawning mouth of Miles Canyon. Willing hands received the lines at the mooring, as the captain showed his skill in making the platform, surprising everyone, considering the swiftness of the water at this point. Opposite Macauley's, on the other side of the river, was Hepburn Landing, which had another tramway that transferred merchandise around the swift waters. But Macauley's Landing was the favourite stopping place.

The passengers were delighted to get off the boat and do some reconnoitering. They soon found the bar at Macauley's and sampled the liquor. Sergeant Joyce was stationed here, a fine, capable officer who laid himself out to do all that he could for the captain and passengers. The captain and crew waited for Constable Dixon, who had just left to pilot a scow down to White Horse. It was not long before Dixon arrived.

Only a few passengers cared to remain on board and run the risk of riding the turbulent waters. The professor and the crowd—who seemed thoroughly comfortable at the saloon—were warned that if they were not at the foot of the rapids by the time the *Ora* was through, there would be no waiting—they would be left behind. Macauley promised to take them down and see that they were on hand. He was doing a nice little business, so he could afford to see to these passengers. He kept his word, although many of the passengers were a little hilarious when they arrived. One lady had stayed aboard, as she wanted to have a little adventure. There were a few preliminaries. Dixon instructed the crew in their different duties. The huge sweeps were placed in position. When the commands "Port!" and "Starboard!" came, the crew were to move the sweeps accordingly. The cliffs were lined with sightseers. At last the words "All clear!" rang out.

The captain was at the wheel. Dixon was on the upper deck, motioning with his hands. At the bow, a crewmember relayed Dixon's orders to the men operating the sweeps. The steering wheel performed rapid motions under the skillful handling of the captain. The water moved faster. They got nearer and the waters began to get narrower. The *Ora* was now ready to go through the "get," from which there was no returning. A shout: "Hard to port!" Then, instantly: "Starboard!" One of the bow sweeps struck the reef and the blade broke into splinters. In they went, through the canyon, into the boiling waters of a basin that looked like the mouth of an extinct volcano.

The *Ora* emerged from the inferno, amidst the shouting and cheering of the crowds who lined the cliffs. In the crowd was the captain of the *Willie Irving*, who had come to get a few pointers before attempting to take his boat through. The steamer continued, into the Squaw Rapids, which were dotted here and there with huge boulders. Dixon shouted "Port!" and "Starboard!" in rapid succession. The craft turned a bend, and there, before it, was the much-talked-of White Horse Rapids. The crests of water certainly did resemble the proud neck of a white steed. "Steady boys!" Nearer and nearer the *Ora* approached. "Hard to starboard!" was the next command, with mighty waters rushing, eager to find a passage through the narrow opening. Crowds still thronged the shore, waiting, expecting to see disaster, such as had happened to many, much smaller craft. Those who knew Dixon, the pilot, were confident he would make it. The *Ora* mounted the arched, rising crest—defiant, resolute, her bow now rising triumphantly. She was christened with white foam. "Port! Hard to port!" Like a swan, she dove into the waters below. She steamed around the basin, coming up to her future quarters amidst the hat throwing and cheering of a joyful crowd.

The BL&KN Company had already erected a large tent warehouse, in which some whiskey was stored. A keg was tapped, and everyone drank to the health of the *Ora*, to the captain, to Dixon, and to the crew. "Say,

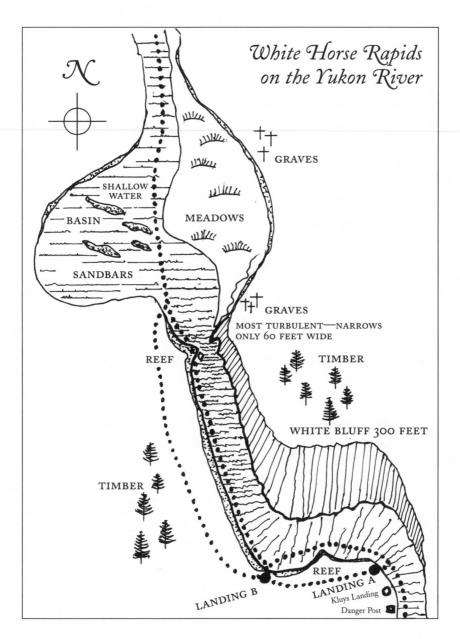

White Horse Rapids on the Yukon River

N

GRAVES

SHALLOW WATER

BASIN

MEADOWS

SANDBARS

GRAVES

MOST TURBULENT—NARROWS ONLY 60 FEET WIDE

REEF

TIMBER

WHITE BLUFF 300 FEET

TIMBER

REEF

LANDING B

LANDING A

Kluys Landing

Danger Post

Between LANDING B and just past the narrows further north, was the swiftest and most difficult section of the rapids. Boats were either portaged over skids for a half mile or controlled by lines on the water as shown. Current is flowing north.

that was a pretty sight," said one. "Did you see her, wheel up in the air? When she dipped, the old wheel threw back the water in the face of the old White Horse, as if in contempt, saying, 'You're not half as bad as you're painted. You're broken and we'll ride you again before long.'" Another remarked, "I can scarcely believe it, after seeing so many scows and boats turned turtle, and lives lost. I managed to save my own life, but my scow and merchandise were wrecked and lost."

The last of the whiskey was consumed. Again, three cheers were given for the captain and Dixon. Around the corner came the passengers, too late for drinking success to the boat. However, by their gait, Macauley had evidently looked after their requirements. "Look here, Dixon," I said, "you've got to accept this little present. This is for tobacco money."

"Gad, I can't accept anything!" exclaimed Dixon. "If the colonel knew what you were doing he would sure be mad!"

"Forget the colonel!" I said. "I'm not paying you for putting the boat through, although goodness knows you do deserve to be well paid for it. This is a present for what you have done for the helpless sourdoughs who have gone before—and be sure to be ready for the *Nora* in a day or two!"

❧

The *Willie Irving* was moored at Macauley's wharf, her captain evidently waiting to see how the *Ora* fared. He voiced his opinion that he would not have done "this and that," if he had put the boat through, and was answered, "If you get through as well, there will be nothing for you to kick about." The *Willie Irving* was a beautiful craft. Her lines were symmetrical and she looked like a swan on the water.

However, there was no time for me to lose in controversy. The directors of the BL&KN Company would want to know of the *Ora*'s success in passing the dreaded rapids. A canoe was ready for the captain of one of the other boats and myself to paddle to Bennett. I gave instructions the *Ora*'s crew to proceed to Dawson with all possible speed and then to return to White Horse, where the steamers *Flora* and *Nora* would meet them.

The canoe glided off, upstream, through a haze of mosquitoes. We were equipped with mosquito netting over our heads and gloves on our hands. In spite of this, the monotonous buzzing became wearisome. We met several boats and scows gliding along, their occupants frantic, many having no netting to protect them. With long steady strokes, we emerged into Marsh Lake and thanked God when we encountered a breeze that dispersed the mosquitoes and enabled us to cast aside the netting and gloves and to enjoy once more freedom from purgatory.

We were attracted by shouts from the shore of the lake, where Indians were camped. We disregarded the shouts, as reports had been received at Macauley's that two prospectors had been murdered at M'Clintock River. We had no time to lose; it would have to be something very urgent to stop us from getting the news of the *Ora* to Victoria. We knew that the parties who were interested in the steamboat venture were anxiously waiting to find out whether the enterprise was a success or failure.

We took turns taking a few short naps, knowing full well we would require all the stamina we possessed to make Bennett in quick time. We reached the Six Mile and made a stop at Fort Tagish, giving the good news to Captain Strickland, who was very pleased and said the success of the *Ora* would greatly help the police patrol the river and keep law and order.

Eight hundred pounds of mail had accumulated at the port here, and was waiting to be taken out to Bennett. The man in charge of the mail wanted help and since the OC knew we were planning to travel quickly, he asked us if the mail carrier could go along—we could have the larger canoe and leave the light one at the port. The mail was to be delivered to Superintendent Steele, who was at this time at Bennett. The captain went to the bow of the larger canoe, the mail carrier went amidships, and we were off again. When we were nearly out of the Six Mile, we heard roars, as if of thunder. "You had better take charge, Captain," I said. "Change places."

"It's nothing," replied the captain. "We'll soon be across Big Windy."

We passed the headland and struck a rough bit of water. "Better turn back, Captain."

"No, it's alright. Head for the Island." The wind grew stronger. "Keep her quartered when the combers are close!" cried the captain.

"Righto!" We had to shout to be heard.

"On we go! Blow on, ye windy gods. Blow; lash into fury your instruments of death.—Quarter her!" cried the captain. "My God, she's getting wild! Good boat! Blow, blast you, blow! Whip into frenzy your galloping waves.—Hey! Quarter her!" We rode over another white crested comber. "Screech and whistle, ye fiends. Screech, you mysterious winds. Blow on, we'll lick you yet! Wreak your vengeance on the towering rocks."

Again we saw a huge comber coming to take toll. The mail carrier rose, having momentarily lost his head, and cried, "My God!" at the sight of an avalanche of water that looked, in the dark, as if it would swallow us. With a swift motion, I drew my paddle from the waters and whacked the mail carrier on the head. He collapsed. Like lightning, I dipped my blade, in time to quarter the canoe. We shipped some spray, and over the crest we went. The worst was over as we glided into quieter waters in shelter of the Island. Old Windy was licked once more. In the distance, we could still hear the moaning and screeching of the wind, like one in rage, foiled in the attempt to wreak her fury on the puny insignificants daring to cross her path to safety.

In the shelter of the Island, worn out by our strenuous efforts, we decided to sleep for an hour. We were awakened by millions of mosquitoes biting and buzzing as the sun appeared from behind the mountain. Our eyes were nearly closed by the bites, but after washing them in the lake water the fever was allayed and we were able to resume our journey. Off we went again, eager to get the good news to Victoria. The mail carrier had quite recovered from the annoyance of being struck over the head in the storm and eventually blaming himself, and shuddering at the thought that his actions had nearly led us into becoming the prey of Old Windy.

We passed Lake Nares, dreading what Lake Bennett might bring. Cariboo Crossing was awake; the sound of the mallet and caulking tools rang in our ears. The campers were giving the last touch to their crafts, ready to be initiated. We entered Lake Bennett. Divided by a narrow range of mountains from Tagish Lake, the water was like a mirror, reflecting the magnificent landscape that surrounded it. "Say, Captain," I said, "those old wind gods are played out. They must be sleeping, or gone on a hunt for cheechakos." We looked across the lake to the Wheaton River. The *Nora* was on the water, ready to get her baptism in the rapids and take her place in the lower reaches of the Yukon, with her sister ship, the *Ora*. There was no time to cross over. We crept along the shores of Bennett and arrived safely with the mail. "Say, mail carrier!" I said, "pay us for bringing the mail safe to Bennett." He agreed readily. "And forget the crack in your head. It saved us all at Windy."

In my office, I hailed my secretary. "Hello, Hildige! Get ready to take a few lines to Skagway and send them by the first boat, special delivery." The gist of my letter was:

Dear Rattenbury,

Ora safely through, nearing Dawson now, if not already there. Tell the mercenaries, who only wanted money for materials supplied to boats, believing enterprise would be a failure, they are fooled.

Firing all pets of shareholders, hiring only competents. Don't send any more money. Boats paying handsomely. Come up and we'll look over the route from M'Clintock to Hootalinka, for which we have charter. Be here in a week from time you receive this.

CHAPTER NINETEEN

Sizing Up the Rush

Bennett was a very busy place, although thousands had passed down the lake following the ice. Merchandise kept pouring in; cheechakos were coming down from Lindemann way. The waters were rising, with many exciting incidents taking place at the rapids. A few boats would come through all right, but there would be a series of accidents. Mule trains were the only means, now, of bringing in freight from Skagway. Some small amounts came via the aerial tramway as far as the White Pass, then transferred to wagon and mules to Lindemann.

Merchandise was piling up, brought in by parties who had gone out from Dawson in the winter to purchase what they thought would be badly needed for the season of 1898. At Dawson, much of this merchandise represented untold wealth. There were bales of tarpaper, nails, blankets, butter, oranges, apples, beef on foot. (Some cattle were slaughtered at Bennett for immediate use, others were shipped, live, on scows.) And there were eggs. One mule train had left Log Cabin with hundreds of cases of eggs, which had survived the ordeals of the rough trails to this point. What happened to cause the mules to stampede no one knows. It may have been the mosquitoes or flies. For some distance, the trail from Log Cabin lay through a growth of stunted spruce. The mules, in their stampede, caused the cases to bump against the trees on the crooked trail. For miles the trail was strewn with broken eggs. This shipment, had it arrived in Dawson, would have meant a life of ease for the shipper, as it represented thousands of dollars.

There were a few coops of live chickens among the merchandise, but what became of these is not known. Perhaps the scow or boat that took them downriver was lost. One of the first chicken dinners at Dawson was fifteen dollars a plate—and there was little more than the smell, at that.

Mike "the lovely Dove" King vied with the transportation company for business, by pushing the sale of his scows. Several merchants fell for his reasoning; he pictured to them the great amount they would save if they took their own freight down the 600-mile route, and later they wished they had not listened to him. Some were wrecked, some were stranded, some failed to reach Dawson in time to dispose of their merchandise at a remunerative figure. Many were good losers, and eventually the steamboats helped them out of their difficulties.

The *Nora*, now ready for transport, made Bennett, took on freight for Dawson, and went through the same ordeal as her sister ship had, at the rapids, also performing well. On her trip to Bennett from the shipyard, however, she had narrowly escaped being wrecked. Her crew said it was the wildest blow they had ever experienced. The wind came down through the gap at Lindemann, blowing down tents and everything in its course. The *Nora*, just below the Island, was on the verge of capsizing, when by a freak wind from the mountain, it veered in the opposite direction and righted her. Then a wind struck her in the stern, lifting her off the water to come down with a smack. Captain Martineau was at the wheel, and his masterly handling of her saved the *Nora* from shipwreck and brought her to shelter and safety.

The storm that nearly spelt disaster to the *Nora* on Lake Bennett took the lives of several who were caught in unseaworthy craft in its wake. Not far from Cariboo Crossing, a young man was found dead, half-naked. His boat had washed in not far from where his body was found. Evidently he had cast off his clothes when his boat swamped and tried to swim ashore. Had he stayed with his craft his life might possibly have been saved. Some of his clothes were found in the boat, along with a letter he had written to his mother. "At last I am on the great waterway leading to the fabulous goldfields. Cheer up! Don't worry. I am writing this letter in my boat, a nice breeze is blowing and I have just fixed up a small sail. We are gliding along nicely. I'll soon be at my destination and will soon send you enough to clear off the mortgage." The letter was half-finished. Perhaps the big blow had struck him. One can imagine the difficulty he must have had in managing the boat, his perplexity about what to do when the big curlers came tumbling over the stern, the buffeting he received—all, only to lose his life in the cold glacial waters. His effects were gathered together and, with an inventory of them, sent to his home.

~

At Skagway, a group met in the sitting room of the Brannick Hotel: William Ogilvie (the first commissioner of the Yukon), Hawkins (the manager of the WP&YR), Mr. Klute, a customs inspector, Superintendent Steele, a professor (a real one this time), and myself (the manager of the BL&KN company).

We sat spinning yarns of our experiences, and estimating as closely as possible the number of people who had gone down the river to Dawson. "If word came that gold was to be found at the North Pole, the old pioneers at Dawson would find a way to get there," said someone. Someone else said the old pioneers could make the planned expeditions of scientists look foolish. Hawkins thought his railroad would be doing a profitable business before the end of the season, and would have steel laid to the summit before Christmas. (It was not to reach there until February of 1899.)

At Dyea, I met Wallace of the Dyea aerial tramway, soliciting freight for his enterprise, but he was too late for the big rush. The tram was finished, as far as the summit of the Chilcoot Pass, and stopped there. The enterprise looked to be a financial disaster, since most of the ocean boats unloaded their freight at Skagway so that the WP&YR could carry it as far as steel had been laid, shortening the route for the pack trains. In fact, the WP&YR was contracting to take freight as far as Bennett.

The little party at the Brannick Hotel had things pretty well sized up. We congratulated Superintendent Steele because, through the efforts of the police, little crime occurred after the Union Jack flew at the White Pass. Yet in spite of their vigilance, lawless characters did slip through and caused considerable trouble. But on the whole, the Yukon was a safe place in which to travel.

Fabulous prices were being paid for articles of which there was a scarcity in White Horse. Everything averaged one dollar per pound. Butter, salt, flour, and staples all sold at that figure. One enterprising individual with a few eggs sold them for one dollar each. Those unfortunate ones who had lost all their merchandise going through the White Horse Rapids paid $150 for a sack of flour (when it was scarce), rather than be delayed any longer. Although there was a big demand for scows (which in June 1898, the BL&KN company, as well as Mike King, were building, to cope with the freight billed for Dawson), the news of the *Ora*'s successful shoot through the rapids caused many to consider taking a steamboat rather that poling their own boats. Although many people were not injured when their scows overturned, naturally, they would lose their merchandise. And those who had no money to buy more supplies became stranded, having to work their passage down. It would be hard to estimate the amount of wealth that was lost in the turbulent waters.

One scow that shot the rapids on its own had a big audience. The sweep with which the owner was steering broke just as the scow was ready to ride the crest. She turned broadside to the current and made a complete somersault. All its freight was destroyed. When the crew was rescued, one of them said, "Let's give up the trip! I've had enough!"

"Like hell!" another returned, "Why, I'm just beginning to like it! Here's one for home, sweet home!" This fellow had been on the trail for six months; he had packed all over the passes, had seen everything destroyed, and was not a bit worried. He continued, "Come on, Frank! We've been pretty lucky up to now." Alluding to a bystander, he said, "This fellow is willing to sell his outfit. We'll buy it. It was no fault of ours that the sweep broke. I want to see what this old river is like farther down, and mean to see it through!" They made arrangements for the other fellow's outfit and away they went, laughing. These were the kind of men who made the Yukon what it was and they would not be conquered.

CHAPTER TWENTY

On to Dawson

The *Ora* behaved splendidly over the rapids. As the steamer progressed down the Six Mile, one of the passengers drew the attention of the captain to the body of a drowned man floating in an eddy. The captain gave the signal to stop. A landing was made, the deckhands took the body ashore, searched his clothes, took an inventory of what was found, and buried the corpse. At the next police post the matter was reported and the boat proceeded on her journey.

The *Ora* suddenly found herself in the river into Lake Laberge. Here, a number of boats and scows were waiting for the wind to die down. They had had their experience on Lake Bennett and Windy Arm and knew what the whitecaps meant out on the lake. At night the wind generally died down, so they waited and took advantage of it. Yet the more adventurous were out in the middle, with square sails filled, and seemed to be enjoying the challenge. Many of the adventurers were old sailors and knew their business, delighted to be off the land trail and once more on the water. Some of those on boats and scows made tempting offers to us to tow them across the lake. (On one of the *Ora*'s trips Macauley, who later became the mayor of Dawson, paid eight hundred dollars to be towed across, but one must bear in mind that some outfits were worth thousands of dollars.)

After passing crafts of all descriptions, sailing and rowing, the *Ora* entered a stretch of the Yukon called the Thirtymile. The trip down was short and swift. The boat was considerably lower at the bow than the stern, which showed how swiftly this piece of water was running. Several craft were wrecked in this river, especially those belonging to greenhorns, inexperienced in swift waters.

There was, in '98, a huge rock about halfway down the river, standing in its middle, a menace to navigation. The passengers who had been enjoying their swift passage were now alarmed to find themselves heading straight for this rock, and wondered if the captain was asleep. They were reassured when the captain spun the wheel and the *Ora*, answering her helm nicely, swung with the current, past the rock. Then it looked as if she would strike the bank, but with dexterous handling of the wheel, she was once again like a live thing. Why not? A swift water captain was at the wheel. Our professor made a note of the dangerous rock, promising to interview the government regarding the menace it posed and its removal; he claimed it could easily be blown out by dynamite. Eventually this was accomplished, but before the rock was removed, many a scow and boat were wrecked at this point.

We now arrived at a junction, where the Thirtymile met the Hootalinka. (Also called the Hootalinqua, it is now called the Teslin River.) Together, these two rivers emptied into the Lewes River (now called the Yukon). Anchored here were crafts of all descriptions, gladly taking much-needed rests. We saw men patching their craft, after having made the rough trip through the lower Six Mile, Lake Laberge, and the Thirtymile. We noticed wreckage of scows and boats floating past. The *Ora* out of necessity had to stop at Hootalinka. The captain, in a voice all could hear, commanded, "Now, boys, if you want to get to Dawson, jump ashore. The mate will give you axes. Start chopping." We had tied up at a clump of dried timber. It was no time before the boat was loaded with all the firewood she could stow. Expert axe-men were present among the passengers and even the professor could wield an axe in a dexterous manner.

While the timber was being loaded, a man came down the Hootalinka and was hailed by a passenger, "Hello, Tim!"

"Why, hello, you old moose!" the man replied. He had just come in from the Teslin Trail. The "Old Moose," on the other hand, had earlier turned his back on that trail of muskeg, making his way to Skagway to catch the first means of easy transportation, namely the *Ora*. "You old devil," continued Tim, "I missed you, and no one seemed to know what became of you, and here you turn up, fresh as a daisy, and me nothing but skin and bones. Say Moose, find out how long before you start."

"It will be fifteen minutes, Tim."

"Tell the captain to hold the boat for ten minutes anyway." Moose asked Tim what he was up to. "Damn it!" said Tim, " To think you are having a good time going to Dawson this easy is too much for me. There is a poor devil back there who had hard luck. I have given him the outfit. He can pay me something for it if he feels like it. If not, what's the difference? This pack is all I'll want until I get to Dawson. And now, Moose, arrange for my passage. Have you got a flask? No? Well, here's off for a good long sleep. Think of you having such a good time and me on that damned trail with no rest, no sleep, rotten bacon and beans, half-frozen and very near scurvy."

Just then the steward came along. Moose called Tim back, saying to him, "The steward will give us something better than flask stuff." One drink was enough for Tim. Moose was to his comfort and Tim did not appear on deck until the last lap to Dawson.

~

The *Ora* travelled night and day, making good time down the placid waters of the Lewes River. A fairly good-sized camp was situated at Big Salmon River (and at Little Salmon). At these junctions, several people forsook their own outfits, glad to take passage on the *Ora* and be rid of the irksome duties of a seemingly endless trail. Those who had no money to do the same, envied the lucky ones who could afford to give away outfits and to avail themselves of comfort, such as it was. We soon passed Carmacks, and, after a few hours' run, sighted Five Fingers. The name was derived from the five channels that were formed by four huge conglomerate rocks, which stood up like sentinels, guarding the entrance to the country beyond. Here, the water rushed through with lightning speed. On we sped, to the Rink Rapids (always a treacherous piece of water), then to the site of the old Fort Selkirk, where we stopped for firewood.

Innumerable islands were scattered between the shores of the river and were many miles in width. One can imagine the surprise that Robert Campbell of the HBC, must have felt when he saw this area. After the company post was built, however, a great jealousy developed between the Chilkat Indians and the Indians of the interior, who favoured the HBC, which made greater remuneration to them for their pelts than the Chilkat did. The Chilkat considered this great country their hunting preserve and came annually to this vicinity. Eventually they found an opportunity to attack the fort, when Campbell and some of the local Indians were away on a hunting trip, and burned it to the ground.

Taku Jack, of the Tagish Indians, told tales of the many times his Tagish forefathers had battled the Chilkat, with whom, at one time, they had hunted, trapped, and traded. As soon as the ice on Lindemann and Bennett went out, they would work down to the Pelly and Stewart Rivers and bring out thousands of otter skins, to trade with white men on the coast. Little wonder Campbell's HBC post was destroyed—the Indians knew that if Campbell remained, he would do all the trading, at his own figure, and their annual harvest would be no more.

Taku Jack's grandfather had told him wonderful things about a river that was named by the Indians, the Yukon. He said that one year the ice did not go out on the lakes. He might not have been exaggerating; some years the ice does not move until July or even the first of August, only to freeze up in the first week in October. Records show that white men who ventured too far up the river from St. Michael (at its mouth) or too far down the river from its source had been murdered. The country around the Pelly and Stewart Rivers seemed to be jealously guarded by the Indians, as it abounded in furs, fish, and meat. One can easily visualize, having once seen this wonderful waterway and enchanting hunting ground, how the different tribes would fight for supremacy over it. Taku Jack was also fond of talking about the cariboo, saying no one could count their number and that it took the cariboo a week to cross the river.

A bishop staying in Selkirk in 1898, was every inch the bishop in his appearance. He came up to see the *Ora*, and one passenger remarked, as he saw the bishop come toward the boat in his stately stride, with

146

about twenty young Indians walking behind him in single file, "Good old boy. You've raised a goodly family." The "family" ranged from six feet in height to three-foot, toddling fellows. They were all charges of the bishop, who was trying to "train" them properly.

The Pelly was sending forth a mighty volume of water at its junction with the Yukon. Here, again, there was a crowd of voyageurs, some with their boats and crafts intact, others busy patching their partially wrecked ones. Robert Service's *The Trail of Ninety-Eight,* expresses the situation graphically.

> But what of the others who followed,
> Losing their boats by the score?
> Well could we see and hear them,
> Strung down that desolate shore.
> What of the poor souls who perished?
> Little of them shall be said—
> On to the Golden Valley,
> Pause not to bury the dead.

A fine fellow, by the name of Marcelles, wanted a job as pilot on one of the BL&KN company steamers. He stated his case.

"I know river well—have just come up. Me? I ran de Ottawa, de Lachine. Me? All say 'One good man.' I go down for you. Me go down with big party. Dey all know, but not de swift water. We go onto de Five Fingers, we call him. Me, dey say 'you sleep—we call you when swift water.' Yes, dey call me—dey wake me up. Dere de Five Fingers. One big mountain ice jam. I jump de sweep. Ah, no time de big water rush under, eleven men in de boat, she go under. Me? I make one big jump, hold onto de ice, pull me up, go to top, look over. No boat, no man, see nobody. I run over de jam de ice. I see not one, no boat, nothing. I stay about. It make me cry. Me, big strong man. Me, I see dem no more. Good men—plenty money and grub. 'Gone! Gone!' de water keep saying to me when she rushed through.

"Waiting, I hear some more. De water say, 'I get some more. You see.' On she rush, laughing, making de awful roar, saying, 'I get some more, I get some more.' She means some more to drown, I know, an me. De good Lord he tells me jump on de ice. Ah, dat was de jump, six, eight, ten feet. I hang on, nearly slip. I see some more scow. Some more de boat way up de river half de mile. I strip. I take off de mackinaw. I wave. I wave some more. I pray do good Lord. I wave. I wave. I wave some more. Dey see me! Dey see me! I call dem. I show dem—dey see. Thank de Lord, dey see me! Dey come into de shore. I catch 'im line and fasten to de tree. We call some more boats. Dey come in too. Some women in party. Dey cry sure when I tell dem story. Dey say, 'So sorry.' Me? Dey make me cry some more.

"We go down see to find some of de men. No man, no boat. Dey say to me, 'You sure?' Me no tell lie. Poor fellows, dey go under. Dey see de big jam de ice. Dey hear de water roar. Dey go under. Me? I say again 'Poor fellows.' I count dem on my fingers, eleven good men. You call dem tears? Dey fall down my face. Den dey believe me and pat my back and say, 'You one good man.' We go down again, de other side. We walk so far, long way. I see my sweep, pick up my sweep, and show dem. Me make 'im Hootalinka my sweep. Pick 'im up and take 'im with me. I got de sweep now—I keep 'im. Help me tink of de good men, eleven. Dey all go! Go! And de waters say—dey laugh, dey roar—'We get some more!' I stay with men half-day, one day, and den by God we hear great noise. We all look and see de jam de ice, all fall away, and de jam de ice we see no more. I go and pilot de scows along to Dawson. Me good man. Dey pay me good. I came here see you. Give de good pilot a job."

The incident that Marcelles related was followed up, but no trace of or sign of the unfortunates could be found. The only thing left was the sweep that Marcelles had and would not part with. The French Canadian kept it as a reminder of his fateful trip.

Selkirk was left behind and a brief stop was made at Stewart. Here again, I was reminded of another intrepid explorer, a daring voyager, companion and clerk to Robert Campbell. He had traced the headwaters of the Stewart River to its mouth (named after himself), little dreaming that argonauts would pass here, by the thousands, in their quest for gold. Yes, even exploring the river itself, and washing thousands of dollars from the river beds while steamboats plied up and down the Yukon, making a regular stopping place where it joined the Stewart. Scores of scows and boats were being patched up and repaired. The sergeant of the NWMP visited the steamboat and asked the usual question, "Any liquor aboard?" Of course there was—a little, enough to accommodate the passengers; the bulk had been left behind at White Horse. The police advised the BL&KN company to leave it there until the permit for it (from Regina) was verified. It was at Stewart that the rumour started about the Honourable Clifford Sifton, the Minister of the Interior, that he was planning to ship in several thousand gallons of liquor in the name of Senator Domville. (At Dawson, the rumour was in the air. Senator Domville and Sifton's nephew were expected any day from St. Michael, with a load of liquor, on the steamer *Domville*. By taking the easier route they avoided paying enormous freight rates over the passes and the risk of losing some of their consignment.)

The sergeant had instructions to hold all liquor that arrived in Stewart. Liquor was scarce in Dawson—as much as two hundred dollars per gallon was offered for it. Small quantities did find their way in, but there was not enough to satisfy the thirst of many of the lucky rich, bringing in their wealth from Bonanza and Eldorado Creeks. The higher the price, the better these prospectors liked it. The *Ora* had to leave behind a few kegs at Stewart to comply with the order that had been issued by Superintendent Steele. Several parties had their permits (issued from Regina), which required a fee of two dollars per gallon. Yet still, whiskey was held up at the different posts. (A thought ran counter to the rumour—if Sifton did indeed have an interest the *Domville* shipment, no one would have a chance to get in on the high prices until their shipment was first sold.)

CHAPTER TWENTY-ONE

Arriving at Dawson

Leaving Stewart the *Ora* pressed on to her goal, Dawson. On the way she encountered unwieldy crafts that had lost their steering gear and were being driven from shore to shore by the currents or stuck on the bars. The steamboat was hailed more than once to stand by and take on board a sick man, suffering from scurvy, and generally, more dead than alive. On the *Ora* went, throwing a line first to one, then to another. At last, Dawson! What a welcome! Crowds flocked the little wharf, sending up three cheers.

At the mouth of the Klondyke, Louse Town (as it was called) was a busy scene. Scow after scow, boat after boat, pulled in. Glad and bois-terous were those who had come through in good health. Sad and dejected were others, in poor health, broken in spirit, dollarless, ready for the hospital.

There was one among them who looked as sick and ill as any, yet in his eyes shone the light of an indomitable spirit as he bustled about and looked after the welfare of the needy. He had come through the rough and tumble of the mountain trail. He knew what backache meant, from pulling his sled, helped over the rough places by noble-hearted fellows. He was a priest, always ready to console and comfort the sick, cheering them on, advising the excited to keep calm and cool, administering from his medicine chest to the sick and weak. Plodding along in his clerical garb he was admired for his pluck in trying to keep up with the excited throng. It seemed as if he were trying to bear the burdens of all. Men whose profanity was shocking to hear respected this little man, who was always sympathetic. Many wondered at a man of his calling making companions with uncouth men. But he knew that, while on the trail, men seemingly rough and profane showed nobleness and courage in emergency. He was to be found on many occasions among men who feared neither God nor Devil. These men learned to admire and respect him. He was an angel of mercy, always at the beck and call of those in distress. He was saving others. Could he save himself? Often his patients advised him to take a good long rest or get some help for his ministrations, as he had practically one foot in the grave through exposure on the blasted trail. (We call it that for many hopes and aspirations were blasted from those who could not meet its requirements.)

His hospital in Dawson was first a tent, then other tents were acquired. Later, big-hearted miners who had received help from him built him a log building for hospital work. Incessantly, night and day, he ministered to the sick and dying, being doctor, priest, and often gravedigger. Beds and bedding and other things necessary for the comfort of his patients were scarce. Many, on reaching their journey's end and arriving at Dawson, seemed to collapse altogether, ambition gone and health shattered. To many, it was the end of Life's Journey. The disease was often a kind of low fever, brought about by drinking river water, which resulted in dysentery. Much time was taken up giving spiritual consolation to those about to take the last, long trail, trying to show them the beacon of light that would bring them to their eternal goal. If ever a man lived and practiced the Christian virtues, he was one. He was a young man, but looked twice his age. Everyone who came in contact with this mild-mannered, heroic man, remembered him, and thanked God they had the privilege of knowing the man who had influenced their lives for good.

Many a good deed was done in remembrance of this good man, known as Father Judge. In the end, he gave his life for others. In the short space of twelve months, hundreds were brought to his little hospital; suffering from fever, scurvy, and all the ills flesh is heir to. For some this was the last rest before they were laid in graves, with none to mourn them but this saintly man. How many sisters and brothers, mothers and fathers, have patiently waited, in vain, for their loved ones to show up, but many died, their names unknown. But name or none, they were all the same to Father Judge. Nature would assert herself. Mortals can only stand so much. At last Father Judge himself took to his bed, and never arose. He had started on that long, last trail, and was taken to his resting place amidst the hills and vales of the great watershed of the mighty Yukon. It was the summer of 1899 when he passed away, beloved by all who knew him.

The Presbyterians had started a hospital, which was sorely needed. It was said that thirty to forty died every day from the fever, yet the great show went on. Dance halls were full, saloons were full, and gambling was rife. Dawson, in the very short time since its site had been selected, had become a modern Babylon.

Fabulous prices were paid for articles that were scarce. A few gallons of whiskey, smuggled in, fetched as high as $250 a gallon. A few bottles of Champagne fetched fifty dollars each, bought by the newly rich to make an impression on some of the ladies at the dance hall. The girls were on the lookout for those whom they knew were vain and who liked to be looked upon as good spenders. Some of these would return to the creeks sadder and wiser men. Who shall say the women of the dance halls did not earn all the money wheedled away from these rough, big-hearted chaps who were glad to relax after being penned up all the winter of '97 and '98 with a scarcity of grub, and to indulge for a while. Some of the passengers of the *Ora* brought in oranges; these sold for one dollar each. Fortunes were made by those lucky enough to have for sale what the human system craved in 1898.

Scows and boats arriving commanded good prices, bought by merchants just starting in the business, to build houses for protection from the cold in the coming winter. One man made his money by pulling out nails from boats, scows, and old packing boxes. He sold the nails for one to two and a half dollars a pound. To him it was as good as a gold mine. One man accosted an acquaintance saying, "I'm going to the shack, grub will be ready in half an hour." Putting a ham under his arm he said, "Only fifty dollars for this little ham." The rate of pay for physical labour was five dollars per hour, depending on the work to be performed.

~

The *Ora*, having discharged her passengers and freight at Dawson, took only a short time to straighten out its business and be ready to proceed upriver for White Horse. (It would be was a prosperous trip for the steamer, which would run around the clock, bucking the swift waters—thanks to the brick-lined fireboxes, which gave the boilers plenty of steam power.)

At the shout of "All aboard!" there was a scramble to get on the boat for the trip out. What gladness and joy, their faces beaming with happiness as they embarked! These passengers, a short eighteen months or two years ago, were eking out a miserable existence. Now they were men of affluence, eager to see their loved ones and break to them the glad news of having enough to live comfortable, and to dispel from the family's mind the continuous nightmare of paying rent, grocery bills, feeding and clothing the little ones, and of counting the dimes and nickels as they slipped through their fingers. Inwardly the fortunate miner was saying, "Thank God." Some, with a carefree attitude, none to care for but themselves, enjoyed sitting in on a game of cards. Others stayed not far from the little cubby hold where once in a while drinks would be set up, for those who cared to join. Could some of these men be blamed that they acted like schoolboys out on a picnic? Had they not gone through hell to attain what they were packing out? Did they not have good claims to come back to? There were others who enjoyed taking a long rest, after the long winter nights spent in saloons, being cajoled incessantly into playing poker, faro, roulette, and blackjack, into dancing and joining in every conceivable game that would part them from their hard-earned gold dust. Night and day the little boat chugged up the waters of the Yukon, one captain taking charge by day and one by night, it being daylight the whole twenty-four hours.

When the *Ora* ran short of wood for the boilers, she would pull into shore, to a bunch of dried-out trees. The boys, without being asked, would spring to the job, using every available axe and saw. Presto, in a few minutes, the boat would be refuelled. Were they not going out with the greatest speed possible, that they might be back again before snow fly?

They certainly enjoyed repartee—given and taken from the numerous scows and boats that passed. They appreciated the position many were in, for had they not all been in the same predicament as those now pulled off bars and shallows? Experiences of what happened at different places en route were exchanged. Truth often was far stranger than fiction, as one listened to the stories told, many of which centred around White Horse. Those were very few who came through this bit of water unscathed. How some of these men managed to get to Dawson, when their scows and boats were frozen solid in the waters, hundreds of miles from their destination could well be told by one able to describe it. The gruelling task demanded a man of iron will, brain, and brawn.

Arriving at White Horse just before the *Ora*, a fine specimen of the human race, who had poled up from Dawson partway and trekked partway, appeared. With him was an elderly man. Reticent at first, they were drawn into conversation and gradually thawed out. The younger man looked after the older as if he were his father. Upon seeing the steamer arrive and hearing that another steamer was to meet her at the end of the portage, the old man said, "Frank, give away the boat to some of the poor devils who are stranded. Buy a ticket for Bennett or Vancouver if you can. Who would have thought, eighteen months ago, when we were nigh dead, that there would be accommodation like this. And for God's sake, get the cook to get meals for two—the best he's got. Never mind the expense. Give him this nugget to hurry things along. We've had enough rough grub—when we could get it—to last a lifetime." What a happy old man. Frank transferred their meagre outfit to the care of the steward and tossed their pokes of gold to him as if bags of marbles.

The *Nora* and *Flora* were at Macauley's Landing waiting for the Dawson passengers. Gold was wrapped up in an old dilapidated portmanteau bound round with old baling wire and rope. Gold in pokes wrapped in gunnysacks; gold wrapped in rough-made moosehide was unloaded from Macauley's tram to be taken aboard the *Nora*. The deckhands marvelled at the weight when handling the small packages.

"Hey, Bill! Give us a hand here," as Jack was struggling to get a small sack aboard.

"Gosh! Aren't you big enough to handle a little bundle like that? Here! Get out of the way!" I attempted to carry the sack myself, but was glad to have Jack's help.

The owner came along and said, "What's the matter boys? It's only 350 pounds of gold!"

What a haul for bandits! But no one thought of such a thing—they were in Canadian territory, where the Mounties would often appear at different places unexpectedly. (All gold handled by the BL&KN company's little boats had a blanket insurance on it handled by a firm known as Heisterman and Company, of Victoria.)

CHAPTER TWENTY-TWO

Frank Smith

The welcome sound, this time from the *Flora,* was heard once more, "All aboard!" The whistle blew, scaring moose that could be heard calling their mates at intervals, and the boat, with her powerful engines, made good time. There was about a ton of gold on board, practically the first shipment out of any size. Each owner of gold had a Winchester rifle to protect himself from molestation on the trail by any of Soapy's gang.

Once the *Flora* was underway, the passengers settled down and the old man told us his story:

"We arrived at Bonanza in '97, following after the ice. Frank was practically three men on the way down. We staked our claims, sunk a hole to bedrock, but got ne'er a colour. Again we sunk, and ne'er a colour, and so on, until eighteen holes had been sunk. 'Money all gone,' I told the boys, 'and no more ground to stake. I've got just enough to take me home to Idaho.' The boys whom I'd hired tossed a coin to see if they should put another hole down for nothing, for they said I was a good sport. I thought I had lost the toss, but Frank shouted, 'The old man wins!' Joe, one of the others, was about to contradict, when Frank, like lightning, knocked him down. 'You know damned well he won!' Charlie, knowing what would happen if he said otherwise, exclaimed, 'You're damned tooting, he won.' Joe agreed that he had made a 'mistake.' Frank said, 'Then let's get started. This is the last hole, and if we strike it I'll see that the old man gives you double pay.' I knew I had lost the toss by the way Frank was acting.

"I started to get the grub. Things flew. Frank had a way that won over even his enemies, and Joe had lost his surliness by the next shift. Another shift came. Shift after shift went by, until one day they asked me to go down and say whether they should continue. I reached bottom and there were Frank and Joe, with gold pans, digging out nuggets, which were falling into the pan—plunk! plunk! I had heard of men's minds going off balance. Well, I felt the same way. There I stood speechless.

"We are now going out to get an apparatus to thaw out the ground so that we can work at it all winter. So far, our best hour's work has amounted to five thousand dollars in gold.—Ah! Here's Marsh Lake! I must tell you about that spot over there.

"Frank and I were sailing down. We heard shooting in the distance. I was telling Frank how nice it would be to have a nice juicy steak, when we saw the campers bring in some moose meat. Frank steered toward the shore. 'Where away?' said I. No answer. Frank beached the boat and saluted, 'Hullo strangers! What's the chance of getting a steak?' 'None. Better go hunt it. We are quite a crowd and can do with it all!' There were four of them. Frank said smilingly, 'Say boys, you see that old man down in the boat? He's dying for a taste of juicy steak.' 'Then you better go hunt it.' Frank, as quick as greased lighting, grabbed two of the fellows by the collars, knocked their heads together, and sprang to the other two before they could get their rifles. He collared them, held them at arm's length, and said, 'I don't want any roughhouse. Where I come from hospitality to strangers was the code. How about it boys?' 'You win. Help yourself.'

"I had just come on the scene, sick and weary, with our guns, using the last bit of strength left in me. I said, 'Want any help, Frank?' 'Sit down and rest, Dad!' Turning to the campers, Frank talked to them in his winning, gentlemanly way and dashed, after awhile, the six of us were sitting down to the juiciest steak I have ever had.

"The campers couldn't do too much for me. From that time on I started to mend. They gave me a quarter of moose, and I can tell you it was a change from bacon and beans. Two of those campers are down on the claim now. Trust them you say—you bet I can. Frank had put the fear of the Lord—or of Frank—into them. He only had to speak and the men would do his bidding.

"You should've heard Frank when a lot of shallow-pated Canadians in the camp began grumbling because so many Americans had good claims, while Canadians seemed to get all the worst ones. Of course the good Canadian didn't talk like that—only the small-minded ones talked about 'Canada for the Canadians.' 'Boys, cut it out,' said Frank, and they all cut it out, at least long enough to hear what he had to say.

"'Do you know that most of the Americans here are Canadian-born, and that they have become American citizens only through circumstances that offered them a better opportunity than was afforded them in Canada? Many of the governors of the different states are Canadians. They were not like a lot of you fellows. They were broad-minded, able, gifted men, who swore allegiance to the country that gave them a living. You do not hear Americans in the States saying "America for the Americans." Men of all nationalities were invited to share in Americans' liberty. Look around us. Some have Swedish names, some German, some Russian, French, Italian—yet they are all good Americans and swear by Uncle Sam.

"'How about Bob Henderson? Cheated out of his discoveries by damned Americans?' 'That may be, boys. But bear in mind that you have the mining laws of Canada, and a body of men representing the law who carry out these laws to the letter, with the greatest impartiality to everyone.

"'Canadians! You are blood brothers to the Americans. I see here two brothers, one a Canadian, and the other an American. Go back as far as you like. Why, you have a good American citizen, Fairfax, who is entitled to sit in the English House of Lords. It wouldn't surprise me at all to know that many of us in this great country are distantly related. Then why these petty jealousies?

"'What better treatment could you get than that met with at the coast? Even Soapy Smith loved everyone, especially their pocketbooks. You were treated as one of their own when passing through their country. We must treat each other here the same. This country is big! Big enough for all, and many of you Canadians should be big enough to embrace all and sundry brothers. The time will come when this great country will provide plenty of riches for all men of different nations. Don't be surprised if the Canadian government tries to people this great country by offering inducements that will keep their young men at home, and will entice Americans, who will become Canadians, into the country. So far, Canada has only been the back door for emigrants to enter the United States, and has paid millions of dollars to people in United States, who were attracted there by better conditions.

"'I hope boys, to live to see a paved road to Dawson from the boundary, yes, and on to the Arctic, too. Many of you know of creeks and bars that would yield good wages, but which cannot be worked owing to their inaccessibility. But with a main road, from which branches could be constructed, freight charges would be reduced and how easy it would be to unearth treasures which have been locked up for ages. Think of the thousands of people who would make their homes in this Far North. Think of the tens of thousands of tourists who would spend millions of dollars to visit this unknown land should such a main highway be built. Think of the gold and silver veins scattered through this vast domain, and copper and other minerals as well. The time will come, boys! As soon as the government wakes up to the realization that the North can produce riches undreamed of, this northland of ours will have a great population. Once that great population arrives, to settle in earnest, this northland will become a great district on the map, and we will all be able to look back, and say, 'I was there 'when.'"

"I'm a Britisher, boys,' the old man went on, "and yet I'm as good a Canadian as anyone here. Speaking of Frank, boys, I'm the only one who knows his last name isn't really Smith. He asked me to ask for some mail for him in the name—by golly, I nearly let it out. He made me swear an oath that I would never breathe it to a soul." Suddenly he called out, "Line up boys, the drinks are on me," and by gum, everyone lined up, English, Canadian, American, Swede, Irish, and perhaps a few others, and drank to Frank's health.

Then I stood treat, then another fellow, and so on, until so many drinks had gone around that all the men were sprawled out on the floor like ninepins. That was the best way of producing a feeling of comradeship that we discovered any night that winter. And probably the saloon made one of its best hauls of the winter, too.

"Whiskey was mighty scarce," the old man went on. "Where they got it from beats me. We paid practically one dollar a thimbleful. Our pokes were mighty slim the next morning, but no matter, we found we had lost track of a day anyway.—Here comes Frank. Now, not a word boys. He's pretty sensitive."

Frank approached with the remark, "Well, Dad, you've got quite an audience."

One of the listeners said, "He's been telling us about the 'Bar hunt.'"

At this cover-up, the old man smiled, saying, "Any man who has gone through what we have been through deserves a drink—Treat 'em Frank! It's on me." Frank refused a drink for himself. The little cubby hold was well lined with the crowd. The steward gave them of his best.

When the old sourdoughs sighted Bennett, they were (to use their own expression), "tickled to death." The boat moored, and a great cheer arose at the sight of the miners packing their gold over the old trail again, to the outside this time. In a short time the pack train was ready to leave. Away they went, rifles on their shoulders, happy as larks, Frank, as usual, in the van, with the old man in the saddle.

The BL&KN company were anxious to know that the *Nora* had gotten through the White Horse Rapids safely. The *Flora*, having unloaded its freight and passengers, immediately turned back for another run to Macauley's Landing. The first news that greeted the ears of all aboard was that the *Nora* had gone through flying, under the able captaincy of Martineau and Waud and Constable Dixon. One more steamboat had passed the famous waters, never to return over the same route again, and by now in Dawson. At the entrance to the Squaw Rapids, the *Willie Irving* lay in the shallows, a plank ripped out of her side. The man who had offered advice, saying he would have done this or that, had slipped on the job of piloting his own boat through the rapids, meeting the disaster which occasioned great delay.

One could see the days shortening. Already it was no longer possible to read at midnight, hence the necessity of not wasting a minute going to and from Dawson. The *Ora*'s engines were now broken in and running smoothly. The BL&KN company had hired the best engineers procurable, to keep the machinery constantly up to scratch. All through the season, engines rarely ever stopped, thanks to the men who constantly nursed them and treated them as their children.

While the *Flora* headed back to Macauley's Landing, a single man rowed his boat down the Six Mile. Everyone watching, at the landing, expected him to come in, as usual, before making the final plunge into the waters below. The passengers and crew of the *Flora* beckoned to him, but no doubt he thought it was a salute cheering him on his way, for he kept on. When he reached Miles Canyon, seeing what was ahead of him, he hauled in his oars and lay down flat in the boat. Everyone thought that he had swooned, and men ran down to the bottom of the canyon, perhaps to help him if they had half a chance. Others stayed on the cliff to watch his fight, mostly expecting to see his boat dashed to pieces on the projecting hidden reef. The old boat must have been guided by an invisible hand, for on it rushed, safely through the Squaw Rapids. However, there was no sign of the man. As the boat entered the swift waters of the White Horse, it seemed as though he was to drown after all, for no one could attempt to do anything for him.

At White Horse, people saw a boat without a helmsman. Several went down to quieter waters to rescue it; they hardly hoped to find anyone alive in it. Now there was just one last stretch of fierce waters. Here she comes! She mounts the crest, she's over the top, the spray subsides somewhat—she is safe! The man straightens up in his seat, waves his hand to the would-be rescuers, places his oars, and continues down the river. Those who had been at White Horse since the ice went out claimed that it had been the luckiest thing that had happened on the river.

The story of the Irishman's luck (for it was an Irishman), in shooting the rapids, so impressed one man who was travelling by himself that he left Macauley's Landing just to see if he could get through the rapids too. He said that if one man could get through by lying down on the bottom of the boat and letting it take its own course, he could certainly get through by giving the boat a little help. He cleared Miles Canyon, and the Squaw Rapids, but when he came to the White Horse, he entered the "wrong" side of the crest, and the boat capsized—another victim of the voracious appetite of the raging waters.

A steamboat, the *Anglican*, was built at Hootalinka, but was wrecked on the river soon after she was launched. This made one less steamboat to compete with the *Ora* and *Nora* on the lower reaches. Can anyone realize the disappointment occasioned by the loss of the *Anglican*? It was not the enormous expense it had cost to build her, but rather the weary plodding, the incessant worrying over getting the material through that muskeg-fed Teslin trail that was worth more than all the money. The *Nora* was to take on many hardy men at the mouth of the Hootalinka River who had straggled in from (as they called it), "that hellish trip." They were gaunt and depressed, and many were half-dead from exposure, mosquitoes, and starvation. They cursed the day—and they cursed Dewdney (the man who had envisioned the trail) for ever thinking of or planning the route of the Teslin Trail into the goldfields. Only those lucky enough to get through to Hootalinka can know the misery that was entailed in getting there. It must be a nightmare when they, in the midnight solitude, happen to turn their thoughts back onto that long, long trail.

CHAPTER TWENTY-THREE

Fox's Tale

Rattenbury and his wife came to Bennett post-haste, upon hearing of the success of the *Ora*. (Mr. Klute, the customs inspector, thought that other names could have been found for the boats, but several of the crew, who knew that the *Flora* had been named after Mrs. Rattenbury, swore that *Ora*, *Flora*, and *Nora* were the luckiest names on the river.) So far, "luck" had been with the three boats, and it remained with them till the end of the season. Some call it luck. Was it? Or was it the skill of the captains and the crew? (Or the application and the foresight of the manager, in the face of those who did not believe that the feat of travelling by boat from Bennett to Dawson could ever be accomplished?)

The BL&KN company acquired a charter to build a light railroad from the M'Clintock River to a point not far from the mouth of the Hootalinka—probably at the mouth itself—so that the rough waters and rapids of the Miles Canyon, Squaw Rapids, Lake Laberge, and the Thirtymile could be avoided. The *Flora*, which had picked up Frank Rattenbury and myself, dropped us off in a small boat in Marsh Lake, at the mouth of the M'Clintock River, to make a rough survey of the route for which the charter had been granted.

A week earlier, at Tagish, a man named Fox had told me a story. Rattenbury had also seen this man, who was convalescing, and was also told the story.

"We had set out to prospect the M'Clintock River for gold, and were about three or four miles from its mouth, when suddenly a shot was fired. As my partner dropped, I saw three Indians, one about to fire again. We were just at a bend in the river, but before I could get the boat around it—thud, my arm went limp. I guessed it was broken, from the way in which it hung. My partner was dead, shot through the heart. I saw the Indians run across the piece of land to the end of the bend. I was faint and dizzy, but when the boat going downstream brushed the other side of the river, I caught hold of some willows on the water's edge and slipped out, letting the boat, with my dead partner, go downstream. I don't know whether I would have tied it up even if I had had the strength to do so. I had all I could do to keep from fainting. I believe it was the toughest job I have ever had—to ward off the oblivion.

"By force of will I managed to keep going, striking off through the woods and brush, guessing at the direction of the NWMP post. It was hard going, and fear possessed me—a fear that hurried me on, putting wings on my feet. Once I fell and struck my broken arm. The pain was excruciating. How long I was travelling is hard to say, but at last I reached Tagish post.

"The next thing I knew, I was helped on to a crude bed of rugs and furs, which seemed to be the next best thing to heaven, just to lie on. As soon as I could, I gave all particulars to the police. The OC immediately gave orders to a constable to 'get his man.' I thought that the police would call it a cowardly action—my having left my partner in the boat. But to my satisfaction, they said that I could not have done otherwise. If I had stayed with the boat, it would only have meant that two more men would have disappeared, adding another mystery to the already far-too-great list."

A few weeks after Fox told this story, the constable who had been sent to trace the Indians told his part of it.

"I entered Marsh Lake, having heard that there was an Indian camp somewhere on its shore. I found this information to be correct, for a few miles down the shore was a camp. I approached warily, and asked the chief how many men were away from the camp. The chief said that he did not know, for it was hunting time to get meat to dry for the winter, and many men were away from camp. After cajoling, threatening, and warning them all, even telling them that the chief would have to come along to Tagish, I finally convinced him that I was in earnest, and he broke down and told me the direction that the three men had taken from the camp. I followed on to White Horse as quickly as possible, but they had not been seen there. At Laberge, I missed them by several days. At Hootalinka, I learned they had been seen there. They had not been seen at Big Salmon River. At Five Rivers near the Tatchum River, there was another Indian camp. Creeping up stealthily as possible, I took them all by surprise. I was armed to the teeth, with the bracelets dangling, and was quite ready for anything.

"First of all, I made the peace sign. Then I told the leader of the party to count his men. He said they were all present. When I asked how many men joined the party in the last few days, everyone was sullen, and not inclined to talk. So I became menacing: 'Chief! When did three Marsh Lake Indians join your camp? You no tell 'em me, my men take you all up to Tagish. I blow this whistle. My men come take you. That will stop your hunting and fishing!' After a lot of jabbering and conferring amongst themselves, the chief gave a young fellow a command, evidently to see how many men I had at my disposal. 'Him come here!' I shouted, and pointed my gun. The chief told him he had better stop rather than be killed. 'You tell 'em all to stay here or you heap sabby this,' I said, pointing to the gun again.

"There was further excited talk, when suddenly the chief pointed to three men. Boldly I walked up to one and held out the bracelets, believing this easy submission was the prelude to a tough proposition. One started to make a break, but he saw my weapon and stopped quickly. I snapped on the bracelet, fastening the other half onto an old squaw. They made a funny picture, those two. Him thin and athletic, and her fat as a porpoise, emitting the most horrible shrieks. One of the three was a mere boy. The other was sneaking after his rifle, but I saw him just in time, and pointed my gun at him. Then I jumped toward the fellow and slipped on the bracelets, undid the shrieking squaw and fastened the two men together. The young boy was docile, and came when called. Soon the three were securely fastened together, and I set out with them for the post, after warning them not to try to escape.

"On the way to the canoe the fellow who had shot Fox, cursed, in his broken English, for being a poor shot and not killing the second man as well. He said they made 'one big mistake' in all three running to catch the boat. One man should have stayed back. They were surprised when they got to the end of the bend and into shallow water to find only one man in the boat. 'We buried him in sand bar, I show you by 'em by.'"

The constable was later taken to the spot and dug up the body of Fox's partner, shot through the heart as Fox had testified. "We arrived at Tagish, and that's that. It was a tough journey, but the order to 'get your man' was carried out."

Fox's story seemed to leave an impression on Rattenbury. Travelling with me, near the mouth of the M'Clintock, he kept watching the bends of the river for Indians. Our instructions were to go upriver until we came to high benchlands. We took turns rowing. When the boat turned a bend, Rattenbury would say, "Is that an Indian?" pointing to a far-away object.

"No, that's an old stump of a tree," I would reply. On we went.

"What's that? There. Just ahead of us. It looks like the head of an Indian."

"You're dreaming, Frank!" I said. "Here, take the Winchester, but for God's sake, don't shoot until you ask me. This is the bend where Fox's partner was shot. That's the shortcut." As we rowed upstream we saw a place where Fox might possibly have scrambled up.

"Do you think, Bill, there are any other Indians about?" Rattenbury asked me.

"Perhaps," I said, "By golly, don't work yourself up to such excitement, Frank. Keep calm, and watch your rifle!"

Eventually we got up into shallow water and found the high benchlands, where we decided to camp for the night. When it started to rain, Frank was most uncomfortable. This was really the first bit of roughing he had experienced. We selected a spruce tree, drove down a few stakes, and by placing and piling a number of spruce boughs on top forming a roof, made ourselves a shelter. Then we cooked supper.

Frank certainly enjoyed his meal after having rowed most of the day and having been in constant fear of being eaten himself. "My!" he said, when drinking his tea without milk, "but this is good." He could not get over the sorry plight his hands were in. The water blisters were painful. I advised him to get a few hours' sleep while he had the chance and the rain was coming down, for once it stopped, the mosquitoes would begin to swarm again. Should anyone think the tropics are the only place where rain falls in sheets, they should have been on the M'Clintock that night! Frank's "Gad!" broke the silence; the shelter was leaking like a sieve and he was literally soaked to the skin. "What bally luck! Gad, I'm cold! Do you think we could get a fire?" he pleaded.

Close by there was dry timber. I lit a fire with much patience—and many matches—then piled on log after log. The rain abated to just a drizzle. It was early morning. Frank thought that with such a jolly fire it would be a fine idea to dry his clothes. "Better let them dry on you," was my advice. "The mosquitoes will be out in swarms if the sun comes out." Frank opined they were in for a day's cloudy weather, for a fog had developed. He was determined to have dry clothes. He built a rack, stripped, and hung his clothes on the rack. Now he enjoyed the fire's warmth. "Don't let the clothes get too near the fire, Frank. You will shrink them," I said.

Frank thought everything was all right. He didn't think there was any hurry to dress, even though I warned him that the fog was lifting. After awhile he started rubbing his leg and pulling at his shrunken stockings. Next his pants. They looked as if they were boy-size. The sun broke out. Frank grabbed his pants, and was some time before he could fit them to his body. The mosquitoes were beginning to swarm and pounced on him as a prize meal. He danced around trying to dodge them. His woolen underclothes would not go near him. He swore and raved. I picked up some willow boughs and tried to keep the mosquitoes off. The willow switch would sometimes come in contact with Frank's skin, and what with the mosquitoes and the switch, Frank's back became a bloody spectacle. At last he managed to get on his woolen garments. It was comical to see Frank's legs and arms sticking out of his shrunken clothes. The tug-of-war came when he tried to put on his boots, also left too close to the fire. I crammed the mosquito netting over him and made a smudge. That nearly smothered both of us, but was better than the continual hum and buzz of the pests. The sun was blazing hot. We managed to get a bite to eat, and after Frank had used up all the available handkerchiefs and cloths to cover his exposed fleshy parts, we set off to survey roughly the route for our proposed light railroad. I will never forget the sight of Frank's white body when first stripped, and afterward, when covered with millions of mosquitoes, red, bumpy, and bloody—and he himself striving to keep the mosquitoes off with a willow switch.

When we resumed our trip, we had gone about a mile or so and were walking, we thought, on solid land—soggy owing to the rain. Every step we took raised an army of what the Psalmist said must have been 'the terror that flieth'. How Frank suffered. How he longed to be back in his comfortable offices, planning other structures. He realized what I had gone through, in being constantly exposed to all kinds of weather to bring the steamer project to fruition.

Our trip had just begun. Ahead of us, about five hundred yards distant, was what looked like an Indian grave. We turned around to take our bearings, and saw, to our consternation, that the ground we had travelled over was now a narrow stream, or rather a ribbon of water. We were on a muskeg, five hundred yards from rising ground. We pressed on. Now we could feel the whole surface spring under our feet. We decided to keep wide apart so as not to put too much weight in one place. Mosquitoes goaded us on. The muskeg was getting worse every yard we advanced. Would we make it? Yes! Only a few yards more to go. The last few yards came near to being our finish, for we sank knee-deep at every step.

I suggested we investigate what was on top of the four poles, to see whether it was an Indian grave or not. Frank, suspicious of Indians lurking near, begged off. His enthusiasm for his light railroad had died. He wanted to go back to catch the steamboat. I was of the same mind. Frank was suffering from the effect of mosquito poisoning, so we started back, making a detour. We gained the boat, and it was now easy going.

In a short time we emerged into Lake Marsh, having had a surfeit of muskeg and mosquitoes, and uttering a cry of thankfulness at our escape from purgatory. The *Flora* was waiting for us. Frank lost no time in changing into dry and comfortable clothes. The steamer trip to Bennett, for Frank, was one of misery. Oil and greases were rubbed into his swollen body to soothe the sores caused by the mosquitoes. He had had enough of the North and realized what the poor devils (as he termed the prospectors) had to suffer on the trails to get to their destinations and the price many had paid in hardship and suffering to get *Ora*, *Nora*, and *Flora* running on schedule. He knew now what the staff had to put up with on the boats—smudges had to be burnt continually, to keep off the mosquito plagues. Rattenbury, I believe, was touched at last, as he sat nursing his head, hands, and legs, swollen and poisoned. At Bennett, a horse was procured for him to go to Skagway, so he might get to Victoria as soon as possible.

Rattenbury asked me to promise him that if one of the English directors of the company came out, as he was supposed to, to take the director over the same route. "I'll make it worth your while. It will show the bally finance men how their money is earned." (Billing, a director, did come as far as Victoria, but had no desire to go further. He was content with the descriptive correspondence and detail I sent him weekly.)

Oral promises from Frank Rattenbury were no good. He was a very smart man—a genius in many respects, but one part of him was so mean he was despised. How it hurts to write of one who was in some things likeable, in others dishonourable. He was unfortunate in his marriages —I believe if his marriages had been happier, his outlook on life would have been altered somewhat.

When he came to Canada from England, he arrived in Vancouver. Finding very little to do in his own profession, he entered the employ of the Bank of Montreal. A prize of five thousand dollars was offered by the British Columbia government for the best design for the proposed new Parliament Buildings (the competition was open to the world); it was Rattenbury who won it. He was rated as a millionaire at one time, but his end was a sad one. In 1935 at Bournemouth in England, he was murdered in a brutal manner by his chauffeur.

This passage in a letter from Rattenbury, written at Skagway, described his experience:

"Of all men I was the most miserable. I tried riding, the trails were too rough. I tried walking, it was just as bad. Some stretches of the trail were so nauseating, owing to the carcasses of dead donkeys, mules and horses, that it overcame me. I simply could not stand it. In the higher altitudes the mosquitoes were scarce, thanks to a breeze blowing. How on earth the two packers stood it is past my comprehension. Asking them how they could put up with it day after day, they said, 'Oh, we thrive on it. It saves us a meal once in a while.' I could not see anything to joke about. Of the two evils, mosquitoes on the M'Clintock, or the Skagway trail, I could make no choice. I must have taken a fever for several days until nearing Victoria. I was sick, which was something new to me. Carry on up there! I can now understand how so many men died on those putrid trails, and know what you have to contend with. I'll remember you. Everything is in your hands."

Captain Goddard, of the steamboat *Goddard*, had a contract with the militia to handle 200 tons of freight for them from Bennett to White Horse. Goddard had his boat below the swift waters and Rattenbury wanted in on the deal, but failed to make any arrangement with Goddard when he met with him. Rattenbury left it to me to negotiate with the officers of the militia to do Goddard out of the contract. Rattenbury's sickness did not seem to make any difference to him when a business deal was on. About this time he made a deal with Pat Burns to handle one thousand head of cattle for him, from Five Fingers to Dawson, at four hundred dollars per head. These cattle would arrive over the Dalton Trail.

In one respect one must take off one's hat to Rattenbury for the indomitable way in which he went after business, and invariably got the best of the deal. He overstepped himself on one deal that would have spoiled his career had the papers around it ever been brought to light, but that will be alluded to later.

CHAPTER TWENTY-FOUR

Burnett's Story

It is a thousand pities there are so few photographs of the ragged, forlorn, woebegone, poor mortals who were buoyed up by the slogan, "Dawson—or bust." Many were "bust" by the time they reached Bennett. But still they were bent on seeing that now famous place. A man called Johnson made good. He had the stuff in him that heroes are made of, but what a price some of those men had to pay. For many, looking back on what they had gone through was like a dream, or perhaps a nightmare.

Whilst in Skagway, on one of my frequent trips there, an old man was robbed in broad daylight by some of Soapy Smith's gang. They took two hundred dollars—all he had left from that fearful Teslin trail—but he was bound for Dawson and meant to get there. This was the spirit that brought so many through, the spirit that overcame all obstacles. He went to Soapy and said, "Look here, Soapy, some of your gang robbed me of two hundred dollars. I want that money back."

"Ah, get along!" drawled Soapy. Before Soapy could draw his gun, the man had him covered.

"Cough up, Soapy, or by the Eternal, you'll get the works." Soapy coughed up.

I felt a tension existing in the populace that would soon come to a head. Soapy had been carrying on high-handedly. The vigilante committee was about ready to strike.

When I travelled over the Chilcoot to Bennett now, I always went on foot. On one trip I met a party of miners on their way out from Dawson, well armed , their pack train of mules loaded with gold. "Did you have a good trip, boys?" I asked.

"You bet!"

"Everything okay with the boats?" I asked.

"Yes. Say, are you the boss?"

"That's what they call me. What's up?"

They told me, "The purser from the *Flora* shot the steward's help, Jim Cowie, on the *Ora*. The skunk deserved it. He claimed to be a prizefighter, and certainly gave the man—Burnett—an awful punishment. Cowie half-starved us, at two dollars and fifty cents a meal. He was selling pies made for us—or rather, pies that should have been for us—to the hoodoos coming out. They would sneak around outside to the kitchen and pay one dollar apiece for them. We did without. Cowie, crew, and all, seemed to be in on it. Graft! It is all graft!"

"Thanks, boys, a lot. When you return, I'll see things are different for you. Look me up at Bennett or White Horse!" I had met the miners climbing the little glacier. As I travelled over the trails to Bennett, my thoughts were concerned with Burnett. He had, at one point, been the cook's help on the *Ora*, and had left the steamer at White Horse. He was a good man, well known and respected, whom I had asked, as a favour, to check over manifests until I came back from Skagway, to give receipts, and to take over all the gold sent out in care of the BL&KN company. Burnett was from Everett, Washington. What would happen to him? How about his wife? Had she heard about the shooting?

My thoughts dwelt ominously on the shooting. Going over everything in my mind, I saw the cause of the whole thing.

At last, Bennett. The crew of the *Flora* repeated the particulars, as far as were known, to me before we left for White Horse to meet one of the lower-river boats. Bennett was still a busy place. Freight was coming forward rapidly. Merchants were continually coming over the trails in haste, to get to Dawson and out again before the freeze-up.

Superintendent Steele was on board. Prior to this trip, he had been appointed to take charge of all the forces in the Yukon. He had booked passage to Dawson, to stop at all the posts down the river. He was an interesting character. We passed the time in conversation on the way to Tagish, his first stop. He gave an interesting history of the early days of eastern Canada and the West, outlining incidents from the period when British Empire Loyalists left the States to settle in Canada, mentioning the hardships they suffered.

This trek into Dawson was nothing compared to what the Loyalists endured, he said, so that they might live under the British flag. In America, there was strife and bitterness. Father fought against son, and relations showed bitter hatred to one another. Superintendent Steele touched on the history of his own family. His father had been a surgeon in the British navy. He was well-versed in Canada's progress, and had at his fingertips the names of all who had played an important part in the making of Canadian history.

Burnett was incarcerated in a log building at Tagish, without any appearance of comfort. He was cold and miserable. I asked to see him, but Superintendent Steele at the fort was a different man than the Superintendent Steele who had been a passenger on the boat. He hesitated about anyone seeing the prisoner, having evidently heard only one side of the story. Word had come to him that Jim Cowie was dead. He knew no more than that Burnett had killed him. Finally, I was allowed to see him, after I had impressed on Superintendent Steele that I had Burnett's wife on my hands and wanted to get a counsel for him. We were allowed ten minutes together. A guard was placed to hear the conversation, and Burnett was warned that anything he might say would be used against him.

Burnett began, "Mr. Manager, I asked you when I left the *Ora* for my time and settlement. You asked me, as a favour, to act on the *Flora* until you could get another man, to take a trip to Skagway, and take care of all accounts and shipments of gold. I reluctantly accepted the job. You gave me a gun, saying it was part of the insurance agreement. I had the gun in pocket. You remember that when you asked the reason I wanted to leave the *Ora* I would give you none. Yea?"

"Yes, yes," I replied. "Come on, Burnett, I have only ten minutes, and want to hear all so that I may act accordingly. Proceed."

"When I went on board the *Ora* to settle up with the purser, Cowie came up and dealt me a smashing blow. I did not retaliate. As I was proceeding to the purser's office, Cowie followed me, slashing all the time at my face. Look at my eyes and face!"

"Yes, I see. Don't worry, I'll fathom this. The passengers on the way out told me the crew were a set of crooks."

Burnett continued, "My body is bruised all over. This happened when I went back to get the manifests left on the desk. Jim Cowie flew at me again. I warned him that if he touched me while I was performing my duty I could not stand any more punishment from him—I would use my gun. At this he jumped at me. I could stand no more. He had me corralled. Many of the crew were looking on—not one attempted to stop him. He landed me terrific punches. I cried out 'Let go!' He redoubled his punching. 'Stop, or I'll shoot!' Still he kept on. So I took the gun from pocket and shot him. That's all!"

"Time's up," said the guard.

"Cheer up, Burnett! Don't worry! I'll send your wife home and clear you. Leave it all to me," were my parting words. I went to the superintendent and asked him to take the manacles and weights off Burnett, and to give him medical treatment.

"So you are sympathizing with a man who deliberately took a gun and shot Cowie!" was the superintendent's response.

"Oh, no," I replied. "The gun was mine. He had to have it to protect the gold. It's no use to say more, major, I know the details, you only know one side of the case. Those laugh best who laugh last! I know you have your duty to perform."

"Yes," said the superintendent, "and I'll see it is performed at Dawson."

The sight of Burnett's face lingered a long time in my memory. It was smashed to jelly. His eyes bulged and blackened down his cheeks, and his mouth cut from the terrible blows of Cowie's fists. Knowing what the passengers had said about the wholesale stealing of the company's food and what Burnett had told me, I was determined to get to the bottom of the affair and to set the wheels of justice in motion.

◿

Back on board the *Flora* (the superintendent back on board, as well), we continued to White Horse, where all the passengers took the trams to Macauley's Landing. Apparently there had been a hot time at the saloon the night before. All, more or less, had liquor in their system. Sergeant Joyce was standing on the bank, watching the *Flora* make the landing. He tried to look sober. He did not know that Superintendent Steele was on board. The superintendent took in the whole situation. He walked up to the sergeant, who immediately stood to attention. The superintendent ripped the chevrons from the sergeant's sleeve and ordered him to his quarters. Norman Macauley and several others were in a state. In the saloon, the mirrors that had been brought in from the outside at great expense were all smashed. Chairs and tables were broken and many men were outside singing, "There'll be a hot time in the old town tonight."

Sergeant Joyce had to report to Tagish, which put the superintendent in a quandary. He himself did not want to go back to Tagish; he wanted badly to get to Dawson. He knew the sergeant was a capable man, yet he had to show his authority. He would not condone lax behaviour amongst his men. Finally, he ordered the saloon closed. All knew that this would only be temporary. Everyone was sorry for Sergeant Joyce. He was well liked. He was ordered to proceed to Tagish, with sealed orders to the OC.

Any constable stationed at White Horse had to be a man who understood men. Such was the sergeant. He had laid down the law to the boys in this way: "Have your fun. Let it be wholesome. Don't overstep the traces. If you do, I'll put a crimp into any carryings on that smell of roughhouse or criminality." It had to be this day, of all days, that the superintendent showed up. The crowd had over stepped their traces, but would have been straightened out had the sergeant had another twenty-four hours in which to act.

Superintendent Steele was indeed making his presence felt, sizing up everyone. His word was law. "Where is Dixon?" he asked.

"He's at the lower end, Sir, just piloted down an outfit with some women aboard. We would not let them go through without him." The superintendent left another constable behind at Macauley's to straighten out the tangle.

Macauley's was a place that required great tact to handle. One came in contact with a heterogeneous crowd. They were arriving and departing every day. Professional gamblers disguised as preachers, merchants, and others—none of whom was the least important to deal with. Some would stop over a day or so, if they had the slightest inkling there would be games. Like other mining camps, White Horse was beginning to be a centre. Many prospectors would start from this point into the interior, obsessed with the idea that possibly just as good would be found in this vicinity as in the Klondyke. This particular day had happened to turn into a roughhouse at the saloon.

Ordinary men and merchants would be inveigled into a friendly game to pass away the time until the next boat. Gradually these games would develop into games of large stakes. Evidently that is what happened the night before. When asked for particulars, no one seemed to know what had happened, not even the sergeant. There seemed to be a certain honour amongst everyone regarding the incident. One employee at Macauley's mentioned, "If we didn't get a bracer once in a while, it would be impossible to stand up to the work of portaging the merchandise, sometimes twenty-four hours a day. What with Jim Cowie passing on, burying him, rescuing cheechakos in the raids, and attending to ordinary business, a little snort is always appreciated."

"Too bad about the sergeant," was another comment. "Anyway, he's true blue. If any sissy takes his place we'll train him. It's too bad there are so many, always toadying to the OC. We'll train him right—we've got no use for a policeman who is a damned sneak."

"Boat in!" came from the lookout, "Leaving in an hour." This put a stop to further investigations at Macauley's. All parties left for the *Ora*, at the lower landing.

I had a talk with the *Ora*'s captain. "What's the meaning of the killing and the rumpus, Captain?" I asked.

"Search me. Bad blood between them, I reckon!"

"Have you heard any conversations amongst the crew?"

"Yes!" said the captain. "They all say Burnett was a damn sneak! They will see that he gets hanged! Where is the other captain, you ask? Why, down attending to the loading!"

I went down and hailed the captain. "Hullo, Cap," I said, "Just a minute. What's all the killing about?"

The captain replied, "The damn sneak deserves to get hung, and we'll see that he is."

"What's your reason for saying that, Cap?" I asked, not mentioning that I had spoken to Burnett at Tagish.

"Oh, blabbing about things," said the captain.

"What things?"

"You ought to know."

"He never blabbed to me about anything. Didn't he tell you anything when he left the *Ora*?"

"Not a thing."

"So you don't know what caused Cowie to half kill Burnett, Captain?"

"No. Not a thing."

"Did Cowie deserve a bullet?"

"What are you talking about, Boss?"

"I want information, and am trying to get it," I said.

"All I know is, he'll hang if we can manage it, Jim Cowie was a damned fine fellow," the captain said.

I questioned all the *Ora*'s crew. The old Scots engineer had nothing to say other than, "It will all come out in the evidence." The crew had been all for hanging Burnett and would have lynched him but for the passengers, who had taken Burnett's part and drove the crew aboard, saying, "He's an American citizen, and you'll not lynch him! We'll turn him over to the police. Burnett is a fine fellow, we knew him on the trail.— Get aboard the boat, Burnett, come on, we'll see you safe to Macauley's." I also interviewed the *Ora*'s steward. He could give no information. He was asked about the receipts of the monies for meals, the amount of provisions taken aboard each trip, the particulars of passengers paying their fares, and other things, all of which I checked.

All aboard! The whistle blew, and away went the *Ora*, with Superintendent Steele, staff, and passengers. I stayed at Macauley's, settling down to check the provisions and stock. The man in charge of the stock had receipts for all the *Ora* had taken for crew's and passengers' consumption. Even though I made most liberal allowance, and included the balance of the stock on hand—what a surprise! When I finished the audit, I found that thousands of dollars' worth of staples had been sold from the boat. By whom?

"Well, Jack! Let's talk," I said to my agent. "What do you know?"

"Absolutely nothing, other than filling the requisition orders sent in. At times it looked as if the orders were for far more than needed and therefore, I think, for a whole lot."

"Tell me all you know," I said.

"Being busy attending to the filling of orders given by the steward, I did not see the fight, if you call it a fight. From what I hear it was all one-sided. Burnett had taken more than I would. I saw Burnett being protected by the passengers from the crazy crew as he left the boat. My God! He was a sight! Battered up beyond recognition. The crew made Cowie as comfortable as possible. Dr. Sugden was called and the constable too, and Burnett was placed in the charge of the constable. Sugden did all he possibly could for Cowie. He was shot in the stomach. Although he was ordered to keep quiet, Cowie insisted on getting up and going after Burnett. A few of us kept him back. Would to God Constable Dixon was at this end. Things would have been different. Cowie became delirious. He kept saying, 'Damn the bandages. Jim Cowie doesn't want bandages.' He ripped them off, and that was the beginning of the end. Anxiously we watched him, and felt that without the aid of a doctor he would die. His end came sooner than we expected."

"Do you think he would have lived had he not torn the bandages off?" I asked.

"Yes, I think he would have. He was a strong man."

"Say, Boss," he went on, musing, "At night I have sat at the foot of the

White Horse, when perhaps all would be quiet for a few hours—which was not often—listening to those turbulent waters incessantly rolling on, splashing the banks with spray, at last losing its force in those placid waters below. And so with me and the others. We were tossed about on the old trail, buffeted by blizzard and storm, reveled in all kinds of devilment, cared for nothing! Then something happens, and like old White Horse, we get swallowed up by the quiet waters yonder. Jim has gone. Hundreds of others have gone in different ways, and still the old river flows on. What does it matter to the river, now and again, if it catches the unwary, and seemingly gloats over its conquest? Laughing in victorious glee if a casualty occurs, as it rushes on? The rapids at night seem to be calling for more victims, as the river roars, constantly roars.

"I lost all by being too confident. Believing nothing would or could happen to me, I found myself in the seething cauldron, struggling to save myself from the cruel heartless waters. Many came through safe, the laugh on their side, and went on to a worse fate at Dawson, to be buffeted about again before passing out of this life's little drama. Do you know they are dying off like jackrabbits when they get to Dawson? Penniless, rundown, they fall into a kind of low fever. The passengers coming up tell of the wonderful work the Presbyterians are doing for the poor unfortunates, yet in the face of all the doctors are doing, an awful number are laid away in their last resting place.

"—Say Boss, excuse me! You were wanting to know about the details of the supposed murder. Well, Jim died. Boisterous and raging, as he had lived. We dug a grave for him. Some wanted a burial service, but who was to perform it? Several dressed in the garb of parsons have gone down the river. Really, they were gamblers, joining in every game that was going on while waiting for the boats. Not one touched or even had a Bible. One of the employees said old Bill had a Bible and said his prayers every night. We went quite a distance to get him, and he seemed pleased to be called on, to perform the ceremony. He read, 'I am the resurrection and the life,' and so on. We were getting tired of his harangue so we abruptly laid Jim in the grave over yonder."

"So that is all you know, Jack?" I asked.

"Yes, Sir."

"Well, I must be off, so long, Jack!"

"Say, Boss, don't you ever sleep? Take a tip from me, stay here for a couple of days and sleep."

CHAPTER TWENTY-FIVE

Vigilantes and Nuggets of Gold

All aboard! I went on board the *Flora*, bound for Bennett, with a crowd of passengers eager for home, sweet home, with their bags of gold. Stopping at Tagish, I was hailed by the OC, Captain Strickland. We had a confidential talk. "Righto Captain," I said. "We'll be seeing you shortly as soon as the passengers are landed at Bennett."

Soon after this trip, word came that Soapy Smith had been shot by a man named Reid, the chairman of the so-called Vigilante Committee 101. Reid and his followers had given Soapy orders to leave the town a few days previously. Soapy answered the order by having a sign painted with the figure 303 on it, to be illuminated at night.

The committee had a meeting on the wharf, and, having been kept listening to the complaints of respectable citizens about Soapy—who was still holding up those who came in boats, bound for Dawson—determined to put an end to his activities. Soapy had heard of the meeting, and he and his gang knew something was about to happen. Undoubtedly goaded on by his lieutenants, Soapy took his rifle and marched to the wharf. A lot of youngsters followed him, also several adults. He swore at them and bade them keep back, and on he went.

He met Reid, knocked him down with his rifle, and then shot him in the thigh while Reid was on the ground. Reid drew his gun and shot Soapy through the heart. Another version, by someone who claimed to have seen it, was that Soapy fired, at a distance, first, and that this shot was answered by Reid, who fell. Then Soapy fell, a result of a return shot of Reid's. In any case, they shot at each other until Soapy was shot through the heart.

This was the end of Soapy's reign of terror in Skagway. Martial law was declared. The gang was rounded up. The dishonest and unprincipled marshals were dismissed. Many who were suspected of being in league with Soapy were rounded up and sent to Sitka (then the capital of Alaska), to stand trial, and were sentenced to San Quentin in California.

Bill McGee, a former resident of Leadville and Marshal, said that he was sorry he had not put Soapy away down south. Soapy was a menace to civilization.

~

From then on Skagway settled down to business and made rapid strides in becoming a town, where everyone was safe. Confidence was restored, public officials were elected, and questionable places were watched. The WP&YR was making rapid progress in overcoming the enormous obstacles in its way and taking freight to the end of the rail. Bracket's wagon toll road was no longer required. The toll collected was no longer sufficient to keep it up and pay expenses. The turns and twists of the mountain railroad while travelling the uphill grade were fascinating, and gave one a splendid view of the country. Gradually the tedious trail made by the pioneers was being wiped out or forsaken and very few were using it. Those able to pay freight did so to the end of the rail. Dyea was gradually moving out of the picture. The aerial tramway was handling a little merchandise, but not enough to pay.

During a trip from Bennett to Dyea, tired and weary, I arrived at the Sheep Creek station of the aerial tramway. I asked for a ride in the bucket to Dyea. The man in charge would not give permission. He telephoned the manager in Dyea, Wallace, and word came back, saying yes—if I would sign a paper exonerating the company of any blame in case of accidents. The bucket was ready. I jumped into it. It was rather small for comfort, but I was glad of the rest. Everything was handsome whilst I took in the views level with my eyes and the bucket. I happened to look down from a great elevation, and there below I saw broken buckets and scattered merchandise, which dispelled the joy of the trip. A little farther on, the bucket stopped. On looking over the side, I found I was suspended over the canyon and was unable to see the bottom. The horror of staying in this cramped position began to take possession of me. Suddenly the tram started again toward its destination. I was greatly relieved when I got out at the station at Dyea, remarking, "Never again!"

Wallace also said, "Never again," for he had not had a moment's peace since the bucket had started its trip.

~

"I want all the employees of the company on board the *Flora*," I ordered. "You will all get two or three days' holiday. Two will have to stay at Bennett. Any volunteers?—Righto! Your interests will be looked after while you stay." Word was given out that the *Flora* would not be going to Macauley's for four days. Any passengers wanting to go on this trip with me were welcome. They were all advised to take their blankets. Only a few who were bound for Dawson stayed behind, as they did not know what the trip was about. Those at the company's mill were given the same opportunities. I went into the wheelhouse with Captain Woodman and gave him instructions.

Instead of instructing the captain to go on to the Six Mile, I told him to turn up the Big Windy Arm of Tagish Lake. We passed a long inlet. The next inlet would be the one we wished to enter. It was as, and where, mentioned. Up this inlet the boat travelled, at the end of which was a swiftly running river. So far, so good. Everything proved as told to me. I called all the crew, employees, and passengers together.

"Boys," I said, "we are going to a creek where there are only two or three parties working. They have found gold. Captain Strickland has given me instructions where to find the creek. We've all got a fair start. I will map out the direction. It looks as if someone will have to stop and look after the steamboat. Who will volunteer?—All right, that's settled. Your interests will be looked after. We must either go up this swift river or make a portage. I believe this is the river Captain Strickland mentioned. However, we shall know, if at the end of it we find a large lake. Someone will have to ferry part of our crowd across and look after things on this side, while the rest will try to find the creek we are looking for. Before starting, let us all eat. We deserve a good meal after the skillful manner in which the captain managed to round up the three moose on the lake."

The story of the moose is as follows. Travelling up that long stretch of water from the route generally taken to the Six Mile, the captain, with the crowd's urging, thought it would be grand to have some fresh meat, and the steamboat gave chase to some moose. All aboard enjoyed it. Gaining on the moose, we began to circle. The captain followed. He circled them many times, gradually drawing closer. One of the moose was to be captured alive. Two were shot, the other was lassooed and taken aboard. Its legs were tied, and it lay on its side. Apparently quieted. The cook had plenty of help dressing the carcasses. The live moose suddenly became frisky. The ropes that bound its legs were a little thick. The half hitches became loose, a final kick loosened the ropes, and over the side it went.

"Don't shoot," said a lanky individual as the moose started to speed away. The man made a flying leap, to its back. He held on while the moose started for shore. The steamboat followed, keeping back a distance to give the man and moose a chance. The moose reached shore. The man got off its back, expecting the moose to charge. Instead, it stood still and looked at him. Emboldened, the man approached and patted its side. Then, when he was ordered to come aboard, the moose followed him! We let the moose go free.

We all finished our meal. I gave the necessary orders to start the journey to find the creek where was supposed to be the discovery claim, and gold. The captain, myself, and a passenger by the name of Douglas were to have the canoe. The crew was to have the ship's boat, and to go up the river as far as the swift waters would allow.

Our canoe had gone about four miles when we came to a drop, about a foot or more, in the river. The crew, which was having difficulty, decided there were enough of them to pack their boat. Finding a light trail, they made a portage. The captain and our party decided to tow the canoe up over the falls, and proceeded to do so. The water at the shoreline had overflowed at this spot, making many potholes. We had to go around a clump of willows. We made an arrangement that when they said, "Let her go!" I would put the canoe's nose out in the stream, from the eddy in which it was sheltered.

"Ready! Let her go!" they said. Out it shot. But the rope slipped through their fingers in an unaccountable manner, or else they were not prepared for the sudden impact of the swift falling water, and the canoe went broadside, on to the fall of water, filled, and over it went. I tried, while under the water, to extricate my legs from under the thwart; the canoe rolled over again, and eventually I freed myself.

There was a bend in the river at this point. I heard, as I was swept down the river, a cry from the captain and Douglas, "He's gone! He's gone!" Treading water, I was carried by the current to the other side of the river. I thought the current would take me back again, for it was now travelling in another direction. The glacial waters numbed my hands. When I reached the other side of the river, I grasped a bunch of willows, but the swift waters snatched me away again, leaving nothing but leaves in my hand. Away I went again. This time, I struck shallow water, and saw a man running to my rescue.

The man reached down and grabbed me by the shoulders, and hauled me up the bank to safety. "Name's Andy Galarno," he said.

"All right, Andy!" I replied. "It won't be forgotten." We both went along the bank to meet the captain and Douglas. They came running through the bush.

"My God! We had about given you up for lost. You had better go back, Boss, and change."

"No, no let's get going." I said. Andy told us that the crew had rigged up a carrier of poles and, with an axe, was making good headway through the woods, packing the boat—an arduous undertaking. The boat, with the crew and passengers, had gone where the going was easier. Our party thought it best to keep beside the river. Mile after mile our little party trudged along, falling into potholes, until each of the other was as wet as I was.

Darkness was coming on just as we emerged from the woods on to the lakeshore. Lake Atlin was its name. We were elated to find that we were on the right track and that Captain Strickland's directions had been correct. (Our destination was Pine Creek, where the discovery claim was being mined.) There was no sign of the other party as yet. They now relied on that boat to take all of them across to the other side. A fire was started—thanks to Andy, who had brought his outfit along—and in a very short time we were enjoying a refreshing cup of coffee, with hard-tack and a few slices of bacon. We had lost all our provisions when our canoe upset. Only those who have experienced sitting around in wet clothes in a freezing temperature can know the enjoyment of the meal in which now we were participating. The sliced bacon, toasted on the point of a stick, was most appetizing. The flare of the fire attracted the attention of the boat's crew, which soon arrived at our camp.

It was now dark. The crowd produced the lunches put up by the cook. These soon disappeared, and we decided to push on, hoping there would be grub on the other side of the lake. We talked things over and realized that this trip would take longer than we had anticipated. Therefore, we agreed that the captain and crew would return to the steamboat, go down the river to Macauley's, meet the lower-river boat, and take the passengers to Bennett. Then the crew would return and take aboard all who were left at this place after they staked their claims, as well as claims for those on the boat. I promised that everyone's interests would be looked after. Those who had blankets rolled in and were soon asleep. Others hugged the fire. When day broke, there would be no breakfast.

In the morning, we launched the boat upon a lake that looked like a mirror. It was impossible to take everyone, so we decided that I should select the first party. I placed everyone's name on a piece of paper, put the names in a hat, and chose a fixed number of names. The mate was to look after the boat and ferry the others across. Douglas, Andy, and myself, not in the draw, would go on the first trip. Twelve were chosen, but this number was found to be too great for the boat. Finally three were ordered back. Even then, the water was only two or three inches from the gunwale. It was still risky. However, the lake was still like glass, and so we started out, trusting that there would be no wind.

We made fairly good time. Two-thirds of the way across the lake, a bit of breeze stirred. Anxious eyes were on the shore. Everyone hoped it would grow no worse. We kept our arms lengthways on the "weather" side, on the gunwale, to keep the little wavelets from coming over. The wind increased. Once in awhile water would curl over, and we had to keep bailing. There was still a half-mile to go, with an increasing wind. Our exertions were doubled at bailing. Could we reach shore without foundering? We feared running before the wind, but it improved the situation somewhat. The question arose, "Can we make it?"

At last we reached a rocky shore, and when two or three gingerly jumped out, catching the boat and steadying it, a sigh of relief arose. The place where we landed was east of an alkali flat. I was in a quandary now. My directions were to go up a creek, but whether the creek was east or west of the place we had landed, I did not know. Finally we was decided that one party would go east along the shore, another, west. If it took all day, and the next, to bring everyone across, not more than six people were to be in the boat at one time.

We split into two groups. The crew set off in the easterly direction. Douglas and I went west. After skirting the shore for a few miles we came to a creek. Believing this to be the one we were looking for, we followed it up for eight miles. It proved to be hard going.

We found the camp of one Fritz Miller, with set-up sluice boxes and several dumps of tailings. He said, "Hullo, there. How did you get here?"

"We followed the creek up from its mouth."

"You must have had a hell of a climb!"

"Say, what's the chance for a bite to eat?" Our clothes were torn to rags from scrambling through bush. "Mr. Miller, I presume," I said.

"Right, but how in God's name did you know?" was his reply.

"I believe you went to Tagish and recorded your claims. You had to give a description of the creek you located on and other particulars. That's how it leaked out. You may at any time receive other visitors. I believe others are on the way. Before we stake a claim, would you mind selling me one hundred dollars worth of gold? I wish to send it to Victoria. If there is to be a rush, and I know there will be, it would be a great favour to me. There will be a steamboat service within twenty-five miles of here, and a big rush will be on."

At first Miller demurred. Then, thinking better of it, and knowing that the inevitable had happened, he weighed out the one hundred dollars worth of gold. It was taken out of tins cans lying around on the floor of the tent. He then gave a short history of the discovery.

His brother had been over this country some years before. He met with accident after accident. Hostile Indians, and trying to elude them, had made his trip hazardous. He intended further exploration of the country, but after returning to Juneau, was thoroughly run down in constitution. With the memory of his hardship and the difficult country he had passed through, escaping death many times, he could not make up his mind to go again, even though he had panned quite a little gold from this creek. He called it Pine Creek because of the thick growth that surrounded it.

In January 1898, when the great rush was on to Dawson, Miller's brother had drawn a map for him, showing this wonderful country and its placer gold. His brother advised him to branch off the Dawson Trail, go up to Tagish Lake, and follow a certain route. (Our party had taken the same route.) His brother told him that by the time he could get to Dawson all the ground would be staked. So Fritz had turned off the Dawson trail, unnoticed by the crowd (since many miners went off the trail for shelter and wood during the cold bitter winter of '97 and '98). He had gone on and on, following his brother's directions, until he came to the tiny, swift Atlin River. (The mouth of the Atlin River is through Graham Inlet, to the south Taku arm of Tagish Lake. Its source is Lake Atlin.) He found Lake Atlin, crossed over the ice, and found Pine Creek and the falls that are near the mouth of Spruce Creek. He found good prospects up to the place where he camped, which became Discovery Claim.

A Mr. Short and his wife were in Fritz Miller's party, and she was overjoyed when she found out their party had visitors. Short was fishing in the creek when Douglas and I arrived. After we had taken a shovel and probed the edge of the bank, and with a gold pan washed the gravel, we found gold whose values averaged seventy-five cents—and more—to the pan.

With the gold we bought from Miller, and with directions for a shortcut to where the boat would be, we set off again to the lakeshore. We had not seen any of the other crowd that had gone east, and neither had the people in the ship's boat, who were waiting for them. These people chaffed at the delay, but when they heard the news of the new gold strike, the delay was forgotten. I lost no time in sending the gold and news of the strike to Victoria by special messenger. Frank Rattenbury exhibited the gold in a jeweller's window, with a card on which was printed: WASHED OUT IN A PAN BY THE MANAGER OF THE NORTHERN DISTRICT OF THE BLKN COMPANY IN TEN MINUTES ON PINE CREEK, LAKE ATLIN. The result was that another rush took place over the old trails to Bennett. From there, men went on to the new goldfields that are today the Atlin gold-mining district.

We now faced a dilemma. We knew that crowds would be waiting at Macauley's for the *Flora*. But it seemed no time at all before a crowd was waiting for transportation to Atlin. We decided to take passengers for Atlin to the mouth of the Atlin River and let them devise their own ways and means of getting across the lake. However, I received word that prospectors who had been bound for Dawson had altered their plans, deciding instead to switch off for Atlin. If boats were to portage from the south Taku arm to the shore of Lake Atlin, a lucrative business could start up in ferrying the gold seekers across to the other side. It was now the fall of the year, the nights began to be nippy and make one shiver, and the rush to Atlin had begun in earnest.

～

One day a man named Joe Boyle rushed into my office. "So, you are the manager! We paid $250 for our passage up from Dawson—two dollars and fifty cents for meals. *You* ought to be kept on them for a week. I feel like getting the value out of *you*."

It turned out that the meals had indeed been rotten, and it had indeed been possible to buy pies for one dollar each outside the dining room. I was overjoyed at getting this proof. I went and got an address for him, wrote it out and handed it to him, and asked him to tell his story to Rattenbury: "A murder has been committed over these meals. The grub the passengers should have received has been sold to wayfarers along the river. If you are coming in again, I think your meals will be the same as you have been getting on the upper-river boats. They have the same material on the other boats, and plenty of it, to give the passengers all they need. The trouble is, it's not only the miners and others who have gone crazy over gold, but steamboat crews as well. There is no doubt that in some way someone is making quite a little cleanup over the grub the passengers should have had. However, I think it is checked for good—or rather, will be, as soon as you return. You know, I can't be too careful in handling the situation, for the crew are under contract, and if they left the boats, who would there be to run them?"

Boyle said, "Well, Mr. Manager, I hope you are right. I am the mouthpiece for the rest of the passengers. Good day. We'll be coming back—that is, most of us." It seemed to be no time before Joe Boyle was back at Bennett, after his trip out, and calling lustily for the manager. With his hand extended, he came running, saying, "Put it right there, I apologize. I take back all that I said when leaving Bennett."

"Very well, Boyle, the least said, soonest mended."

"Hell, man, I haven't said anything yet. But wait until I get on the lower boat. They will hear plenty. I know what you are doing for the poor dog they have in the pen, accused of murder. You're right, everyone is crazy. It's gold, gold, gold. I've been down and got a wood concession, which is as good as any gold mine. I guess I'm as crazy as any of them. My partner, Slavin, the prize-fighter, will be tickled to death when he hears it." (A few years later, Boyle was interested in the Stewart River dredges. When the Great War started, Boyle led a contingent of Klondykers to the front. He gained notoriety when he saved Queen Marie of Romania when she was fleeing for safety. She, after the war, when visiting London, England, inquired after and wished to see the "brave

Colonel Boyle." The message was delivered to him. Through loss of money and misfortune, and having sunk low in poverty and sickness, he was unable to pay a visit to the beautiful Marie. He gradually sunk lower, and departed this life after a hectic career.)

What I did for "the poor dog"—Burnett—who lay lingering in jail at Tagish, was as follows: I wrote to the Minister of Justice.

> To the Honourable David Mills,
> Minister of Justice, Ottawa
> Dear Sir:
> Allow me to bring to your notice a sad case of a man accused of murder. This will reach you before any record is sent to Ottawa by the North West Mounted Police.
>
> Will you kindly use your authority to see that the accused is treated in a different manner than at present, as I can assure you that the police have been given a wrong impression, by an unscrupulous body of men who are bent on finding him guilty.
>
> Everything the accused did in this case was in self-defence. The accused was employed by me to take my place while I was off to Skagway on very important business. Had I been set upon as he was, by a crowd of bullies, I should have done the same.
> Yours very truly,
> The Manager of the Bennett Lake & Klondyke Navigation Company

I received a letter in reply.

> Sir:
> Your letter received, re: man accused of murder. Am taking the matter up with the police. A judge will be sent to Dawson. The man will have a fair trial. Justice will be done. I have the honour to be
> Your obedient servant,
> David Mills
> Minister of Justice

Visiting Burnett again at Tagish, I found him nearly recovered from the terrific beating given him by Cowie. He was given comparative liberty but was locked up at night. There was not the slightest doubt that an order from the Minister of Justice, asking them to be careful in this particular case, had had its effect. Captain Strickland however, was a humane officer, as was Major Wood.

CHAPTER TWENTY-SIX

Bound for Atlin

The steamboats on the upper waters were now kept busy night and day attending to passengers for Dawson and Atlin. Not one hour could be spared. One captain would be on duty for eight hours whilst the other was off. This was kept up till the close of "the season." Hotel and cafe proprietors were returning from Vancouver, Victoria, and Seattle, bringing in up-to-date material, trying to outdo one another in the race for modern service and equipment. They hoped to reap a harvest from providing services during the upcoming long winter, during which many miners would leave their claims and come to Dawson and spend their hard-earned gold dust.

Numbers were still coming to Bennett, bound for Atlin. Many believed it would be cheaper for them to have their own boats than rely on a steamboat, so Mike King was busy building boats for them. If they should be lucky enough to stake a claim, they would want to come out before freeze-up.

On one of the *Flora*'s trips to Atlin an awful wind sprang up on Windy Arm—one of the worst she had experienced. We arrived at a place near Mount Olive. There was no shelter. The people on the steamboat noticed two men on a rocky ledge, waving frantically. Their canoe was badly battered and they had hauled it up out of reach of the angry waters.

The captain went to their rescue. He got as near as possible to the shore and by careful seamanship launched the *Flora*'s shore boat. The men who operated this boat were old sailors who had spent much time on the sealing schooners on the Bering Sea. All on board admired the way they handled the boat. Eventually they got the two marooned men on board. One of the marooned men was Captain Cartwright, the son of Sir Richard Cartwright, a minister in the Laurier cabinet. The other's name I have forgotten. They were both members of the NWMP. It was actions such as this that the police did not readily forget. To describe the picture of the raging waters tossing and pitching the *Flora* about, combers, one after the other, incessantly breaking board, would be a hard matter, especially the little rowboat with four men aboard, dodging comber after comber, gradually working its way to the shelter of the steamboat. At last they made it and the four men got aboard, eager hands hauling the rowboat to safety. Captain Cartwright was profuse in his praises for the manner in which the rescue had been effected, and also thanked the two who had successfully managed the boat which took them off the precipitous rocks.

The trip to the so-called "Golden Gate" was rough. On entering it, we found calm water. The Golden Gate was so named because it led up to the gateway of the Atlin goldfields. One could scarcely imagine that a small sheet of water like Windy Arm of Tagish Lake could turn into a raging sea of combers in the space of a few minutes.

The passengers were all unloaded, some with merchandise, some with liquor, preparing for the great rush that would take place in the spring. Ever in the foreground was the ubiquitous vendor of liquors, ever exploring for more avenues to dispose of his fiery and trouble-making agency. On their way out, patiently waiting for the *Flora*, were those who had already been in and staked their claims. New creeks had been prospected and good pans found. The creeks were named Spruce, Birch, Ruby, St. Mary's, and later on, McGee. All the samples taken from these creeks were of purer gold than any that had been taken from the Dawson district. It was only a few weeks after I had sent the gold purchased on Pine Creek to Victoria, that Atlin was proven to be a promising gold field.

Those who were returning to Bennett from Atlin did not relish the idea of having to go to Macauley's first to meet pick up passengers from Dawson. They wished to be taken directly to Bennett, so they could go to Victoria, Vancouver, and Seattle to outfit properly and get ready to go to the Atlin Camp over the ice. Sometimes one would think they would get their way by the attitude exhibited. Often it took a firm hand to deal with the situation.)

At Macauley's Landing, amongst those waiting for the upper-river boat, there would be bitter haranguing. It was a heterogeneous crowd— some from the Maritime provinces, some from the United States and other countries, some going in, and some going out.

"Yes! I know—you're fine fellows all right, you fish-eaters! You bluenoses! What you want is to rub up against some real men. Men who have a broad outlook on life. Men who have pioneered this western and northern country. You are narrow in your outlook on life. You're cheap down to the last nickel. Those men are risking their lives to pilot you through waters you won't risk yourselves! You, with your scows and merchandise! Yet you'll drink and guzzle."

"You take that back, Mister!" said a young French Canadian.

"Hold you, he's right," said another. "I know them. Me. From Quebec. I know. We was same. Me all same as Bluenose. I come west and to de North long ago. See me, messieurs. I sail de sea. I roam de west. I mine de Circle City, and de Fortymile. Me one different man now. Me. I make 'im good on de Bonanza. I give you all de drink. Come on. You, Ontario, come on you all. By 'im by you all do same as me. You de mean man now. You close. You do up everybody. You wait. You get 'im de hard knock. You small man now. Five, ten year maybe, you be big man lak de Big Alex. He spend de money. He mak de money. Drink up on de Frenchman. I spend de money. I mak 'im. Aye, Jim. When we spend him de money on me. She say, by 'im by, Jim spend 'im de money."

"Come on boys, just another." This was an American. "Never mind the haspars who want Canada for the Canadians! Why, blast it, my old man was a Canadian. He told me when I was a kid of the small, petty way of the Easterners, and he often wished his brothers would come out west and have a little sense knocked into them. The West, and the North, where everyone would become a man."

"Right you are, Yank!" said a Englishman. "This country is big enough for all. Green! Was I green when I first struck Canada? I had some money. Was I tricked? Hell, the remittance boys from the Old Country made the Northwest. They were the only ones who circulated money. The early settlers would have starved to death if it had not been for the remittance men employing the Easterners to break their lands and to do their chores. Do I know what the Yank here is talking about? I should know! I've been in lumber camps, in mining camps, and here I am with all the ruddy polish knocked off me, and in the scramble for Dawson. Got all I went after. Now, no fighting boys! What Canada wants are men like Bob Henderson. Broad-minded men, whether they be Americans, Germans, French, or British. Quit the 'Canada for the Canadians' stuff, and drink hearty. Fill them up again, barkeep! Here comes the boat, fellows. Come on!"

The Mounties, listening to all the talk, were ready to settle any disturbance that might arise. Talks like this were frequent. Those coming out from Dawson were all pals, forgetting their hardships and intent on having a good time when they got outside.

It was during this trip that a few prospectors brought out some good-looking samples of gold from the headwaters of the Big Salmon River, which runs up toward the watershed of the Pelly River. Samples that differed in colour from Dawson gold were also shown, from Thistle Creek and Selwyn.

～

Once word about nuggets that had been found at a new discovery claim drifted into Dawson, a stampede from there into the area ensued. The nuggets had come, supposedly, from above the falls on the Stewart River. A Mr. Fisher was appointed recorder for this area, which the two original prospectors had mapped out. Although hundreds left Dawson in boats, poling and rowing to the Stewart, they could find no sign of the place.

Winter was fast approaching and the disappointed stampeders returned to Dawson, some to Thistle Creek. Fisher stayed on. The winter snows came down, and the waters started to freeze. During this time, a band of Indians came along and stopped in Mr. Smith's vicinity.

Before they left, the chief said, "Huh! huh! You stay all winter, you want pemmican," and left the recorder with dried moose meat, hard as rock. Fisher threw them in a pile on one side of the little hut and forgot their existence.

Scouring the country on snowshoes, he could find no trace of the two prospectors who had caused the rush. He stayed on, but toward spring his flour, bacon, and beans gave out. He then lived on fresh moose meat for a considerable time. As the sun got higher in the heavens, the meat became warmer and fly-blown. He determined to leave the area as soon as possible, but had to wait until the ice went out, as it was not safe to travel on. His boat was below the falls; he would be able to travel down the river in it.

Meanwhile, the only food he had was what he could bag with his gun. Occasionally he would get a grouse. The moose all seemed to vanish. Then, recollecting the dried pemmican, he brought it out, for he was in dire need of subsistence. Chopping chips off it, he soaked them and boiled them. Happy day. His mind returned to the Indian chief who had said, "Huh, Huh!" That despised pemmican saved his life. The Indians had known that when the spring came, his fresh meat would soon spoil—the only thing that would be left to eat would be lumps of dried moose meat. At last the long-looked-for day arrived. The ice went down the river. He soon had his boat fixed up for the journey.

Since Fisher had not shown up at Dawson in the fall, those who had been with him were questioned. All they knew was that he planned to stay till the last minute in the fall, to try and locate the trail of the two prospectors. A search was made. All the country around the falls was scoured, but there was no sign of the recorder. He had built his hut a long way from the falls. The recorder had a life insurance policy, and his relations and friends put in a claim for it, but the company would not pay until his death was definite.

At Stewart Post the Mountie saw a boat coming downstream. He beckoned it to come in. The man had a beard down to his chest and was burnt black with frost and heat. He made for the shore and jumped on the landing stage. When he gave his name, the Mountie said, "Fisher! My God, man!" The police had all been notified to look for him. "Where have you been? The insurance companies would not pay anyone until they were sure you were absolutely a goner."

"Say, give me a meal, a cup of coffee," said Fisher. "I haven't had bread or flaps for two months. Then I'll talk, and I'll be on my way, to quieten the fears of everyone. What a meal!" Did he smack his lips, you bet!

CHAPTER TWENTY-SEVEN

Partnerships on the Trail

William Ogilvie had been "outside"—that is, to the East and to Ottawa, and the government appointed him Commissioner of the Yukon Territory, its first. Toward the end of the summer, he brought to the Yukon a staff of clerks, nineteen in all. Amongst them there was a postmaster for Dawson and officials for other departments.

A contract was made to take the party to Dawson from Bennett. Mr. Ogilvie was an estimable gentlemen, who was evidently concerned about some of his staff, for there was a particular understanding that the men were not to be advanced as much as one dollar without Ogilvie's consent. All went well until arriving at Macauley's where, as usual, a game of cards was going on. One of Ogilvie's staff asked me for a loan. Politely I, and one or two others refused him, whereupon he told me what he thought of me, but not in exactly refined language.

There was a delay at Macauley's because the Dawson boat was a little late, and during it several of the staff sat in on the card game. Their eastern city smartness was not good enough to win them anything from the roughly clad gentlemen who were gathered together. When the game ended, the Easterners were sadder and wiser men. One had to be pretty well versed in the art of card playing to win anything from the bunch at Macauley's, rendezvous for many, when a game was on. Missing a boat was nothing to these men, compared to missing a game of cards. They came from every part of the world. The Easterners had already, having travelled only this far from the East and civilization, found these rough-garbed boys could hold their own in anything and in any way—in any subject, game, or brawl. Ogilvie, again, told his story of Captain Strickland's paddling to his camp—out of breath, puffing, and blowing, for he was getting very stout—and between puffs, saying,

"My God, Mr. Ogilvie, they have struck it the big, big—big—biggest thing in the world."

∼

Once again the *Flora* landed at Bennett, with many interesting individuals aboard from Dawson. The greater part of them were miners and they were packing large quantities of gold. It was reported that in September 1898, over three tons of gold were taken out. This must have been a very conservative estimate, for in September alone the *Ora* had several hundred weights of gold on board each trip. It would be hard to estimate just what the gold amounted to in September. No one experienced a lack of gold nuggets and any kindness was rewarded with a nugget of gold. Even individuals who were not miners could show interesting gold specimens.

Coming off the *Flora* this trip was a man named Cirs, in the charge of a constable. "Hullo, Cirs, what's up?" I asked, having always thought highly of him. Cirs begged the constable for permission to have a few words with me and was granted it. This was his story (which was confirmed by a passenger).

"I well remember the rough and tedious times we had going over the trails to Bennett, and I was pleased at the prospect of being at the head-waters of the Yukon, and able to enjoy the well-earned rest and sleep we had all looked forward to for so long. For days we enjoyed the sight of the rugged mountains. The magnificence of it all! The sun rising. The glow and beauty of the colours cast upon the mountaintops. The busy scene of teamsters and pack trains unloading. Boats being built. The never-ending procession of dog teams and mushers going along the lake will ever live in my memory.

"Alas, that I should fall for a verbal presentation to me of a rich piece of ground away up the Stewart River. The glowing account was given by a man who had been there and wanted a partner. Everyone was after riches. I thought of home and what wealth would do for me in the East. We followed the ice as it went out. It was life! Exhilarating! All worries were dispelled by the constant vigilance of piloting our craft over dangerous waters. The joy of it all, as bend after bend of the waterways opened up new vistas. The peace of it all."

"Excuse me," I said, " I must attend to things."

"Just a few minutes, for old times' sake." Cirs went on. "Great valleys stretched away for miles on each side of the river. It made one feel how small and insignificant we are in this great land."

"Hurry up, Cirs," I said, at the same time thinking the poor fellow a little strange.

"As I was saying, it was grand floating downstream, but another matter when pulling and poling up the Stewart. My partner became morose, sullen, and quiet. Nothing of beauty or grandeur interested him. It seemed he wanted me as part of his scheme, to get me into his great treasure field as help only. We arrived at the place and it was as he pictured it. The country had been prospected. The man had fine samples of rich ore of silver and gold. At last, having arrived at the place of his destination, he became surly.

"It seemed everything had to be done his way. It mattered not for the sake of harmony how much I tried to please. It just made things worse. He insinuated it would be better if some people were put out of the way. What full-blooded man would let a statement like that go without explanations? He reached for his gun but I was a little quicker, and now I am charged with murder. It was a matter of him or me. I have had plenty of time to think over what I have done and have come to the conclusion I would do the same thing again under the same circumstances. So you see, all my beautiful visions of wealth and happiness have come to naught, unless I am found not guilty."

A tap on the shoulder by the constable and the command, "It's time to hit the trail," ended the conversation. The words of Robert Service suitably express my meeting with Cirs.

"This is the law of the Yukon, and ever she makes it plain:

Send not your foolish and feeble;

Send me your strong, and your sane—

... Send me men girt for the combat, men who are grit to the core ..."

∾

One would have no hesitation in saying, after witnessing many fights on the Yukon (some arising out of very trivial matters), that a good many partners have disappeared, some through jealousy, some through carelessness, and some through greed and selfishness. These cases have passed into oblivion.

Another man, having been told Cirs' story, told of his own experience coming up Lake Bennett in a canoe. It was blowing a gale. Making for a small shelter, in which was moored a scow, he caught hold of the scow, to work around its side for shelter. The owner of the scow, whether sane or drunk, took up a large piece of wood that was lying on the deck, and hurled it with all his strength at the fellow's head. Luckily the fellow ducked, or it would have killed him. Pulling out his revolver he shot, hitting the scow owner in the arm. The canoe owner saw that the man was a bully, for he was whimpering. Like a good many others, he could give but not take. In other words, he was yellow.

His partner bobbed up after the shot, saying, "It was coming to him! I've felt like doing that myself. I often wished he would quit or jump into the lake. One day he will find himself floating down the river, a corpse."

However, most of the sourdoughs were fine, splendid fellows. There were never better. It is a pleasure to live it all over again and remember many of them, men of sterling character, honest and generous to a fault. Under their rough exteriors breathed noble spirits and hearts. Yet there were now and again met with, despicable men as well, who were lawless, selfish, and ready to murder for a song. Many of these, the "spawn of the gutters," as Service called them, did get their just desserts, either by being shot or by beatings. Many realized that the environment of just and honest men in the North was no place for them.

Miss Smith, with the dogs Yukon and Alaska, after hearing of the gold find at Atlin, made up her mind to cut across country and stake a claim. She had already performed many services of mercy, and run the rapids with the pilots when occasion arose, merely for the sheer love of the thing. She decided that before leaving she would like to have one more jolly ride down the White Horse Rapids. The time came. Alaska and Yukon were aboard. All set, and away they started.

Everything went well until they approached the White Horse. The scow and a fallen tree with outspread roots happened to meet just at the base of the crest. The pilot shouted, "Everyone for himself," and occupants and merchandise were thrown into the boiling waters when the scow overturned. The pilot, in the seething waters, cast a look around for the young lady. She had already reached the bank with the two dogs. All were good swimmers. When she looked back, and saw both the pilot and the owner in difficulties, she immediately sent the dogs to the rescue. Obedient to orders, one dog went to one man, the other to the other, and soon all four reached the shore. She was full of sympathy for the owner and his loss, and expressed herself accordingly. "Now Miss, don't worry. It's all right. The outfit is gone, but there are plenty of outfits at Macauley's, or even here. I can buy from them that have cold feet. I esteem it a privilege to have had your company on our ill-fated scow. We could not help the blasted tree wanting to make the passage at the same time we did."

It was not long before the young lady appeared again from her tent, looking spic and span. After attending to those who needed her help she prepared to go across country, to the Atlin goldfields, with a young man and his wife, who were up in the North for their honeymoon. The dogs had saddlebags made to pack provisions, but an old prospector told the party that it would take too long to make the trip, so they decided to take the boat at Macauley's and follow the route the others were using. They were ferried across Lake Atlin by one of the many boats now plying the waters. Here again the services of the angels of mercy were called into play, for even strong men were laid up by some strange sickness that was brought on by wrong food and hardships.

By this time nearly all the country adjacent to Pine Creek was staked, but merchandise kept pouring into the new town of Discovery. Close to Millar's first camp, a man named McKee had discovered a creek which he named after himself. On Spruce Creek, he found that at its head the water ran off both ways. Following the creek to its mouth, he discovered some very coarse gold. Later on, Lord Claude Hamilton became interested in this property and in other quartz-mining properties.

Miss Smith returned to Bennett and said, when asked, that she was waiting to meet someone who had been greatly delayed on the outside and so had not gone through to Dawson. Her description of the Atlin camp, now assured of being permanent, was indeed fascinating. She had left the honeymooners behind. They were now on an exploration trip around Lake Atlin.

In 1899, the honeymooners, having settled down to a regular, routine life of domesticity, decided to visit the enchanting country again. This is their account of that trip, an overland one from Atlin to the outside.

They hired one of the many boats that were on Lake Atlin. They took the boat to Moose Creek (which flows in what is now Surprise Lake, east of Lake Atlin), another creek the roaming prospectors had found. Caching their boat, they each took a pack, with the necessary provisions. They believed they would encounter very few obstacles in travelling the old Bennett trail to Skagway and that the trip would be a short one. They came to the Llewellyn Glacier, which impeded their progress. Travelling over part of the glacier they experienced many difficult tasks and sudden drops.

Eventually they made the right of way of the WP&YR, in the vicinity of Log Cabin (now a depot of the railroad). This was the start of the trail for winter travelling to Atlin; it cut out the difficult route they had just traversed. They found a very undulating trail that led to the south Taku arm of Tagish Lake, fairly easy going, opposite Graham Inlet (the Golden Gate). Thousands used this trail in the winter.

One would have thought that the honeymooners would have had enough of roughing it, especially over that particularly rough piece of country. Yet there they were again in 1899, and I was reminded of Service's words: "listen to the wild, it's calling you!" The wild had called them once again. In '99 they were seen drinking in the intoxicating, breath-taking splendour and grandeur of the Atlin trail and on down the mighty Yukon River, all the way to its mouth in Alaska on the shores of the Bering Sea.

∿

In '98 the days were getting shorter in the month of September. The nights were colder; merchants and miners, in feverish haste, wanted to reach Dawson before the freeze-up. Merchandise piled up in Bennett. Scows were in great demand to take the freight downriver. It was night and day work for all. Cattle were brought in and slaughtered, then loaded in scows—the weather now permitting this method of transportation. Bales of blankets, fur-lined coats, warm clothing by the ton—all for the requirements of the now big population of Dawson to replace the clothes worn out by the argonauts of the spring. Many came along the river also in need of winter clothing. Quite a few colonies were set up at the mouths of tributaries entering the Yukon. Ever-increasing quantities of equipment and liquor arrived, to supply the demand for the coming winter, during which time many propositions would shut down. The easy money from the well-paying creeks would be easily spent.

There was no lack of money, yet hundreds of unfortunates had no work, no means of surviving the hard winter months. There were no mining claims. Suffering was rampant. Many of these unfortunates went to their graves in Dawson, their deaths brought on by rundown constitutions contracted during their long journeys down the river with not sufficient, or the right kind of food. Dance hall ladies gave liberally to the helpless who now came in from the creeks. Mining apparatus was eagerly awaited so that winter mining could be carried on successfully in thawed-out ground. Many scows and boats destined for Dawson, owned by individuals hearing that all and everything had been staked, and of the illness and scarcity of work, sailed on to Fortymile, Circle City, Tanana, and other points further down the river instead.

Throughout September the boats were thronged with passengers going outside to spend the winter. Some had made good—ladies among them. There were, however, also many who had spent their all to get to the goldfields but had arrived too late to stake a claim. They were broken financially, broken in health, broken in spirits, and they were on their way home.

Many were indignant over the manner in which the mail was distributed. Long lines of men would have to stand for hours waiting for mail. Those waiting to catch a boat would give anything to know if there was a letter for them. Graft soon started up. Those desiring to get mail in a hurry were accosted by some in league with the postmaster, who offered to get their mail for them for certain considerations. The nuggets acquired by this method amounted to a considerable sum. It was said by some that a small amount would be refused. If the steamboat was known to be leaving, bills of large denominations were handed over for immediate delivery of mail.

~

The steamer *Domville* started from Dawson with a number of passengers, among whom was the Senator Domville. It was rumoured that the *Domville* would be another boat to ply its way between White Horse and Dawson. She had negotiated the river nearly halfway up the Thirty-mile. The boat, drawing too much water, was hard to navigate in the swift current. At a difficult point she swung around, and broke her back. This was the end of the steamer *Domville*.

The *Nora* took the passengers off the wrecked boat, including the senator, who arrived at Bennett. The senator came to the BL&KN company's office, accompanied by the purser of the *Flora*. The senator introduced himself; he wanted "the courtesy of the company" by being given a free pass. I could not see my way clear to doing this, and forthwith gave my reasons. The senator was taken by surprise—he, a member of the Senate, refused a free pass! He said he would settle with the directors at Victoria.

"I'm sorry, Senator, you must pay for your passage before leaving Bennett," I said. At this statement the senator became far from acting the gentleman. "Now Senator," I said, "I want you to look at things my way. Rumour has it your company includes a very powerful member of the government, whoever that may be. We had a permit for our company's liquor. Our permit carried with it the same privileges as your permit, but our liquor has been stopped all along the route. It has cost us a lot of money to protect it, by watching and guarding it continually. Why? You can answer that, Senator, if you wish to do so. After the highhanded performance of the police, who are carrying orders they say are from a Member of the Cabinet, we want to make up a little of the money we have lost by charging you and your outfit passage. Anything against the fairness of this, Senator?"

"We'll see about the fairness of this later."

"Good. But you'll pay for your fares before you leave, and if not, the police will stop you for beating your board bill and fare." The senator drew a wry face, produced his pocketbook and paid the fares.

"You'll hear more about this, young man," he said. And so the BL&KN company got back just a little of the expenses it had spent on the care of their liquor during orders given to hold it up. Had the company the same break as the senator, it would have sold the liquor when the market was at its highest, and consequently, the senator would have been treated as other members of the steamboats were, being given a free pass. In the fall of the year, the company gave many a poor, woebegone fellow a pass for the outside, with the understanding that he would chop wood to pay for his passage on the way up the river.

CHAPTER TWENTY-EIGHT

Percy Smith

Frank Smith returned from the outside with an outfit to thaw out the frozen ground, so that it could be worked during the long winter months. He saw Miss Smith (and her two dogs, Alaska and Yukon), of whom he had taken more than passing notice at White Horse. Going to the captain he asked to be introduced to her. Frank becomingly acted the gentleman. The rough exterior obtained by constant mingling with a rough-and-ready environment, when logging and in mining camps, he readily cast aside. The two were soon on the same level socially, both in speech and manner.

In answer to Frank's question, she said yes, she was going to Dawson: "I'm waiting and expecting my brother today or tomorrow." Her brother had been delayed. She had everything ready and was sorry that they would not be able to go down the river with Mr. Smith. After a while Frank "suddenly" found that he had other freight to round up, and told the purser he would have to take the next boat.

The next day, the trail was watched eagerly by Miss Smith for the long-looked-for brother. Her vigil was rewarded by the sight of him entering Bennett with his long, easy stride. She went to meet him. "Hullo, Gwen. Say, you look fine." After a good hug they went down to the wharf.

Gwen said, "You see that man over there, Percy? I was introduced to him yesterday. His name is Smith. Be sure and remember that our name is Smith as well. That is the name I was introduced by."

"He's stayed behind to have your company down the river? Strange, isn't it? Now Gwen, take hold of yourself. Watch your step!"

"Oh, bother you! You are always thinking horrid things of your sister. Come, I will introduce you."

By this time Frank had turned round and was coming toward them. "By all that's holy—Frank!"

"Percy!" The recognition was instantaneous.

"Eight years since we parted from the boat, Frank—you for Texas, I for British Columbia!"

"I see, Mr. Smith, that there is no need for an introduction, you seem to know each other quite well."

"Forgive me, Miss Smith—it is a very popular name, isn't it? However, for certain reasons, I had better retain it."

"You two must have a lot to talk about," said Gwen. "I must get everything ready." Frank's eyes followed her, as many others had done, while she was on her errands of mercy. Having had some little experience in a Vancouver hospital, she was worth her weight in gold. Many, in after years, would look back and think of this wonderful woman, nursing them back to health and strength.

"It's good to see you, Frank!"

"It certainly is good to see you too, old boy."

"Tell me, what have you been doing the last eight years?"

"That won't take long, Percy. I was a cowboy for a big outfit in Texas, which knocked all the shine off me. I became as tough as the crowd. It helped make a bit of a man out of me. I drifted to British Columbia and found men, tough as they make them, all around me. Soon after, it was mining camps along the coast. Then Alaska. When word was passed around about gold in the Klondyke, a lot of us early in '97 went over the Chilcoot. At Lake Lindemann I came across an elderly fellow having his work cut out getting a boat ready to go downriver. He offered to let me have a half-interest if I would throw in my lot with him, or pay me five dollars per day until we got to Dawson. 'Forget the pay, Mister. I'm seeing you down.' We were late, we thought, for good ground, however, the old chap staked on Eldorado. I staked as well, and threw in with the old man. We built a hut, sank hole after hole, until the old man was broke, and then some of us boys put down a hole for nothing for him. We struck it rich. Boy! We had it rough getting to

Dawson. Say, Percy, old chap, you can throw in with me if you have no other plans. Now, old boy, how have you been making out?"

"Jolly tough, lately. The gov'nor bought a ranch for me. Later my sister came out. Gradually the markets for our produce disappeared. We intended to go to the Klondyke, Gwen and I. We had a farewell dinner party, and wound up with a game of cards. One of the crowd, who should not have been there—a rather common fellow—was caught cheating. Borlase, who married Gertrude, gave him a crack. The fellow didn't know who or what hit him. He had pull with the authorities. We were all pulled up for assault and battery. I saw it would go hard with Borlase. Knowing Gertrude would take it hard. I pleaded guilty to the whole thing, and here before you stands Percy ———, son of Sir ———, a jailbird. Our tickets were already in our hands. It was decided Gwen, being well able to take care of herself, would go north. Everything was ready, down to training the dogs. She was to wait for me at Bennett. The thought of staying around, knowing I was in jail, was distasteful to her, although Borlase and Gertrude would not hear of her going away. Gwen is a fine girl—a trump. She tells me her accumulation of nuggets is a sight to see. We are now ready for a fresh start."

"Tut, tut, my boy. I had to quit Texas for just such a jamboree. I wonder what the Earl of ——— would say, to see me here. There is only one fellow who knows me here, and this is old Selky, whom I entrusted to get a letter for me. We had better stick to the name of Smith until we have made our pile. And by jove! It looks as if it's good. Say the word, Percy, and we are partners."

"That's ripping of you, Frank, but I have no money to put into the venture."

"Don't mention that. Then we will still be Smiths? Tell your sister. Shall it be Granville to her, or still Smith? Ah, here she comes."

Time did not hang heavily on their hands. There was much to talk about. Nationality was forgotten in Bennett—it had imbibed the spirit of the West and of the North. In fact, this was what the great Yukon called for, to quote Service:

"Sired of a bull dog parent, steeled in the furnace heat.

Send me the best of your breeding, lend me your chosen ones;

Them will I take to my bosom, them will I call my sons;"

～

Miss M. (the famous Belinda Mulroney) and Count Carboneau had just arrived at Bennett from the outside, with modern fittings and furnishings for her hotel. (Later, rumour said that the "count" was just an ordinary adventurer from Montreal.) There was a doctor at Bennett, and Miss M. went to him for advice. She was suffering from a headache, no doubt brought on by overexertion on the trail from the nauseating conditions that prevailed. She had had a very short stay outside, and the great amount of freight, now on the wharf, had evidently taxed her strength. The doctor said she would have to stop at Bennett for two weeks at least. (He intimated to a few that he would make a few dollars himself, as she could well afford to pay.)

Miss M. repeated to a few friends what the doctor had told her. "The idea!" she said. "I'm not sick. He tries to make me believe I have a fever. Why, when coming in over the trail for the first time, I felt a whole lot worse than I do now." The captain of the steamboat had heard both stories and he went to his medicine chest, found headache remedies, and advised her to take a rest. So she did. She left orders that no one was to disturb her, not even the doctor. She had been on the go ever since she had left Dawson.

Next morning the doctor visited her. "Well, doctor," she said, "I am perfectly well and feel fine."

"Ah, that is the symptom. Take this draught and keep very quiet. Be sure and take it three times a day." She did not take the medicine.

She chuckled to herself, and said "Does that greenhorn think I am as green as he?" There was one person who was troubled—the count. He told everyone that he believed she was ill. Several believed he was hand-in-glove with the doctor to fleece Miss M. of a large fee and go fifty-fifty with the doctor on the proceeds.

The boat arrived, and with it a crowd of boys with their packs of gold for the outside. A vast amount of gold was taken out during the season, and no record could be kept of it. It was great to see the happiness of the boys. This was their holiday. They were enjoying it. They were going home, and acted like all the others who had gone out before them. Yes, home to see mother, wife, and sweetheart. Brave boys. Comrades all. For had they not braved dangers together, saved each others lives, when travelling was not so easy as now? "Come boys! Just one on me, here's old Bennett and Lindemann. Methinks I hear the twang of the saw, the sound of the hammer and caulking mallet, the ring of the axe on the frozen timber, the hauling of logs to the sawpit. Was it worth it, Jim?"

"You're darn right." And away they went with a light tread to Tom Gagar's (the Yukon Hotel), to say hello to Tom, whom they had left behind to cater to the wants of others coming along the trail.

"Drink hearty, boys."

"Keep the change, Tom, you deserve it." Elated, yes. No more rebuffs of regular occurrence, as had happened in the past year, trying to hold down jobs, driven from pillar to post. They had wrestled from old Mother Earth some of her treasures, hidden for ages, and now had a competency for life.

I was told about Miss M. and the doctor, and immediately sent a messenger to Miss M., asking her to come aboard. I offered her my cabin, and she went in and locked the door. Once more no time was lost. The little boats were constantly on the move, as any day a bitter and hard frost might come and congeal the great waters, closing the easy route to Dawson. All aboard! The whistle blew. The doctor had called on his patient while the boat was loading, and when she could not be found, he hurried to the ship, but she could not be found there either. He told the count. The count was very worried and did not know what to do. He warned me, and begged me to hold the boat for a little while, but we cast off. The count jumped aboard, and the doctor stayed ashore. As the steamboat drew away, Miss M. emerged on the deck, and shouted, "Goodbye, Doctor." Chagrin was markedly shown on the doctor's face when she blew kisses to him. And so once more, an interesting crowd was on its way to Dawson.

At White Horse, Frank Smith, Percy Smith and Gwen Smith, all debated whether or not to run the rapids on a scow that was going through. They decided they would do so. Frank asked the owner for permission, saying that he would put her through for him, as he had done it before. Without hesitation, the owner gave the sweep to Frank, and away they went.

They passed the Miles Canyon, went on to the Squaw Rapids, and then went on to the final leap. Strong arms were at the sweep. The scow answered the powerful handling of Frank as pilot, gauging to a nicety the exact position. She hits the comber at the proper angle. Interested eyes are upon Frank, full of confidence that every movement of his is correct. He rides his mount, the White Horse. The scow is received by the swirling waters below, and is steered and snubbed up to the bank in safety. "By Jove, Miss Smith, we had to go through safely. I could not afford to make a bally poor job of it, with you aboard. You know, the water is cold!"

"You did it wonderfully. This was far better than a few weeks ago, when I went down. It was no fault of the pilot, though—we hit a tree at the time the scow was ready to make the leap. We were all thrown into the water."

"Great Scott—you, in those boiling waters!"

While Percy was busy at the warehouse arranging his freight, which had been waiting for him for some time, Miss Smith was telling Frank all about her frequent running of the rapids.

~

Word came up the river that the *Canadian* and the *Columbia* were to be laid up, owing to the shallow water. These boats had been put on the run to the upper reaches by Maitland Kersey, former manager of the White Star Line in New York. He left his lucrative position to put these boats on the Yukon, bringing them to Dawson via St. Michael, but was too late to make any big money in the season of '98. Whether he would make any money in '99 was also questionable, as the draught of these boats was too great for the many shallow parts of the river. (This river is of a great width—miles from shore to shore—with innumerable sandbars.)

The *Canadian* and the *Columbia* steamboats were quite an acquisition to the Yukon River service, with comfortable berths and good service. However, these advantages were offset by their great draught, which delayed them in shallow water. They were stuck on sandbars so often that the smaller boats made better time (although the accommodation on these was far inferior). When the small boats were stuck on a bar, out came their grasshopper legs, and in a few minutes they were on their way again.

The grasshopper legs consisted of two stout poles with strong chains. The poles would be placed in position on each side of the boat, leaning out upright toward the stern. The chain was placed under the hull of the boat. If a clump of trees happened to be handy onshore, a cable was attached to the trees and the windlass. When all was ready, orders would be given for "all steam ahead," and the grasshopper legs would gradually obtain an upright position. With the aid of the water, the wheel, and the windlass, the boat would steadily lift as the grasshopper legs straightened. Over the sandbar the boat would hop, once more into deep water.

In the fall the river waters fell rapidly, owing to the night frosts that sealed up the small rivulets and streams that fed the great river. A number of scows and boats were caught on sandbars toward freeze-up. These bars could have been avoided, in many cases, had it not been that novices were handling the boats. The novices could not readily discern the shallows. Several boats and scows were stuck on bars, to remain there until the next spring. It was impossible for steamboats to get near enough to pull them off. The steamboats were cursed for not coming to the rescue of the smaller craft, but even the company scows had to be left to their fate in the fall. Every minute meant dollars to the company and passengers. The risk of helping anyone could not be taken, for fear of the intervening sandbars to be crossed. Many of those stranded would have to wait until freeze-up and make the trip over the ice. Most of those who were caught on the bars did not know the regular route of deep water. It was not so bad for those near shore, as a shelter could be thrown up rapidly amongst some trees, where they would be fairly comfortable until the ice was strong enough to travel over. Tales were told of suffering by some of the unfortunates who did not dare to leave their merchandise. There were prowlers on the lonely wastes, ready to pounce on anything that could easily be gotten.

CHAPTER TWENTY-NINE

True Love

Once more the shout, "All aboard." Frank and Miss Smith came running.

"Close shave, Frank," said the captain.

Percy had become anxious at the disappearance of his sister and his friend. "Where in God's name have you two been? We were about to sail without you."

"It's all right, Percy, old boy. Just having a bit of a stroll. It will be beastly cramped up in the little boat; we thought it nice to stretch out our legs a bit." Gwen was glad to have a bit of a rest, and sat down beside Miss M.

"You came near to missing the boat, Miss Smithy."

"Yes, indeed, but it was a lovely walk."

"It must have been, I'm sure. Forgive me if I'm rude, but do you know the man you were walking with?" Gwen was on the point of politely telling Miss M. that it was none of her business, but instead, calmly and coolly answered the question with another, "Do *you*?"

"Indeed I do! I should know him!" Gwen was instantly on the alert, asking herself, "What can this woman know?" Was Frank to be thrown down from the pedestal on which she had placed him, as one of the few men she had taken any notice of in a way that appealed to her? Was she to hear something horrible about the man whose company she seemed to desire?

"Will you tell me what you know about him? Is it to his credit? Otherwise I do not wish to know."

Miss M. replied, "Since leaving Bennett, I have noticed that you are very interested in him."

"Oh, indeed, you must be a very observant person." Gwen was on the point of leaving this inquisitive woman, but inwardly yearned to know as much as possible about her new-found acquaintance. She swallowed her pride, and the topic continued.

"You will excuse me, Miss Smith. Will you allow me to give you my thoughts from the first time we met? We are the only women on board. It would be nice to have someone I can really confide in—they are few and far between in Dawson."

"I certainly shall respect your confidence," said Gwen.

"Then, while the men are busy below, we will have a heart-to-heart talk. I shall be pleased to know more about Dawson; it will be interesting. I met Count Carboneau on the trail. I am wondering if he really is a count. Like many another young American girl, I thought it would be great to go to a mining camp, after reading so many stories of the 1849 California gold stampede, and the fortunes made in business with the miners. I decided to go to the Klondyke and engage in business in a small way, and perhaps, find romance."

"Did you go in on the trail in ninety-seven, Miss M.?"

"Partly in ninety-seven. Very early in ninety-eight we arrived in Dawson. Shall I ever forget? Oh! Those poor men! What they suffered! My poor services were appreciated by the sick and dying. Arriving in Dawson, I opened a restaurant. I made a lot of money. Today I am enlarging my establishment, trying to bring about a high-class, clean-dealing hotel!" Gwen asked if she thought it would pay. "Most certainly. The boys appreciate service in return for the large amounts of gold they pay out when they go to town."

Gwen was eagerly awaiting news about Frank, yearning to know the worst about him, feeling that any time it might come from Miss M.'s lips. Her fond hopes and ideals might be shattered. Had she been making an idol of him? Again the picture of him came to her mind, going through the rapids. Those rippling muscles handling the scow, guiding the sweep in such a masterful manner. The easy way in which he accomplished everything. The handling of freight, the manner in which he ingratiated himself with everyone. Her heart was speaking. No. He could be nothing but clean and manly in every respect. She tried to stem her feelings for this man, but ever and again the thought possessed her, "He is my ideal."

Gwen was awakened from her reverie by Miss M.'s remark. "I know you won't mind my saying, when first my eyes looked upon you, my thought was, 'Can a young woman like this be going to Dawson to join that Hell on earth? Can she be going to an early grave, the Dance of Death? Can she be falling for the alluring gold?'"

Gwen drew a long breath, quivered, and felt nauseated by the picture drawn for her of that den of iniquity started by greedy, unscrupulous individuals. Past masters, from all parts of the world in similar pursuits, preying on the credulous to get from those who possessed gold, riches dearly won. Still she dreaded to hear something not-very-nice about her idol. She had met him under such peculiar circumstances—a friend of Percy's, and therefore a friend of hers.

"I was delighted to find that you were travelling with a brother and friend," Miss M. continued. "My thoughts of what would become of you were dispelled. In Dawson three beautiful women came to see me to get refreshments. Two of them were gold diggers and used to the tinsel life of dance halls. They tried to persuade the third to join them in their revels, but failed. She appealed to me for help and advice. Today she is happy in the thought that temptation was resisted, and now she is the wife of a good man. Could you know the mean, detestable methods used to get women to throw their lot in with the low, degenerate dancing crowd? The low, miserable skunks that will do anything for gold? You would loathe their kind forever. Be careful, dearie, of those men, polite, courteous, and acting the gentleman. Shun them. Also, look out for dope. Yes! Up in this far country, women are unconsciously doped into the lives they are leading. *Some* are leading, I should say."

"Yes, I know," said Gwen. "I had a little experience in the hospitals on the trails. If it had not been for a good man who knew of a trap to ensnare me made by a low ring of men controlling the abominable traffic you have alluded to, I perhaps would have been doped into submission to their vile life. Who knows if I would have been in their power today?

It makes me shudder when I think of those unfortunate girls."

"One beautiful woman awoke in a dance hall, having been treated by dope. Oh! The tears, the remorse, after finding what had happened. Today she is drinking her life away. How soon she passes away, she cares not. All this is going on and the rotten rascals are gathering in their ill-gotten gains by the thousands of dollars. These rascals know that it is the women who goad on the men to wine and whiskey, and thus, the miners' hard-won money flows into the coffers of the unscrupulous devils."

Poor Gwen. She still dreaded hearing the worst of her hero. The man who was different from any other man she had ever met. The bell rang for lunch, however, and the conversation stopped. Percy and Frank joined the women at the table. Several men were stretched out wherever they could find a place, and would not be disturbed. They had come through on the Teslin trail, and seemed not to be able to get enough rest. "Let them sleep," said Frank, "they have earned it. I know what it's like. The pity of it is that the poor devils will get disappointments. There are now thousands scattered amongst the hills and creeks far from the Dawson district in search of gold that they will never find. If ever it is found, it will be deep. I firmly believe that in years to come, far richer wealth will be found, when machinery will drill to a great depth."

"I say, Gwen, this is stunning. It is splendid gliding down this magnificent river," said her brother.

Gwen brought her brother's mind back to British Columbia by saying, "I do hope Hamilton will buy the ranch."

"Now don't you bother about that, the ranch will take care of itself. Frank and I are going to make it rich."

Frank chimed in, "You two watch each bend of the river. You will be surprised at the wonderful country each bend will unfold to you.—Say, Percy, this is altogether different. This is paradise to what we experienced going down in a bally old scow, which leaked like a sieve. We often stopped and caulked the seams with moss, especially after we had run the Five Fingers and the Rink Rapids."

After lunch, there would be the intermingling with passengers, some dressed quite respectably and generally called "Professor" or "Colonel." One could pick them out, especially the professors, who would continually suggest a game of poker to pass away the time. Some of these gentlemen were going in for the first time, to inveigle some poor miners into games in order to fleece them. These professors were very polite to Miss M. and Gwen. Frank met a couple of them whom he noticed were paying great attention to Gwen, who in her ladylike way eschewed their company. On one occasion Frank had to remonstrate with one who's persistency for Gwen's company was repulsed by her. Frank had to be drastic with him.

"Look here old boy! Just lay off the lady. I'm giving you fair warning. None of your flipping handkerchief stuff around here. Handkerchiefs sprinkled with dope! I know your abominable tactics. Just keep away! Keep clear! The lady does not wish to have your company."

The man's hand gradually went toward his shoulder. Frank, quick to notice it, caught it, and with a dexterous twist, took his gun from him and threw it overboard. "Smart, eh!" said the man.

"The next time, look out!" came from Frank. "There will be no fooling."

Percy was on hand if any others attempted anything. "They know better now than to start a rumpus," he said. This little episode did not stop Frank and Percy from settling down to a game of cards with them again. Frank warned them that if there was any crooked work there would be a roughhouse. It is surprising how genial and jovial a gambler can be when he knows someone has a whip hand over him.

The ladies were again by themselves, and had much to talk about. Naturally the conversation drifted into channels interesting to Gwen. "You asked me if I knew Frank Smith," resumed Miss M., "This is how I know him. There now. Don't look frightened, Gwen. Allow me to call you that. I can see you have a soft spot in your heart for the man. I have noticed it for some time."

"Indeed! I think you must be imagining a lot," said Gwen.

"Now don't get mad, dearie. I am going to tell you all I know. One afternoon the boys came in from the creeks with a lot of gold. They had given me their pokes, for which I gave receipts. Each man had his name on his poke. Big Alex was there. They all wanted something good to drink. I happened to keep it. It was good quality, and better than they were used to. I saw some were getting all they could stand. Big Alex was after buying claims, and trying to get them from some of the boys who were drinking. Some in their muddled state accused Big Alex of being a cheapskate. I was beginning to get worried, knowing that inevitably this would end up in a roughhouse. They were all getting ugly.

"Frank was the only one who was sober. He seemed to know when he had had enough. 'Come on boys, the lady is getting worried,' he said. 'Damn the lady,' said one. 'She's here to do business with us. We're paying for it.' Frank just took the fellow to the door with ease. 'Come on, boys! Come on, Alex!' 'Say, who are you ordering around?' Emboldened by Big Alex, the others became uproarious and started to put Frank out. He, waiting calmly for the onrush, grabbed two of them by the collars as they arrived, and knocked their heads together. Big Alex waved the other fellows back, and was about to tackle Frank when Frank sidestepped and caught Big Alex by the arm. His jiu-jitsu experience soon had Big Alex just where he wanted him. Frank turned around just in time to miss a bottle thrown by one of the other men. That finished it. Frank caught the fellow in his powerful grasp and hurled him against Big Alex. They both went to the floor." Gwen drew in a long breath and inwardly gloried in the power of Frank, still dreading to hear of something not to his credit.

"Big Alex got to the floor and held up his hand to stay the other fellow's. He held out his hand and said, 'Shake. You are the first man to put it over me. Now boys, one drink more and we will be going.' They all drank to Frank's and my health. 'Say Frank, I'll double the price for your claim. How about it?' 'Thank you Alex, it's not for sale.' I think Frank Smith is one of the finest gentlemen in the North."

A gasp came from Gwen. "Thank God! Then I am not mistaken."

"You admire Frank. Who would not?" asked Miss M., and Gwen, blushing, asked to be excused. She wished to be by herself.

"Before going, allow me to thank you, Miss M. You have taken a great load of doubt and anxiety off my mind." She spontaneously kissed Miss M. This was the beginning of a lasting friendship between the two women.

The dogs, Alaska and Yukon, had the run of the steamboat. They were constantly near their mistress. Gwen was enjoying a quiet communion with herself, looking far off, on some of the low, open tracts of country. Lost in thought, she was disturbed from her reverie by one of the slick fellows who had previously been warned by Frank to lay off and to be mighty careful of his behaviour to the young lady. This fellow slyly talked to her of the beautiful trip and gradually broached the subject of the gaudy butterfly life of the ladies in Dawson. In his sophisticated manner pictured the glowing life a lady could have. "Leave me this minute! Here Yukon!" From the tone of Gwen's voice the dog sensed that something was wrong and that his mistress was in trouble. He sprang at the man and bore him to the floor of the deck. A piercing shriek was heard. Percy and Frank rushed to the scene just in time to stay the fangs of the faithful dog, about to close on the man's throat.

Frank raised him up and said, "Get up. Damn you. You were warned. The next time any of your party are found hanging around the two ladies on board, so help me, I'll throw you overboard!" Frank and Percy went to Gwen and learned the cause of the trouble. "He will not trouble you again. I shall be close to you, don't worry." How sweet those words were to Gwen. It was all settled at that moment, when their eyes met. It was a look of understanding for both of them. Frank left the scene. Gwen had made a decision, and whispered to herself, "Yes, I love him." Thus on the Yukon riverboat, a girl had found the meaning of true love.

CHAPTER THIRTY

The Arctic Express

I was surprised when my mailman handed me a letter containing all the particulars regarding a company that had been formed to handle the United States and Canadian mails. A man named Richardson had a contract with the United States government to carry mail through, during the winter months, for eighty thousand dollars. The contract was, of course, too big for him to perform successfully alone. He knew that the BL&KN company could handle it as far as Dawson. He would then be able to look after the other end—St. Michael to Dawson, and the intervening points. In this letter, I was appraised of my appointment to the mail contract and of my appointment as manager for the Arctic Express. I felt that a Herculean task was being imposed upon me, but the directors of the BL&KN company, knowing of my work so far, agreed that I was the one to supervise this latest enterprise.

The contract was drawn in Richardson's name, and he left Victoria with a launch and eighteen thousand dollars' worth of supplies, to look after the lower reaches of the Yukon. I was to look after the upper reaches, from Bennett down, by building Arctic Express posts every thirty miles, or by making arrangements for mail with someone located thirty miles from a post. This project entailed building scows, procuring good axe-men and mechanics, and supplying the necessary lumber, doors, windows, stoves, heaters, and other things for the successful carrying out of the enterprise. Honest men had to be found to run the posts. Thus, the Arctic Express was started to handle the American and Canadian mails.

Uncle Sam was liberal in seeing that the delivery of mail was carried out promptly and as expeditiously as possible. The Canadian government acted exactly opposite. They were parsimonious in their dealings and wished the Arctic Express to carry their mails gratis, for the "priv-ilege" of allowing American mail to be taken over Canadian territory. The Arctic Express company had presumed that the Canadian gov-ernment would come through handsomely when they found out what a boon it would be to get mail to Dawson. The BL&KN company had, up to this time, handled mailbags for the police and government with-out remuneration.

A Mr. Lynch, believed to be a Canadian government agent, told me that he would take the matter up in Ottawa. He would show them that the building of the Arctic Express posts was an advantage to the public and to the government. He was on his way out and believed that he could get an appropriation. He realized the enormous expense attached to the enterprise.

It was reported that Clifford Sifton had been to Dawson in the fall of '97 and that he had come out with Major Walsh in the spring of '98. (This was never verified, and is doubtful.) However, many complaints were made of the manner in which the Canadian government acted in the Yukon. Had Sifton been in Dawson, he certainly would have seen that more money was allowed. Many felt that the head of the postal ser-vice, as well as the heads of other departments of the government, had allowed only a ridiculously small amount for the proper running of the country. They did not allow for risks taken by those handling their busi-ness. In many cases, very high wages were paid by companies to men to undertake the arduous task of delivering their goods.

Money flowed like water in the initial stage of building the posts and scows and buying provisions and other incidentals. One hundred tons of provisions had to be distributed between Bennett and Dawson, so that those coming out over the ice during the winter could be fed. Many who found no work in Dawson took this means of travel to get out of the country, some trusting to luck. They had no money. The Arctic Express company promised Richardson that the men he had hired in Seattle as mail carriers would be looked after and financed until they reached their destination. Wives of the men were to receive monthly allowances.

Another great expense was the buying of suitable dogs. Forty beautiful malamutes were bought in the East and shipped to Bennett. An Icelander named Charlie took charge of them. They had to be fed. Fishermen were employed to catch fish sufficient to feed them for the winter. The fish had to be dried. It was an interesting sight to see thousands of fish drying adjacent to the dog corrals. Charlie had a wonderful way of handling the magnificent malamutes, some of which were savage animals. It was indeed risky to approach the dog island without a whip and the knowledge of its use. Sleds were procured, suitable for carrying the mail, made to order. Now ice was forming, and travelling was difficult and expensive. Boats had come close to having their planking at the bows cut through by the razorlike, thin ice.

∾

Everything possible was done to make the Arctic Express company a success, but, like a bolt from the blue, word came to me at Bennett that Richardson had misrepresented the cost of the enterprise. Orders were sent to me to stop payment of wages and other expenditures on the Arctic Express, and to recoup as far as possible, by transferring everything to a new company that had been named Relay. The reason for the BL&KN company's attitude was partly because the Canadian government would not advance the Arctic Express any monies for carrying mail. They relied greatly on the NWMP to attend to the mail.

There was still a great quantity of merchandise that could be rescued from the Arctic Express by speeding downriver post-haste, and seizing it in the name of the Relay Company. I still had the dogs, the sleds, many of the scows, and a great quantity of provisions. It took a great deal of time and energy to follow up the parties which had gone downriver to locate and build posts. Night and day was consumed in overtaking all who had been engaged under the name of the Arctic Express. However, by the time I reached Dawson, all employees had been overtaken. Richardson's men were notified to look to him for wages. A halt had been made. Those hired by the Arctic Express swore and cursed. They were going to take legal action, but in this Far North country they found it was not so easy. The men who would not hire out to the new company were paid off. The posts were built and arrangements made for the convenience of hundreds—if not thousands—who would be travelling over the ice for the outside and home.

Frank Rattenbury, chairman and promoter of the BL&KN company, the Arctic Express and the Relay, had gone to England out of reach of Richardson's attorneys. Richardson was about to start a lawsuit. I had my hands full in trying to pacify the enraged mail carriers who were to serve the lower reaches of the Yukon. Some were six hundred miles inland and would now have to wait until the waters froze over. The new company was composed of men of substantial means. They were mostly from Victoria; some of them (and their contributions) listed here. Others promised big amounts, if the venture was reported okay.

Lake Bennett Company	$10,000
Sir C. H. Tupper	$1,000
A. J. Galletly	$1,500
C. A. Holland	$1,500
F. J. Pemberton	$1,500
E. B. Marvin	$500
J. Muirhead	$2,000
Dr. Jones	$1,000
Dr. Kaker	$1,000
A. E. Langley	$1,000
P. Burns	$2,000
D. Burns	$1,000
Thomas Earle	$2,000
C. F. Maran	$300
The Honourable E. C. Pooley	$5,000

My task was no sinecure, now that there were three companies to look after. Some men—good men—wanted to quit. They thought they had put in all the time they wanted in the North. Some said they wanted their pay—and that they were not going to freeze to death in the God-forsaken country. Some wanted to be paid every week, others wanted money for booze. Some wished to go to the Atlin goldfields. "Jack was as good as his master." Nearly all looked upon themselves as persons the company could not do without. Several obnoxious employees were discharged. This created disturbances that were only quelled by the knowledge that I had a gun and knew how to use it. The enormous amount of investment had to be protected. The steamboats had to be kept running. The mail drivers had to be looked after. Posts had to be provisioned. Men had to be installed at them. Inventories had to be taken. Honest men were few and far between, for everyone was in the North to get the best of the deal.

Many noble characters were met with on the trail of 1898 and also many despicable ones. There were men who would not stop at anything if there was a chance to gain anything. One day two men came to me and asked if they could travel on the steamboat for half-fare, promising, of course, to pay the rest on their return. They said they had a business deal to put through. The North was a country of chances, and the men received their tickets.

One month later they returned and paid the balance of their fares. "Thanks a lot," they said. "We did the business." One of them told me their story.

"It was this way. We left Bennett on your boat. Before reaching Dawson we had skinned everyone on the boat of their loose change. Oh yes, there were NO GAMBLING notices on the boat, but no-one paid any attention to them. We made about two thousand dollars during the trip. Not much, but it seemed to be all the change aboard. When we arrived at Dawson, we settled down in a gambling hall. We started a friendly game with each other. Along came a miner who gave the barkeep a good-sized poke of gold, and asked for one thousand dollars' worth of chips. Will rose up from table, and said, 'Ted, you've got my pile. Come on, it's your treat.' The psychological moment had arrived.

"I rose up from the table, went to the bar, and said, 'Barkeep, the drinks are on me. This fellow (indicating Will) thought he could play cards.' And then, to Will, "'You don't stand a chance, playing with me. I can trim any man at poker.—Say, Sourdough, What's yours?'

"'I'll take whiskey,' replied the sourdough.

"'Drink hearty, boys. Do you know, Will,' Ted said to me, 'I feel like breaking the house tonight. If there is anyone who wishes to try me out, now's the time before I leave.—You, young fellow, you seem mighty confident. I'll take you on! Unless you can play poker, I am telling you, you are up against a player. I've just skinned Will here, and he's no slouch!'

"The bait worked. We went to the table. Play started. The sourdough was five hundred ahead. We called for drinks. 'What's yours, miner?'

"'Whiskey straight.'

"'Same for me,' I said. The drinks were brought over, but mine, as we had arranged, was just ginger ale. We both spluttered at the raw stuff! The miner was one thousand dollars ahead. Drinks were served again, mine again being ginger ale. This time the miner lost two thousand dollars. His poke was good for a few thousand yet. 'How about it, want to quit?' I asked.

"'Say, boy, play on! I'll get that back.'

"I was now five thousand ahead. 'Want to quit?'

"'Not by a damned sight!' The miner got ten thousand dollars' worth of chips. He was well known and had a good claim. The drinks came regularly, mine always ginger ale. Thus the game went on until the miner was so far gone that he threw up the game, the loser by twenty thousand dollars. I was still as sober as a judge.'"

"I've heard enough," I said, interrupting the story.

"Just one minute, I'm not through yet," said the fellow whose name was Ted.

"Be quick then, I'm busy!" I snapped.

"Well, then. We roped in about half a dozen of these suckers until we had to be moving. It was getting too warm for us. Pretty good business trip, eh!"

"Say, I've just remembered you, Ted," I said. "Why weren't you sent down to Sitka with the gang?" Teddy's hands went to his shoulder, but he was stopped by his partner. He would have been stopped anyway— I was always on the alert for such emergencies. Less vigilance was taken of those going to the interior. Many of those going in at this later part of the season were very circumspect, until on the boat and past the scrutiny of the police. In reality, many were the spawn of the devil. They were "hale fellows, well met," until the opportunity arose to carry on their nefarious business. Everything in the North was a gamble. Those who were not fortunate enough to get a claim often went to the Devil. Different circumstances brought out the best and the worst of those who went down the river and over the trails in 1898. To quote Service, there were men who were "Steeped in the slime at the bottom, dead to a decent world." But there were others, of sterling qualities: "Men with the hearts of Vikings, and the simple faith of a child."

CHAPTER THIRTY-ONE

The Mail Carrier's Story

"We left Dog Camp after receiving orders, a canoe and taking on provisions that had been left for us by the steamboat. The winds were beginning to penetrate our bodies, foreboding the wintry blasts yet to come.

Jack and I had the task of going upriver as far as possible, before being frozen in by the waters, to chart and map shortcuts on the winding parts of the river. Everything we wished for was supplied, from fur caps and sheepskin coats to moccasins, mukluks and other necessary provisions. As we neared the island on Big Windy, Jack noticed what seemed to be a log. But as we neared, it proved to be a human body, floating. We had been instructed to take note of things and to report on them.

'Say Jack, what are we going to do?'

'I suppose,' said Jack, 'We shall have to take the body to the island. We must give the poor devil a decent burial and see if any valuables remain on him.'

We towed the corpse to the island and, after searching his clothing, found roughly two thousand dollars in his belt, but no sign of any name. The money and belt were put in the canoe on some old wrappings so that they would taint nothing. The smell from the decomposed body was far from pleasant. We buried the body and piled large clumps of grass on top. Then we disinfected our hands so that there would be no reminder of the unpleasant job.

'Well,' I said to myself, 'This is a nice start.' Somehow I sensed that evils undefined were yet to be experienced. On we went in an uncanny silence that seemed to pervade the atmosphere. Jack, usually talkative and humorous, was for some reason quiet. At last he broke the silence.

'Joe, you are not fool enough to part with that money are you?'

'Why sure. We've got to do it,' I replied.

'Not me, or you either.'

'Say Jack, are you crazy?'

'Not a damn sight! Damn'd if I'm going to part with the dough for others to put in their pockets. I've got it here by my side and here it will stay. We'll disinfect it and divide. What do you say, Joe, how about it?'

'I can't do that Jack, it won't be right.'

'You'll do it, or one of us will be the same as that other fellow we've just buried!'

The $2,000.00 had a sinister influence on Jack. We were nearing the Tagish Post. I was heading toward it.

'No you don't Joe! It's dark. We'll slip by the post. Keep going. My gun is on you! Shout and you are a goner!'

We passed the post and on we went. Good God, I thought, what kind of partner is this? At the camp he was a "hale fellow, well met" and liked by all. Strange how fellows alter at the sight of money, knowing it can be theirs by taking it, and knowing that no one will be the wiser.

'Say Joe, it's no good being sulky. Look at this thing sensibly. Here's a bit of luck, and you want to pass it up to those fellows who'll put it in their pockets. I say findings keepings. If you want to be a pal, it's okay, if not, then it's just too bad.'

'Look here, Jack. We belong to the same order. You know your obligations.'

'Damn the obligations! We are in this cruel rotten country where it is every man for himself. And you can just bet I'm going to keep that money. And say, you didn't know it, but I've cached a case of whiskey under the provisions, with my outfit. That will bring me quite a sum. Say the word and you're in it. There is an Indian camp down the lake where we can get $25.00 a bottle for it, but we must watch our step.'

The camp was found by the glow of the fire on the shore. Jack made for it. There he saw the Chief sitting beside a log with women squatting down beside him. On the other side the younger men were lounging around. Then there were two logs about one foot apart with a fire between. It was not a big fire, as one of the cheechakos' that warmed the front of a person while his back would be freezing. It was surprising, the warmth that radiated from it.

'Take a drink, chief!' Jack gave him a taste. Immediately the Chief was alive.

'How much him cost?' asked the Chief?

'Thirty bucks!'

'Too much!'

'O.K. Goodbye Chief!'

'Hi! Hi! Give you twenty.'

'No, twenty-five.'

'O.K.'

The twenty-five were produced and Jack departed.

I wanted to go, leaving Jack with the Indians, but didn't. Would to God I had! Jack came to the canoe, but when about to push off; some of the young bucks came rushing to the beach. 'My God,' I said, 'we'll be shot, just like Fox and his partner. They are after the whiskey. Push off!'

'Scared,' said Jack.

'You'll bet it will go tough for us if we're found and tougher for us if we're killed for the whiskey!'

'Aw! Go chase yourself,' said Jack.

'No, I'm pulling out.'

'Damn you, move and I shoot you! I'm staying. They want some more.' Several bottles were sold, until evidently the Indians' money was gone. Then Hell burst loose. Jack jumped in the canoe. An Indian with a rifle was about to raise it, when Jack got in the first shot and hit him in the gun arm. The rifle dropped.

'Paddle toward the river! Giver Hell!'

And away we shot in the dark.

I said, 'We'll be caught before morning.'

'Hell, we'll travel all night.'

'How about the rapids at night?'

'Of all the yellow pups to travel with, you're it!'

'All right,' I said, 'put me in at Macauley's.'

'You're crazy Joe! You don't think for a minute I would put you off there. You're going with me. The moon will be up by the time we hit the canyon. You're good at the rapids so off we go.'

The moon came up. We were nearing Macauley's. There were shouts of revelry heard from the saloon; no one was at the wharf to see us go by. Into the open jaws of the canyon we went, out into the Squaw Rapids. What a damn fool I was not to have wrecked the canoe right there! Somehow it seemed like second nature for a good canoe man to guide his craft to safety, so on we went. Thundering ahead was the White Horse, resplendent in the moonlight. A few dexterous strokes takes us over the main and into silent waters. Not a sound from the warehouse. More than likely they were revelling with the crowd in the saloon at Macauley's. All was peaceful.

'Keep her going,' said Jack. On we went down the balance of the Six Mile; never was a quicker trip made by a canoe.

We knew that if any questions were asked at Macauley's the answer would be, 'No! No one has passed here!' The same answer would be given at White Horse. In my mind there was no doubt but that the shots had been heard by someone. In the morning sometime we sighted LaBerge Post, built for the Arctic Express Company or the Relay Company. We hailed it. No one was there. Jack would not stop for a cup of coffee. There was a following wind. He set up a small lugsail and hit straight for the Thirtymile. The Devil's luck was with us—we sighted the "Ora" coming in the distance. We tacked inside the island and had a bite to eat while the boat was passing, for Jack did not want to be seen. When the "Ora" had gone a safe distance past us, we went off again, reaching Gauthier's at the mouth of the Thirtymile. We waited awhile, but no one was there. Very likely the old man had gone to look after his nets.

We passed into the Thirtymile. Down we went with lightning speed. After passing the big rock, Jack took a swig at the bottle.

'By God,' he said, 'That was a narrow shave by the rock. My fault!' I was remonstrating with him, but it was no good.

'Oh, shut up Joe! Here, take a swig of this!'

I refused. Jack had evidently taken more than one swig from the bottle, as he suddenly shouted, 'You damned waters, we've got you licked,
and you know it. You licked the poor devil at Windy, but not me! Rest in
peace, old boy! I'll make right use of your $2,000.00.'

We emerged into the Lewes River. The old Hootalinka was getting
low at this point. Everyone seemed to be busy preparing for the winter.
Boats were still coming down the Hootalinka from the Teslin Trail. We
paddled down the Lewes. Jack took another drink. How it happened, I
do not know. We must have both fallen asleep. They said they found us
both on the bank. Jack was dead, the canoe upside down and I was
unconscious; I didn't come to, until arriving at Selkirk.

For a long time, when I tried to straighten things out in my mind, no
remembrance of anything would come to me. Eventually a man looked
in upon me, and I asked him 'Where is the canoe?'

'Wrecked,' came the reply.

'Did you save any of the outfit?'

'Nary a thing!'

'No whiskey?'

'No!'

'Any money?'

'None.'

'Am I dreaming?'

'You are at Selkirk,' said the fellow.

'Give me a cup of coffee,' I said.

'All right, just you keep quiet.' The coffee made another man of me.

Weak? I'll say I was. I fell back when I tried to stand up, and there I
was. It was three days before I was able to be about.

Eventually I got to Dawson. To get my mind off my late experience,
and on finding that my inside money belt had not been taken, I began to
visit the dance halls, the saloons, and other houses reputed to take away
the worries of life. After joining in some of the wild orgies, nothing was
too wild for me. Some of the boys from the creek were spending gold
dust as if it were sawdust.

The suave bartenders with their scales on a deep plush, weighing the gold dust with their carefully kept long finger nails would pick up the gold from the scales if it was overweight. The small gold dust adhering to the fingers between the flesh and the nail would be disgorged when the gold was put into the poke at the back of the bar. When the plush was shaken, it was a means of obtaining great profit to the bartenders and proprietors. Every little trick known was practiced in this particular business.

I became tired of the dance halls, the girls, and the booze. The route was as far as Weare. We were experiencing a cold snap. Everything was ready and away I went to the Fortymile. For a bed, I slept on Uncle Sam's mailbags. I started the next morning for Circle City. A couple of miles out I heard a shot. Looking back, I saw a dog team coming for all that was in them; another shot rang out. There was another man racing after the first team. Another shot rang out and I saw another man racing along some distance behind.

There was a ledge running out at the bend of the river. I dodged behind it, leading the dogs, and this gave me the advantage over the other teams racing pell-mell. Peeping out from my cover, I saw that the head team was about to turn into the ledge.

As it came, I shouted, 'Up with your hands!' Lo and behold, it was my old partner Jack.

He shouted out, 'You dirty low-lived skunk! Leaving me for dead. You stole the whiskey and the money!'

'You've got it all wrong, Jack! I've got no money or whiskey! I woke up in Selkirk after days of unconsciousness.'

The second team came up. It was an Indian. He stopped in his tracks when he saw that I had them both covered with my gun.

'So it is you!' Jack exclaimed.

The Indian in his broken English spoke, 'You stole me good Indian dogs to what for? Oh! Know you heap now. You the man in canoe upriver. You two boys sleeping in canoe. Good Indian sneak up on you, crack'em twice on head. Leave you for dead. Other man I take him to

Selkirk. You come live. Too bad! He not have money or whiskey, I took'em. I steal other team to catch'em my team. You steal'em my team last night. Now other man he shoot me steal'em his team.'

Around the bend came the third musher. He started to talk but I held up my hand for silence, still covering them all with my gun. The Indian and Jack were watching each other closely, for they knew that this was a showdown.

'Me, I wanted whiskey. You good man shooting old White Horse at night. Me, too! Me good man, me shoot'em night White Horse. You stole my team,' said the Indian.

'No,' said Jack. 'Borrowed them to catch up to this man I saw last night! So it was you, you dirty Indian,' he went on, 'who stole my whiskey and money.'

'Me! You call dirty Indian. Me, belong to the Tagish Charlie band. Me! I hit you two on head you sleep in canoe.' Quick as a flash Jack's gun was out; the Indian's rifle was in his hand. They both shot at the same time; both were fatally wounded. Jack gurgled, blood streaming from his chest. I rushed to Jack. He saw the end was near. In a weak voice, Jack said, ' Joe, I take it all back. This dirty Indian ...'

'Any message Jack?'

In a whisper, Jack said, 'None, Joe, none. Wouldn't want them to know the end was like this.'

'Any address?'

'No.' That was the last of Jack.

The Indian lasted a little longer. The third musher was attending to him. In his broken English, the Indian whispered to him; 'Too much whiskey, ... too much white man.' And so he too, passed away.

The third musher and I introduced ourselves.

'The Indian stole the money and whiskey from old Jack here. Jack thought I had stolen them. The Indian left Jack for dead on the upper reaches.' I explained 'Maybe the Indian has Jack's money on him.' We searched the body and found a wad of about $1,000.00. The balance he had evidently spent.

'Good God, man, the money is tainted!' said Barnes, the third musher.

'Yes,' I replied, 'in more ways than one. Jack found it on a dead man's body on Windy Arm. Instead of turning it into the post, he decided to keep it himself. He did say, though, that if there had been anything to identify the man, he would have notified his relatives.'

'Do you claim any of this money, White?'

'Say, brother, you just take it and use your own judgment as to how you dispose of it. You take the bodies back,' I said, 'and I will give you a statement.'

Done on the back of my mail receipt book it read as follows:

> Jack, other name unknown, was accused by an Indian, name unknown, of stealing his dogs. They had words, and shot each other in my presence, and in the presence of one Barnes. Barnes came after the Indian who had stolen his dogs in order to go after the man named Jack.'
>
> Signed, White, mail carrier. Signed, Barnes, mail carrier.

As I left, I said to Barnes, 'You can do what you like with the money, Barnes. If you don't wish to give it to the police, give it to the hospital. Whatever you decide on doing, I am in perfect accord.' That was the last I heard of Barnes, or of the shooting.

From then on I felt like another man. A load was taken off my mind. It pays to do the right thing. Jack would have been living today had he done the right thing."

So ended the mail carrier's story.

CHAPTER THIRTY-TWO

The Dalton Trail

The Dalton Trail was used as an overland trail to drive cattle to Five Fingers, Selkirk and Dawson. It was covered with bunch grass, which has good fattening qualities. Several small groups of cattle were driven over this trail in 1898. Some arrived not far from Dawson on the other side of the river. Others arrived at Five Fingers, there loaded on scows and steamers, and from thence taken to Dawson. These herds fetched good returns. Inspector Jarvis was stationed at the Dalton post for some time in 1898. He was respected and liked by all who came in contact with him. This trail had to be closely watched as many attempts were made to smuggle in liquors and other taxable articles.

Pat Burns, ever ready to take a gamble, shipped in a bunch of steers over this trail in 1897. They were gladly welcomed as there was not an over-abundance of provisions. People were constantly arriving in Dawson over the ice after being caught by the freeze-up on different parts of the river. The Dalton post was a lonely one, nevertheless the trail had to be guarded. It was imperative that shady characters be stopped from taking this route.

It was no picnic driving cattle so many miles. The starting point was Haines Mission, situated on the Lynn Canal. There was generally a sigh of relief from the cowboys when their destination was reached. No wonder they relaxed and gave themselves up to the enjoyment of the dance hall, saloons, and gambling dens of Dawson, spending their all, speedily, at the exorbitant prices then charged for everything. After a couple of days they would have to borrow to get to the outside. Some would remain and were lucky in striking good claims.

"Hullo, Dave!"

"Why, Hullo, Feero, how's tricks? How did you get in?"

"Drove in a bunch of cattle for Pat. Say, Dave, for old times' sake, when we rode night herd for Pat (which we'll never forget), lend me your dogs. I've got to git. All my money is gone."

Dave answered, "How about your claim on Eldorado, Feero?"

"Oh, it'll keep till I come in again, Dave." Dave let him have the dogs on condition that he keep them in good shape. He was to look after their feet, feed them properly, and return them before the ice broke. Feero received the dogs, a dandy team. The trip out was a hard one. Some parts of the river were hummocky, making tedious travelling. Still, he was making good time, considering he would go all day and sometimes into the next without meeting a soul or any place he could get a bite.

He fed the dogs, however, and at last arrived at Skagway. Here he sold his old partner's dogs and saved enough out of the sale to buy a ticket to Victoria. Arriving at Victoria he found himself again without funds and sold his claim on Eldorado for three hundred dollars. The purchaser of his claim, on arriving at Dawson was too late—the claim had been restaked. Dave was out a team of dogs and the purchaser of the claim was out his money. Many others who had loaned money to the faithless ones never received payment. This was another case of misplaced confidence.

Poor old Dave! He thought a lot of his dogs. They were faithful beasts and by their patient toil had helped him out of many a predicament. They knew instinctively when danger threatened and had saved his life in many a blizzard. He could hardly credit that his malamutes were gone. Never really tamed, yet always ready to hit the trail in the morning, they would faithfully see him through the day's journey. At its end they would watch at the campfire for the pieces of bacon rind cut from Dave's supper, the morsel of fish, or their rations of boiled rice and tallow. After feeding they would dig themselves a hole in the snow, and curl themselves up, unmindful that the temperature was sixty degrees below. Dave could feel safe and sleep without fear of molestation, for they were always on guard, alert to the slightest sound.

Strange animals indeed, part wolf and part one-knew-not-what.

Faithful unto death, caring not for caress. Men fought over them, alienating friendships of long standing. Dogs were seldom stolen. No-one will ever know the fate of many who were guilty of this crime in the Far North. No, not even the police. It was as well to assault a man as to molest his dogs. Dave was inconsolable over his loss and went a thousand miles to get them, but was unsuccessful in his search.

~

Clamouring to get their freight to Dawson before the freeze-up, returning Klondykers were busy from Skagway to Bennett. Everyone was anxious to at least catch the last boat. The White Pass was now handling freight to the summit, and from there to Bennett by mule trains. Blizzards were again raging over the mountaintops, precursors of the coming winter. It was becoming hazardous for those who had stayed too long on the outside. Up went the price of packing. Snow was lying in the foothills, to remain until the next spring. With feverish haste, freight was coming for Dawson and the packers were earning their money. Those who had tasted the sweets of travelling upriver by steamboat anticipated the joy of going down by the same method. No more tramp, tramp, and relay for them. No more harrowing experiences such as those of '97 and '98. Everything was hustle and bustle. Fingers were tingling with cold from the icy winds coming down the draws as through a funnel.

Bill McPhee was a steamboat passenger, with his precious freight of whiskey. He guarded it as if it were worth more than gold. A few police were passengers too, with a great quantity of freight for Dawson. They were in the charge of Inspector Belcher, another good man of the NWMP. Word had reached Bennett that Captain Ritchie was going to tie up the *Ora* for the winter. I heard this and ordered, "all aboard" and ordered the scows to be filled with the merchandise, straining every nerve to get the *Flora* to Macauley's before the *Ora* arrived at White Horse and was hauled up for her winter quarters.

"By Gad!" shouted Bill McPhee, as soon as we landed at Macauley's, "We're here first!" The first scow started through the rapids with a load of valuable merchandise, and got through beautifully. On came the others, all getting through safely. Several passengers going in for the first time took a chance and went along in the scows to be near their merchandise, should anything happen to it. It was great to hear some of the greenhorns giving their experience as the scows rushed through the rapids.

"Holy smoke, that was the greatest trip of my life," said one. "Wouldn't have missed it for the value of my freight. Those pilots know their jobs! It was worth double what they charged. Hip! Hip! Hurrah! Here comes the *Ora!*"

As the crowd of passengers watched, the *Ora* made the landing and miners came ashore with their baggage and packages of gold. The dunnage of the captain and crew was ready to be unloaded. They had decided the *Ora* was not to make another trip. Maitland Kersey, the manager of the *Canadian* and *Columbian* approached me, in his patronizing manner, saying, "The captain is not going to make another trip."

"What do you know about it?" I asked.

"I guess you are all afraid of a little cold weather and have got cold feet."

"I'm running these boats and I want no interference from anyone. Your *Canadian* and *Columbian* have been failures and you would like to see ours tied up. Nothing doing!"

The Dawson agent of the BL&KN company was also going out. Led away by the suavity of Kersey, his excuses were low water, ice forming on the quiet waters, and so forth. I asked the captain if he was going to make another trip, and he said, "No, I'm taking no more chances."

Bill McPhee spoke up and said, "Hell, Captain, you can make two more trips yet. I know the old river. Been up and down since eighty-five."

The captain said, "Alright, I'm going out, and that's all there is to it!" And, followed by the rest, he started off. Three Indians and the accused man, Burnett, were being escorted to Dawson for trial on the charge of murder. Seeing the smiling, insinuating manner of Kersey, I told the crew to get lively before they were arrested for stealing and selling the ship's grub. The crew, taken by surprise, did not say anything. The police heard all that passed. Judge Dugas was also standing by and heard the conversation. He heard me accuse the crew of sending an innocent man to be tried for his life, simply owing to their greed and avarice. I said, "Now then, boys, who is going to volunteer to make another trip, at double pay?"

"Double pay? I'm on. I'd hate to see the boat without an engineer," said Mac.

"How about you, Cockney?" I asked.

"Sure, I'm with you."

"And you Jack?" I asked.

"I'm with you."

"Okay, I've got a cook," I said, and sent a messenger, for Captain Martineau and three good men he could trust. The old crew wanted to be paid off, and a pass to Victoria was issued to each of them, with instructions on how to get their pay when they arrived there. By the time the freight was aboard, Captain Martineau, a swift water man from the Columbia River, jumped aboard and in a very short time there were plenty of men to cut cordwood.

Judge Dugas remarked, "You must have had your hands full, Manager, keeping those unruly men in hand all summer."

The judge heard, as others had, such remarks as, "Damn the manager. We can do without his pay until we get to Victoria. We've made our pile." I was glad that the leaders of the crew had gone outside, as they had been instrumental in causing the death of one of their number, Jim Cowie, and they were witnesses in the affair that caused the arrest of Burnett. Burnett was pleased that the police and Judge Dugas were present when the crew were accused of stealing the company's provisions.

This trip, on which we had started, was fraught with great anxiety, not only for the *Ora*, but for a number of scows which had left previously. Captain Martineau's stentorian voice was heard: "Cast off." Once again, we were on our way down to the land of gold on a fast-falling river. It was said that the first shipment from the Klondyke was on the

Portland—a ton of gold—and that was what caused the great stampede. There was over a ton of gold on the *Ora* the trip before the last, and several tons on many of her previous trips. Word was left with the warehouse man at Bennett to have all Dawson freight ready to load on the *Nora* if she came in. It was getting very cold at nights. The *Nora* was to make another trip, if humanly possible, after arriving at White Horse.

Only one stop was made on the Six Mile. That stop was made to bury a corpse floating by an eddy. There was no identification—just another unfortunate whom the old White Horse had dealt with unkindly, another waited for by yearning hearts, who would never return to cheer their lives with dreamed-of riches.

It was a jovial crowd on board. Everyone was in good spirits when entering Lake Laberge. The waters were placid and beautiful. The boat made good time on this sheet of water. The different groups were engaged in conversations of every kind and the judge took great interest in everything. One old-timer knew the man after whom Lake Laberge was named. At the mouth of the Six Mile, provisions were unloaded at the Relay post. The next post was at Gauthier's at the end of Lake Laberge. Provisions were left off at this point. All hands were attracted by the sight of a vast school of lake trout, keeping pace with the boat as it entered the Thirtymile. Gauthier, the fisherman, brought aboard a wonderful specimen weighing over fifty pounds. It was bought and handed over to the cook to be placed on the table for supper and everyone anxiously awaited the sound of the gong. When at last the welcome sound was heard, Judge Dugas was first in his place. Inspector Belcher and several constables, Smith (a young lawyer), and Potts (a clerk), were amongst the passengers. They had been sent up from the firm of Tupper, Peters and Potts in Victoria to prosecute at the murder trials. Also, there were several merchants from the outside, and miners bringing in with them different kinds of apparatus to thaw out the frozen ground, to make winter mining possible. They were all loud in their praises of the fish dinner a Newfoundlander prepared.

After the meal was over, the table was cleared as usual, and nearly everyone settled down for a game of blackjack, the favourite game for a crowd. They tried to get the judge into the game too, but he would not join them. In spite of the notices NO GAMBLING ALLOWED, which were all around, the constables were just as ready to play as the others. Prosecutor Smith and young Potts were in their element, but were soon cleaned out of their ready cash—however, it was all done in a gentlemanly way. Thus, the long evenings passed away. The boat travelled night and day, using headlights to find her way through the difficult channels and sandbars at night.

CHAPTER THIRTY-THREE

Evening Yarns

During these evenings some would huddle around the boilers yarning about their experiences down the river in the first rush. One miner told this story.

"After days of constantly watching each bend of the river in hope of finding the goldfields, one day we discerned a few scows and boats tied up at the bank. Happy day! We made for the spot and found several men busy unloading their supplies. The place was called Louse Town. There were three of us, with only the clothes we stood up in. Our boat had capsized at White Horse when running the rapids. We had been working top speed to get to Dawson before the freeze-up. We were looking forward to a good cleanup when we reached our journey's end. By the time we reached Louse Town we were all half-crazy.

"Why? Well, the days were blazing hot on the way down the Lewes from Hootalinka.

"One day I noticed lice crawling around the neck of one of the other fellows. He examined us and found that we were in the same fix. Lice on all of us! What were we to do? We had lost our soap and medicine for such an emergency when the boat had capsized. It became unbearable. We stripped, and flung away our inside garments. We tried to wash our outer clothes, but when dry they were still unclean. When we had an opportunity, we would take turns plunging into the quiet waters and would drag in the water behind the scow. We dared not stop. Often, in the daytime, we would be naked. When the evening chill came on we had to don our filthy garments. We had no lotion to exterminate the filthy pests. You can imagine with what joy we pulled into Louse Town. No wonder we were half-crazy!

"We heard a welcome shout, 'This way, boys, for a good cleanup!' The three of us dashed off to the rendezvous where we were scrubbed down with coal oil, and then had lotion applied to the hairy parts of the body. Clean clothes were brought to us and although they were misfits and we had to pay plenty for them, they were worth it. We were given ointments for future application, and once more felt fine. They charged us one hundred dollars apiece, which cleaned us out except for a few dollars. But had it been two hundred dollars each, we would not have demurred. We were not the only ones who had been in the same fix. No! Dear, no! A lucrative business was done at Louse Town.

"You can thank God, fellows," he finished, "that you didn't have to climb the Chilcoot, and sleep in your dank, sweaty clothes, and then arrive at Louse Town in the same condition that hundreds of us were in. This is no dream! Most of us went through it. The cleaning up took us out of purgatory. There are hundreds of boys on the creek right now trying to get rid of them. It's not a nice story. But why mince matters? You wanted to know our experience, and it would not be right unless you heard the unpleasant part of it as well as the best part. Fortune favoured us. We got hold of some good ground. It was sight for sore eyes when we beheld our first cleanup. Ah! that was worthwhile!"

"You surely earned your gold," one listener remarked.

"Gad! What a beastly experience," another said.

Huddled around the sheltered part of the steamboat there was always a group swapping stories. Judge Dugas enjoyed listening. It gave him a glimpse of the kind of life the early pioneers went through, and what they were still going through. The only warmth to be had on the three little BL&KN boats at this time of the year was to be obtained from hugging the kitchen or the boiler house. The judge was getting a little experience on this trip. He was meeting a class of men with whom he would later have to deal with in his professional life. He realized that they were nearly all good fellows at heart, and he began to understand that when they kicked over the traces, which was often, they really were entitled to a little recreation. Another miner told a story that was about the Teslin trail, as full of horror as the one we had just heard.

"The Chilcoot may have the name of testing a man's fitness to survive the difficulties of the trail, but if ever there was a nerve-breaking, back-breaking trail, it was the Teslin. I've seen men lie down and die. Yes, and I've buried them just where they lay. More than once I felt like giving up. Every morning there was the same old urge—Dawson, or die. We often felt more like dying. Sometimes a thaw would occur, and we would wake to find our stuff in a pool of water, or on a muskeg, and it would have to be abandoned.

"At one place on the trail we espied a little shack, evidently belonging to some of the earlier argonauts. Some of us went over to say hello. There was the axe and kindling outside but no one came out to say hello to us. We noticed that the axe blade was rusty and thought that perhaps the shack had been deserted. We opened the door, and looked in. There were three bunks, all of them occupied. We thought that the men must be asleep, until we saw a note which had been left on the table. On it was written, *'Scurvy got us. Too weak to go for help.'* They had fixed up the shack for winter and had died in their bunks. Until we arrived it was evident that no one had passed this way to find them. They had been among the first to take the Teslin trail. Thank God, I survived it all—and what's more, I struck it rich."

Among the men on the Teslin Trail was a "sky pilot", John Pringle. His cheery word and his never-wearying help, enabled us to keep on to the end. I take off my hat to him, surrounded as he was by hardened cases, hearing language the like of which will never be heard again. He kept on, helping whenever he could, never rebuking us for anything. Once he told a bunch of us that he had been in the ministry for a number of years, but that he never really knew God until one day when he climbed up the Little Tal Tan. He would hear some of the followers swearing and cursing, and he understood. He would get a crowd together on a Sunday—those who would listen—and it was through his influence on them, if only for a little while, that he really began to know his God. One Sunday he preached a sermon during which he used a Hebrew quotation. Afterward, a rough came up to him and politely told him that he believed that the minister had misquoted the passage, and gave him the correct quotation.

'Why, bless me, you are right,' was the reply, 'The thing didn't sound exactly right when I said it. Well, well, I'll never judge a man by his coat again.'

'My dear sir, forget it,' the man replied. 'You are doing a far greater work than I am. You see by my bedraggled appearance that underneath a rough exterior may often be found something you would not expect.'

This was just one of many stories told on the boat. Those going down the river for the first time were very persistent in urging the pioneers to tell yarns. Some of the pioneers refused to say a word, for they would rather forget their harrowing experiences.

Whilst going down the Thirtymile, we passed the *Domville*. Her back was broken. She was an old boat and had not been able to stand the strain of the swift water of this short river. The captain had swung her to shore with difficulty and there she lay, the prey for whoever wanted to plunder her. Judge Dugas asked if someone could tell him her history. No doubt, seeing the name had reminded him of the senator back east. More than one knew her history. Judge Dugas had quite an education whilst on his way down the river to Dawson. Some said that the *Domville* had been insured and rumour was rife that her braces had been tampered with. Others said they guessed the owners were masterful men, and had done a masterful stroke of business.

⁓

Another Relay post was provisioned at the Hootalinka and arrangements were made to put up cordwood during the winter months. Posts were also provisioned at Big Salmon, at the mouth of Little Salmon, at Carmacks, and at Five Fingers. At Five Fingers, the pent-up waters rushed at a great rate through the five channels. It was exciting to go through these waters. Up to this point the captain had been cheering on the scows and boats, and shouting orders to look out for shallows. At Rink Rapids, the steamboat found a ticklish bit of water to navigate, but the captain espied a channel of deeper water than the one generally used, and he successfully made it, remarking that "The Rinks are devil-ishly shallow."

The next stop was at Williams Creek, where another Relay post was established. Between Williams Creek and Selkirk, the Yukon was inter-spersed with innumerable islands, and the water was very shallow.

Bill McPhee and the captain would often have a few drinks together. Bill didn't know that after very few of them, the captain would be very much the worse for wear. Once, when he was very drunk, the boat approached a narrow opening, just wide enough for the boat to pass through. Drunk as he was, he dexterously flew the wheel around, and over we rushed. It was quite a waterfall, and we merged once again into the main body of the Yukon. Few knew of the captain's condition. Our luck was short-lived, though. The passengers were beginning to feel fine after their plunge over the falls, when suddenly we struck a bar. The rum had taken such effect that the captain's vision was beclouded. The steamboat, stopping suddenly, seemed to bring him to his senses. He shouted, "Out with the legs, getsh the chains!—Jack, you old shuns of gunsh, over you goesh. Throwsh the chainsh under midshipsh."

The passengers, seeing at last that he was drunk, began to bewail their fate. They plied me with questions, and I told them to keep quiet. The captain, thinking that the crew were taking a long time to obey his orders, came down in a fury. He went into the water, up to his waist, and helped to hoist the grasshopper legs. The water completely sobered him. Once more on board, he rang, "Full speed ahead," but the boat did not budge. "Jack, bend a line to the mainstay. Get across the snub to a clump of trees.

"Ferry over the passengers to the shore. It will lighten her a few tons," he cried. "Shift the freight forward, you deckhands!" All the passengers were taken onto the Island. It was cold, but in a short time a fire was going, around which everyone huddled. There were six inches of snow on the ground. The old-timers helped with the crew as much as they could. Judge Dugas was still aboard, and you could see by his face that he was wondering whether or not he would have to tramp over the ice.

This time when the order, "Full steam ahead," was given, the boat moved imperceptibly. The captain rang, "Astern, a bit," then again, "Full steam ahead." This time she moved. The grasshopper legs attained a vertical position. Then over the bar the steamboat went. Down fell the legs, to be picked up and stowed away for future use. The whistle blew, she made for the Island. The gangplank was lowered. The passengers came aboard with a mighty cheer, and in half an hour they were on their journey. McPhee promised not to let the captain have another drink. The captain asked me for just one more nip of rum: "Just to keep from taking cold. I'll promise to take nary a drop after that!" I got the flask and poured out "just one drink."

"I know you want this, or I would not give it to you," I said.

"Ah! That's better," said the captain.

"I'll take one with you," I remarked. "Here's to Dawson!" The captain held out his great paw and we shook hands. Not a word was said, and not a hint as to the mishap. After a change of clothes, the captain went on duty again. The boat was once more in capable hands, and Jack, the indefatigable, went below to change his clothes.

At this time of the year everyone had to be on the *qui vive*, for the waters were getting low. Everyone settled down, in good spirits again, once the boat was on its way. The judge and the inspector had regained their equilibrium and all were jovial, feeling sure that the boat would not be stranded again. They were all loud in their praises of the captain and of the way in which he had handled the boat. Bill McPhee took the blame for the boat's getting stranded on the bar, saying that in all his ups and downs on the river he had never known of the piece of water we had just been through. Orders were given that not another drink was to be served to any member of the crew until they reached Dawson.

The next stop was Selkirk, where another Relay post was provisioned. Supplies were unloaded for Major Bliss and Lieutenant Bennett of the militia. Considerable time was consumed in looking after the police and militia business. The officers wanted drinks badly, so a case of Champagne was taken aboard the *Columbian*, which had tied up here for the winter. It was surprising how many of the passengers followed that case to its destination. At this point Champagne was twenty-five dollars a bottle.

Business having been completed, the boat set off. It was night by now and pitch dark, but that made no difference, for the boat was equipped with strong headlights. Even then, it required skillful handling of the wheel. In this district there were some treacherous waters. Still, the game of blackjack went on into the small hours of the morning.

Between Selkirk and Selwyn Creek, where the river is dotted with small islands that form innumerable channels and sandbars, several scows were stranded. Cries, appealing for tows, were heard. The captain essayed to help, but came near to disaster himself. A police scow was amongst those stranded. Inspector Belcher wished the boat to stand by, but this was impossible. We were too far away to be of any service, and could not safely get any closer. The passengers said that there was no use in everyone being stranded, and the judge concurred. He promised to use his best endeavours to get a steamboat or a launch to rescue them. The pioneers aboard said, "Gosh, they are in no worse a plight than we were when we first went down! Let them use their heads! They have axes and plenty of trees are near. They'll get off if they use their heads!"

At breakfast time the subject of the price of meals at Dawson came up. One old-timer, who had come up as far as Selkirk, enlightened them. "Say boys, it all depends on your pocketbook. You can have a meal for fifty cents to keep the pangs of hunger away. I've tried them all, some good enough for the most fastidious. You can go to Louie's and get the best coffee and cake in town for one dollar. At another place you can fill up on pea soup for twice that much. If you want a light snack there's a coffee shop where you can get a small piece of lemon pie and a cup of coffee for fifty cents, but it will cost you two dollars and fifty cents before you get through. The lemon pies are great, but they never saw a lemon. They're made of lime juice and extracts. Then there is Millar's place. The specialty is Irish stew, and believe me they must work night and day to keep the pot boiling, owing to the incessant coming and going. You have to wait your turn, but it's worth waiting for—the most satisfying meal you can get for the money. The chef at this place takes his thirty bucks every night and goes to work in the morning dead broke.

"It takes some money to hold up your end in Dawson. Years later, after the gambling was closed down, Millar went down the river and lost his fortune. His wife came to the rescue saying, 'Never mind, Charlie, I have fifty thousand dollars I saved on the side and you never missed it.' The boys generally paid in gold and gave good weight, with sometimes an extra nugget for Mrs. Millar. She was cashier and always decorated herself with nuggets of gold. She even used nuggets for buttons on her dress. Another place you can get a good square is at McCormack's. You can get your fill, but it costs. Then there is Chisholm's. He ran the Delicate Esson in Seattle. A bunch of us went in there one day for a meal. The first chicken brought into Dawson was advertised. We had plenty of dough, but didn't get much chicken. We ordered all we could get away with for a treat. It cost us nearly fifteen dollars apiece for that meal, but it was exceptional. Chicken was scarcer than gold. Another place is Timmins', where you will get nice clean grub. Timmins is a helluva nice fellow. It was rumoured that when he was an editor of a paper down south he shot a man in self-defence. He put in a little time in San Quentin, but was liberated when the case was tried. You will find him as straight as a die, and his wife is a fine lady."

The next Relay posts to be provisioned were Selwyn Creek and Crouch Island. Some good samples of gold were taken from Selwyn Creek, but the bedrock was very deep. Men were coming and going night and day, intending to sink to bedrock. The Mining Recorder, even at this late date, was doing quite a business selling licenses and recording claims. Boats were being poled up the river to Thistle Creek, following rumours that gold had been found in paying quantities. Many paid fifty dollars to men going in to have claims staked for them. Some claims were staked at the mouth of the creek, where one would have to go hundreds of feet to bedrock.

The next stop was Stewart River. There was plenty of water on this run as the White River entered the Yukon between Thistle Creek and the Stewart. White River derived its name from the colour of its water. It was a great stream flowing through a country composed of soft, white clay. Its creamy white waters discolour the Yukon for many miles. The Relay post at Stewart was provisioned in a short time. Many boats were met here coming from the upper waters of the Stewart, no doubt on their way to Dawson to spend the winter after a season's prospecting. Two more Relay posts near Dawson were provisioned, one at the Sixtymile River and one at the Fortymile River.

CHAPTER THIRTY-FOUR

Winding Up Business

Dawson at last! All on board were delighted to have escaped being frozen in. A crowd had congregated at the little wharf and cheered vociferously when the boat docked. Maitland Kersey had announced that there would be no more trips that fall, but he had reckoned without the management of the BL&KN company. The crowd shouted, "Good old *Ora*," and when she left the next day, there was another wild cheer.

The weather was turning very cold at this time. Steamboat tickets were sold to capacity for the "up" trip and many ladies were included among the passengers. They had made a little pile and were going out for the winter to enjoy a milder climate. Boys from the creeks with their stakes were going out too. It did not take long to unload the freight, and the crew were given leave for the night.

The *Nora* was well on toward White Horse. The *Ora* had passed her at Rink Rapids on the way to Dawson and it looked as if the *Nora* would be able to get in one more trip. Tickets were sold conditionally. The steamboat was taking a chance, the passengers would also have to take a chance. There would be no coming back on the company for damage or expense. Merchants who had come in on the boat, sold everything through the night and returned the next day. It was quick work. Everyone was preparing for the winter. One merchant claimed he had made double the profit he expected on his merchandise.

At Dawson, the judge was looked after by the police department. He was probably the only one of the jolly crowd that came down on the steamboat who was not seen through the night taking in the gay and sometimes rowdy proceedings in saloons and dance halls. The crown prosecutor and I had a few minutes' conversation over the case of Burnett. The prosecutor was told he had no case. His witnesses had left the country. They should have been subpoenaed before they left. The case had been aired freely and the facts widely discussed, especially on the boat, in the hearing of the judge.

I had an interview with William Ogilvie, settling all the business done with vouchers in connection with the commissioner's department. His office was a crude affair. He was a difficult man to contact and only those with business of the utmost urgency could get an appointment to see him. He was a man of outstanding integrity. The coal showings on the bluffs going down the Yukon River could easily be seen. There was a good seam showing on the shore opposite Dawson. I was negotiating at this time for coal concessions.

Before the *Ora* left on her return trip, I had to go to the dance halls and saloons to find many of those with whom I had business matters to settle, and they were usually found in one or another of these places. What hells they were! Passengers who had been on the steamboats posing as "wives going to their husbands," could be seen on the dance floor, and were now known as Tootsie, Flossie, and so on. Old men, young girls, young men, old girls, were there in a half-drunken state. In the gambling dens, men who had come to the country without a dime could be seen with ten thousand dollars' worth of chips in front of them. Drunken men scattered gold dust over the bar. They were all obsessed with the spirit of squandering as if the supply of yellow metal was never ending. At the Victoria Hotel, an orgy of drunkenness was in progress. Included in the company was a civil servant, who, without a cent to bless himself with a few short weeks ago, was now exhibiting his pass book, with a heavy balance to his credit. He was lavishly spending on the girls fawning upon him in his drunken debauch. Thus, a busy day and night were passed winding up the season's business.

~

On October 26, 1898, the *Ora*'s whistle blew at Dawson, announcing its departure for the last trip upriver. It was surprising to see everyone hurrying to complete their business in order to take this last trip to the outside before freeze-up. They did not intend to be cooped up until the next July and have to take the arduous trip over the ice to Bennett or Skagway. The overland trip was lightly regarded by the hardy pioneers with good dogs, but to the uninitiated it was a dreaded ordeal. A great crowd assembled to say goodbye to those fortunate enough to have the means of getting out. This would be their last touch with the outside world for months. At this time sickness was rife in Dawson. It was apparently due to impure water and took the form of a low fever resulting in many deaths.

William Ogilvie came hastily down, asking for me, and introduced to me to an elderly gentleman, a colonel from Tanana. Ogilvie said, "He is an old friend of mine and just arrived upriver. He unfortunately had his camp burnt up, and with it his pocketbook, and is without funds. He wishes to catch this boat so that he may raise funds for a big proposition." The boat just then was casting off.

"Righto, Mr. Ogilvie, righto," I said.

"It's just the same as if you were doing it for me," said Ogilvie.

Shouts of goodbye were many as the old boat bucked her way upstream. The crowd remained at the wharf until she had turned the bend. To many of them it would be a winter of discontent.

The passengers were rounded up and bundles of gold labeled with the owners' names were thrown at the feet of the purser, while scales were set up to weigh the gold dust for those who paid their fares in this way. One noticed the characteristics of the different individuals. There were great open-hearted men, all glad to be leaving the scene of their arduous efforts, for the first time able to spend money freely without having to bother about where the next dollar would come from. They poured dust from their pokes onto the scales, until the scales touched the stand with a thud. A little spoon was always there to scoop up an overweight and put it back into the poke. "Hell," some would say, "Let her ride. We're going home, aren't we?" Others were not so free, and would scoop up all the extra weight very carefully. When the fares were checked, it was found that there was a large surplus of gold above the total sum of fares. "Well," I remarked, "it will help to pay the passage of some of those on board who have no money, and who begged to be taken outside in time to escape the winter." One passenger cursed the world in general. He was having to work his passage out. He had gambled away a fortune and when everything was gone, had been kicked out of the saloons. Now he had convinced himself that he was tired of life.

The steamboat touched at the Sixtymile River. At this point boats were scrambling down the river to Dawson to hole up for the winter. Some of these prospectors had made good, even though there was no phenomenal strike at Dawson. Many would loosen up during the winter and find themselves broke once more before the spring. What else could be expected, when there was nothing to do but amuse themselves till spring?

At length the steamboat arrived at Selkirk. Here a passenger bid goodbye to a girl who had accompanied him so far. She had decided to go back to Dawson to spend the winter. She was only a gold digger. He peeled off five one-hundred-dollar bills from a roll and handed them to her. She did not hesitate to take them, and tucked them in her stocking.

Just as the boat was leaving, another passenger peeled off one thousand dollars from his wad, gave them to me, and asked me to send them to an address in Chicago. I was about to give him a receipt, but the fellow was already ashore. "Hell," he said, "I'll only lose your receipt. We all know you. It will get there all right. I'm going back with the girl! She's true blue!" The other fellow looked on. Perhaps he felt a fool?

Scows were still coming down the river. We recognized among them those who had been stranded on bars, yelling for help when the steamboat had been on the way down. They had pried themselves loose, and joyfully greeted the boat as we passed.

The day after the steamboat had left Dawson, I was taking a breather, after having straightened up the business of the *Ora*, when I espied the gentleman who had been introduced to me by William Ogilvie. "Well, Sir," I said, "I hope you are comfortable."

"I'll get along," said he. Linking arms with him, I took him off to the kitchen, and asked the cook to give us something to eat. I listened, while eating, to a most harrowing experience in the Yukon. The man had had great faith in the Tanana country, but now all his prospects were gone—everything destroyed by fire. It looked like robbery. In fact it must have been, for the gold could not be found anywhere. However, he predicted that Tanana would prove to be a wonderful placer ground. (This ground, in Alaskan territory, eventually did become famous, for there was a rush the next year.) I told the steward to see that this fine old chap was well looked after. He was an educated man and very interesting. Furthermore, he never intruded upon anyone. At Bennett, he was going to trust to luck to get to Vancouver. I noticed him starting off for Skagway. I called him back, and handed him a pass for the steamer *Amur*, good to Vancouver.

Long afterward, I received a letter from Pennsylvania, with a cheque for a nice little sum enclosed. The letter contained only a few words: "Cast your bread upon the waters and it shall be seen after many days. Captain W———." It took me some time to connect "Captain W———" with the interesting old chap I had helped at Bennett.

The *Ora* now approached the Rink Rapids. The captain scanned the wide stretch at the rapids and found that one place was as good as another to go through. Cautiously he entered the rapids, with all hands holding their breath. The boat scraped a rock, but passed over it, only to be struck immediately. "By the Lord, Harry, we're stuck!" a passenger exclaimed.

As the boat seemed to be well stuck, the passengers were sent ashore to lighten the load. The old pioneers aboard took a boat rope with them, which was fastened to the bow. Onshore they commenced a tug-of-war but still the boat held. Then they realized that the angle at which they were pulling would hinder, not help the boat. So they waded into the icy waters up to their knees, cheering each other on and, by bending their backs to the task by a mighty effort, straining and tugging, they moved the boat. We heard, "Now then, once more!" and "She's coming, boys!" It was a sight, to see those boys up to their knees in the freezing waters cheering each other on, and calling out to the landlubbers to lend a hand. The boat was once more in deep waters, and at last the rope slackened. The whistle blew.

The captain shouted, "You fellows who are dry, make way for those who aren't." The cook had a good meal ready, and those who had been in the water had the first table reserved for them until they had time to change their clothes. Free breakfast for everyone on board! And so the Rink Rapids were passed once again. I started to thank the men, but they shouted, "Cut it out, Boss! We'll get her to White Horse if we've got to pack her!" These men of the North never said die.

~

"Laugh, damn it! I couldn't help laughing!" the captain said. "One of the fellows tripped on a rock and fell flat in the water. That fall made the rope taut, with his weight hanging on it. That started the first movement of the boat over the rocks. Why didn't someone take a picture of those fellows splashing through the water?"

On we went till we reached Five Fingers. The captain chose, as he thought, the best channel. The water was coming through like a mill-stream and although the whistle blew for all steam possible, the boat's nose met the fall of the water without making any headway. In fact, she was finally forced back. The captain shouted and cursed for more steam, but the engineer answered back, "You've got all I'm allowed to give." When told to give her another twenty pounds, he replied, "Not by a damned sight. I don't want to go to kingdom come." The captain tried to send the boat up again, but it was no good, she couldn't make it.

The captain said, "These boilers are three-eighths steel; they'll stand another twenty pounds of steam. If we don't get it, we can't get through."

"I'm not going to lose my papers because she blows up!" returned the engineer.

When I was called, I heard this, and blew up at the engineer: "Hell, Mac! You're not on a deep sea boat now. We're on the Yukon, and it's freezing up like hell. Give us twenty pounds more—she'll stand it easy."

"I won't do it," said the engineer.

I said, "You're fired, then, Mac. Go to the steward and get your money."

The captain asked if any of the other fellows happened to be engineers. There was no reply. The stoker was a cockney. The captain promised him double wages to get the boat through by applying the extra twenty pounds. He said, "Lor, blimey! You bet."

All those not wishing to stay aboard were to walk around the bluff. Charlie and all the pioneers stayed on board. The nervous ones and the merchants walked around. They firmly believed that the boat would blow up. "We'll only die once," said Charlie. "How does it go?—'Cowards die many times before their deaths; / The valiant never taste of death but once.'"

The cockney and I watched the gauge. It was soon up to 160, then to 165, and then to 170. The bell rang. Orders rang out to cast off and to give full steam ahead. The captain knew his business. The old boat drifted downstream for a few yards, and then, as if alive, she jumped. The old wheel turned with terrific speed, throwing spray all over the deck. After a few humps she was through and once more in deep water. "Bravo, Captain!" Three cheers for Captain Martineau were given with gusto.

Mac was asked if he wanted his job of engineer back again. He grinned and said, "Righto!"

"You can report that a bunch of miners chucked you out of the boat and took charge. And say, Mac, if you raise any fuss, and are still on the job next spring, we *will* chuck you overboard." Mac grinned again. He took charge and all was serene once more.

> Yes, we go into the night as brave men go,
> Though our faces they be often streaked with woe;
> Yet we're hard as cats to kill,
> And our hearts are reckless still,
> And we've danced with death a dozen times or so.

CHAPTER THIRTY-FIVE

Autumn Tales

The cold had increased in intensity. The ice had formed in quiet waters. Now it could be seen how wise it was to cover the boat to the waterline from bow to stern with sheet iron, otherwise the planking of the boat would have been cut through. Hootalinka at last, where a number of craft were tied up for the winter. The boat entered the Thirtymile, those on board a cheerful, happy crowd. This time, old Mac did not object to being asked to give it more steam, for the Thirtymile was a stiff climb. We entered Lake Laberge and met a stiff, cold, freezing wind and a heavy sea. Finally came the Six Mile, and at last, White Horse. Here we had to wait a couple of days for the *Flora*, which had been delayed owing to an increase in business on Tagish Lake. Many passengers were bound for the Atlin placer grounds.

Inspector Moody, who had taken passage on this boat, had arrived at White Horse feeling his old self after a terrible trip over the trail from Edmonton. He was a remnant of a party and was emaciated to a great degree. He lived the last three days before arriving at Dawson by chewing his moccasin strings. He was sent to the coast to recuperate, and his trip upriver had started him on his way to recovery. Later on another man, a French Canadian, travelled over the Edmonton trail by another route. This is the story he told.

"I was fired by an American party, for I was used to swift waters, and their craft was built and ready to sail at Lesser Slave Lake. They wanted to sail at once, but I told them that there was too much wind, a big storm, and that it was no good to cross today. They laughed at me, and said I was yellow. I would not go, so they left me behind with an axe, a gun, and some ammunition. I saw them pull away from shore and, knowing that they were not used to boats, I was anxious about them. I watched for hours and saw them in difficulties. Finally the boat cap-sized. I waited for a day or so to see whether any of the party would turn up alive, and then saw the craft making shore, miles away. I went to it, but there was not a single soul alive of the party of ten. I hauled the battered boat onshore, and found a sack of flour and some other provi-sions. There was a coating of half an inch of flour and water around the sack, but the inside flour was still good.

"They said I was a coward. Me! I'm no coward. I know bad waters. The Erie, the Huron, Superior, they don't fool me, and neither did Lesser Slave. I have nearly drowned too many times. The next thing was to get to Dawson. I had no maps, only my judgement to follow. I did meet others en route, but many of them scarcely knew which way to travel. I selected my own route and at last stumbled upon a large river. I didn't know whether it was the Yukon or the Mackenzie, but I decided to build a raft and sail down it anyway.

"My grub and my ammunition were nearly gone. I built a raft of dry logs, held together by willows, and what I could find of use in my pack. I thought there would be a better chance of meeting someone on the water than on the land. I poled off into deep water and drifted down the river. Grub all gone, I kept on drifting. Unable to keep my mind from wandering, I fell into a state of unconsciousness, and knew nothing more until I opened my eyes and saw a father of the Catholic church bending over me.

"He gave me something to drink, and then I lapsed back into uncon-sciousness again. The father watched over me constantly until I became stronger. A full three weeks. He told me that the mission children had drawn his attention to the raft with 'a dead man on it.' He put off, and brought it safely ashore. I stayed at the mission until freeze-up, and fully regained my strength. In the spring of the next year I again started out for Dawson with a new outfit from the mission. I eventually reached Dawson and, not being afraid of work, I have never since been out of employment."

While waiting at the White Horse for the lake boat, I met a Mr.

McMillan, of the Canadian Bank of Commerce. He was ready to go down the river in a canoe. Everyone advised him to wait to see if the *Nora* showed up, so that he might get information as to the state of the river. Although he had a bad cold at White Horse they could not prevail on him to stay. So, off he went with the best wishes of the crowd. It was to be his last trip down the Yukon or any other river—with the exception of the River Styx. He did make Dawson, but on the way he contracted pneumonia, from which he never recovered. He was liked and respected by all, but like so many of us mortals, he thought that things could happen to the other fellow, but not to himself.

On November 3, 1898, scows were still coming down from Bennett. If one kept in the centre of the current it was still safe to travel. By rigging up a canvas for a covering in the stern and erecting the little telescope Klondyke stove, one could keep fairly comfortable. Mr. McMillan, of the Bank of Commerce, would have fared better had he thrown in his lot with some of the old pioneers still going down to Dawson on scows. They were rigged up for warmth. Many a pioneer suffering severe cold favoured the simple remedy. Stay under cover, no matter how cold outside. A severe cold was the forerunner of pneumonia. These pioneers would soak their feet in hot water, warming their blankets in the meantime, and then curl themselves up in everything available, developing a good perspiration. In the morning, the cold would in all probability be broken up. Many victims of spinal meningitis recovered after treating themselves in this way.

One of the passengers on the *Ora* during the trip up told of his experience.

"We gathered up all the oxen and horses round Bennett, buying them as cheap as possible, and believe me, they had to be cheap. Then we bought a scow and loaded the oxen and horses, and set off for Dawson. No sooner had we started than we were struck by a heavy wind. Lake Bennett was no longer 'Beautiful Lake Bennett.'

"The wind howled, the old scow creaked, and started to leak, and we had a devil of a time. We dare not put into the shore, for fear of going to pieces. Treacherous whitecaps came rolling over the stern. We let a piece of canvas down and fastened it to the corner posts, and that kept the scow from swamping. We saw the island just ahead of us and wondered if we could possible make the passage, which narrowed considerable at this point. We thought that once we were on the shelter of the island we would be comparatively safe, but we had no such luck. The wind grew and blew intensely. A fierce gust blew over our tent onto the frightened animals, who shuffled over to one side, nearly capsizing us. We had thought the tent anchored sufficient to stand any wind. How the boat ever righted herself is a mystery to me. Pulling the tent away from the terrified animals was, in itself, nearly fatal to us. We passed the island but found no shelter. Still, on we went, before the wind.

"We kept two men at the sweeps to steer and one at the pump. It was a question of whether we would be able to make Cariboo Crossing into Lake Nares. If we could only keep down the water! Nearer, nearer, and just in time we made it! Now in quieter waters, our next job was to beach the scow, and then to unload. This done, it took us a full week to fix up the old scow. We had no oakum, so we caulked the leaky seams with moss.

"We did not want another experience like the one we had just passed through, so the question was, 'Shall we go on, or quit?' We tossed a coin—heads we go on, tails we don't. Heads it was. The horses and oxen were now in good shape after their week's rest amongst the luscious bunch grass. Loaded once more, we went through Lake Nares and into Little Windy with just a nice gentle breeze blowing. We had made a sail out of the tent, so the going was pleasant. After passing Big Windy we unloaded, for feeding purposes, at the mouth of the Six Mile, and eventually landed at Macauley's on the Six Mile. There we unloaded and put the scow through the rapids without the animals. We shipped them again at the end of the portage and made the end of the Six Mile without mishap. The sail was raised and merrily we scudded along, with a breeze coming off the shore. We were thinking ourselves fortunate in the weather when up came a hurricane.

"Did we travel? Did we take water? Did we work the old pump?—I should say we did! We were like drowned rats with the spray and spume flying over us. The animals were mute. The poor dumb brutes evidently knew that their end was in sight. The scow was gradually sinking. However, we never said die; we didn't quit. The old pump was worked faster than ever, but to no avail. Another mile. 'Keep her afloat, boys,' shouted one of them. One-half a mile, and still she floats. One quarter of a mile, and a cabin in sight. She is sinking. The waters closed over her, but the scow rested on solid bottom in shallow water—just the depth of the scow's height. It did not take us long to get the animals unloaded and onto good feeding grounds, nor did it take long to hitch a team onto the scow and to sink a good, round, long pole under the bow. By prying the boat, we soon skidded her up onto dry land. We bored holes in the planks to let the water out.

"Now we pondered whether to go on with the live cattle, or to kill them and take the carcasses down to Dawson. We decided on the latter course. It was cold at nights, and fly time was over. We were kept busy butchering. The horses looked to be fine meat, the oxen excellent. Before the butchering had been completed, a group of Indians came upon the scene. They said they had smelled the killing miles away! We told them to help themselves to the offal, so there was an orgy of feasting. In return, they turned to and helped us load the meat during the night.

"Our scow was in better shape when we finally started off again than it had been when we had first shipped the cattle and horses. We had not a hitch all the way to Dawson. Once there, we sold the beef for one dollar a pound, the horsemeat for fifty cents a pound. We had earned the money. We felt fine once more—we had full pocketbooks again. We had a hot time in the old tavern.

"We'll be in again next year with another cargo.—Say, look at the teepee! Damned if that isn't the hide of old Buck. And there's the hide of old Bright. They weighed a ton apiece. I can tell them a mile off by the spots. Hurrah! Here comes the *Flora*. Happy Day!"

⌁

Hovering around Macauley's were some average-looking Indians: morose and sour. They looked as if they would not hesitate to put a knife through one. Several of the miners went over to the camp where the Indians were squatted around the fire, amongst them women, young girls, and children. A couple of white men wanted to take two of the young women for a walk. This came near to precipitating a fight, and but for the timely arrival of the police, who knows what might have happened. The Indians seemed to be Stick, from the Stikine.

The *Flora* discharged her passengers from Dawson. It looked very much as though we would have to wait until freeze-up and go down over the ice. This would mean good business for Macauley should we have to wait. But after a few days of lively times at Macauley's, the *Nora* showed up from Dawson with another batch of passengers and the news that she was going to attempt another trip. She did ultimately get to Dawson, and tied up there for the winter. This boat paid for herself many times over.

A silent man who had not told his experiences before was asked to do so. He told of his trip in 1897 from Dyea to Dawson.

"It was like this. You have heard my partners tell of their hardships, so here goes. The steamboat arrived at Dyea. Our trip had been like a pleasure outing. We started up the river. Halfway up we crossed, as the going seemed to be easier on the other side. There was never a slip. We got to the Canyon. Everything was hunky-dory. On we went to Sheep Creek, then up the Scales. It was as easy as falling off a log. We went over the Young Glacier, then onto Lake Lindemann, where we built our scow. I could outdo any man in cutting lumber. Everything was just lovely. Away we sailed, down Bennett past the celebrated Windy Arm, and ran the rapids. Laberge was like a sheet of glass. The Thirtymile was easy, so was Five Fingers, and the Rink Rapids. Finally we struck Louse Town, everyone in good health and clean. We went on, struck a rich claim on Eldorado, and here we are, with never an accident."

"Of all the damned liars, you are the ace!" exclaimed one of the men. "Listen to *me*, boys. Aubrey here was one of our crowd. I wouldn't interrupt him until he was through. We had just left Dyea. A few miles up the river a bridge had to be made by felling a couple of trees.—No, you don't Aubrey. You stay here and tell them that I'm telling the truth.

"We came to the bridge, then Aubrey started to walk across. Halfway over he fell in. We pulled him out, minus his pack. We didn't do too badly after that, until we got to the Scales. He was halfways up the Scales, when suddenly he came tumbling down, and was only saved when the rear boys braced themselves and stopped him.—That right? Aubrey?—Here, hold him, Jack. Let him face the music.

"While cutting the planks in the sawpit he ruined a whole log by not following the line. His planks were half an inch in some places, an eighth of an inch in others, and in some an inch and a half. And he had posed as an expert pit man!—Right, Aubrey?

"Well, we built the boat and came down the Lindemann Rapids. Damned if he didn't lose his balance and fall over! We saved him by the skin of his teeth. Lake Bennett was calm and fine. Aubrey fell asleep, and I'm damned if it didn't blow great guns as soon as he woke up. That was very nearly the end of us. We talked seriously among ourselves, for we thought we had Jonah aboard, and that perhaps we had better throw him overboard."

"That's a new one on me," said Aubrey.

"We gave him another chance, and got through Windy, but we had a hell of a time. He was on watch when going down the Six Mile, and was told to watch out for Miles Canyon. Damned if he wasn't just a bit late in calling us. It was evening, we were snoozing. We got hold of the sweeps just in time to get her through and save her from going broadside. We told him to turn in and sleep. He went out of sight. Away we went, taking the wild waters like a swan. As soon as Aubrey showed up again, up bobbed a dead man, drowned, just as we entered Laberge.—Right, Aubrey?

"We put in and buried the poor bloke. When we struck the Thirty-mile, we told Aubrey to turn in again, for everything was going all right, and we wished to keep it so. In the Lewes River we got him to help steer in that nice stretch of water. Bell crawled below to get some tobacco, and when he returned to the deck, Aubrey was in a tangle with some trees floating down the river. The roots spread out and stuck up like the arms of an octopus. It took us some time to get clear. Strangely enough, everything went all right while Aubrey was sleeping or cooking, although once he upset the little stove and nearly caught the scow on fire. Thank goodness, we made it safely through the Five Fingers and the Rink Rapids.

"One fine day we left Bell and Aubrey to pilot the scow through the maze of islands. The water was deep. Bell went to find something. We were all sleeping. Aubrey took the moment to run the scow high on a bar. It kept us all busy loosening gravel from her bow. She moved. Aubrey, working like a slave, had not noticed the movement. It was too late when he tried to jump aboard the scow. The current took it into swift water. We turned a bend, and although Aubrey swam to the island trying to make a shortcut, we passed him. He waved frantically, but someone said, 'Let the Jonah be.' We snubbed the scow at the first possible place, and caught sight of Aubrey plunging through the undergrowth of the island. He still had a channel to swim, and being Aubrey, he nearly swam under the scow. But Bell was getting so attached to him that he bent down and collared him and hauled him aboard. He was a sight for sore eyes. Pants torn to shreds, shirt gone, and laughing like a Cheshire cat. After this he kept below, getting meals, and sleeping. Nothing happened while he was sleeping—and could he sleep! Sometimes he slept the clock round.

"At last we arrived in Dawson. We struck it good on Eldorado. Aubrey had us all tuckered out working one of the claims. He was the first to spy the golden streak. He could work hard as any two of us. We went into Dawson for a little recreation and to treat ourselves. Aubrey here was able to look after us, taking drink for drink. He broke the bank at the gambling hall. It was Aubrey who piloted us to camp, with fifteen thousand dollars' takings in his pocket.—Right Aubrey? If any man said that Aubrey isn't the best man that ever went down the river, I'm ready to take him on. Let's have a drink to Aubrey!"

Aubrey called on the boys to have another. "Here's health to you all. I leave it to you, gentlemen, to decide which of us is the bigger liar!"

When they got near Bennett, one fellow was heard to remark, "Gad, it's like a dream. Here we are, at the place we started from in our scow. At that time it was the great unknown. Now we have our pockets full, our sacks full, and in a few more miles we'll be enjoying the good things of life."

Charlie and his partners were bent on going out from Bennett over the Dyea trail. They were told that Skagway was the better route, for they could take the train from the summit of White Pass. "Hell! We don't know the Skagway trail. But we know every foot of the Dyea." They hired mules, packed their gold and set off."

"How are you going to get those mules down the Chilcoot?" someone asked.

"Leave that to us. We know the old trail, and we want to have the laugh once more at some of the dilemmas we were in."

CHAPTER THIRTY-SIX

Trail Packers, a Thief, and a Trial

One event saddened all of us that fall. Some of the boys who had been on the early trail took passage on the *Nevada*. She foundered in the Lynn Canal. Not a soul was saved. Those brave boys and their hard-earned fortunes were lost, with no one left to tell the tale. The BL&KN company were busy winding up the season's work. It was late in November. The nights were bitterly cold.

An old packer named Feero, who had hit the trail to get all the papers and documents to settle with the steamboat company, was caught in a terrific blizzard and not heard of the next day, in Skagway. A search party started out, and by accident one of the men stumbled on a bump in the snow. Scraping it away, they found poor old Feero, frozen. He was a fine chap, who had weathered many a blizzard with his mules. Blizzards such as the one he was caught in seemed to come from nowhere, with no warning. You turn a bend in the trail, to be confronted by an impenetrable wall of sandlike snow. Like many others, Feero may have been worn out by incessant plodding over the rough trails, for he could no longer brave the storm.

Years afterwards, Joe Brooks, another old packer, who had settled in California, thought that he would like to trek over the old trails once more. In 1933, he and a few others set out. They arrived in Skagway and started out, equipped in the old way, to go over the old ground. They camped on the spot where Feero had lost his life in 1898. Just before turning in, Joe told the others the story of having found Feero right in this very spot. He also told them of their experiences together on the trail.

It had been a tiresome day for this little party of men, who were not as young as they had once been, and they slept soundly. Next morning, one of the men was up before the others. When he had the breakfast ready he called them. Joe did not wake up. He never woke again. Joe knew the life in Skagway and Dyea as well as the rough-and-tumble of both trails. He often spent his hard-earned money, fortunes, in a game of poker. He had made big money and recklessly spent it, but always with an eye to recuperating his spent fortunes. Joe took his last rest in the same spot where his old friend and rival had taken his. He crossed the Great Divide, as he had done so many times before, for the last time. Thus, another of the old pioneers passed away. Not many are left now. One can imagine Joe's thoughts, as he made up his mind to traverse once again the trail, along the same lines as Service's: "There's a land, Oh! it beckons and beckons— / And I want to go back and I will!"

How many of the thousands who travelled the trail of '98 and left the scenes to others, men who have settled down to ease and comfort in sunny climes, have not felt the urge to tread the old trails once again? The willingness is inwardly there, but alas, the physique is not equal to the task. The past is gone, but memory never dies. Some have been surfeited with this world's goods and have often wished that once again they could be in the hurly-burly climbing the trails, leading to something beyond—something, they knew not what. Ease and comfort is not suitable for some. As Service says, they wanted, "A trail to break, and life at stake, and another bout with the foe."

❧

The year's work of the BL&KN company on the Yukon was gradually getting straightened out. Every night I slept in the tent with the strongbox. Many thousands of dollars in gold dust were kept in the steep box. One night, after rolling myself in my buffalo robe (it was intensely cold), I was startled by a very stealthy movement. It sounded as if one of the hold-down ropes of the tent walls was being loosened. I listened. It was deep midnight. For once, Bennett was quiet. Snow lay on the ground. The strongbox, where the gold dust was deposited, never entered my thoughts. Again there was a slight sound, as if the rope was being rubbed. Silently I lay waiting and listening. I heard the canvas slacken, and then heard someone breathing softly. My ever ready gun was once more brought into use. I fired at the top of the tent. Instantly, there was a rush of running feet. Springing to the opening, from my bed on the floor, I saw a figure just rounding the other sleeping tents. Strangely, the shot had not awakened anyone, but then, card games often continued all night. The sound of a shot was hardly likely to arouse attention.

The next morning nothing was said; no one even mentioned the shot. There was one man whom I thought my friend. He was one of those smooth, oily-tongued individuals. During the day's routine he was given the job of staking the strongbox to the ground so it could not be moved. He was more exuberant than usual. I had hired him after he had given me a hard luck story during the very busy time. After this night's incident, I watched him very closely. I arrived at the conclusion that the fellow had betrayed my trust. My suspicions were confirmed. The man's manner became insolent. People began to mention the man's strange way of trying to establish himself as a good fellow. "Boss," said an employee, "look out for that double crossing son of a gun. He claims to have pull somewhere. See he doesn't cut your throat. He's a dirty, low-lived specimen of humanity. I can see now how easy it would be to shoot down someone of his makeup. You've been too good to him, Boss!"

Another attempt to get the strongbox was made. During the days, the stakes had been loosened. I feigned not to have noticed. It was getting late. I told the boys I was retiring. Going to my tent, I bustled about for some time, but at last put out the light. On the side of the tent, away from the strongbox, I slipped out under the wall. I knew that if anyone was going to attempt to steal the box, it would be this night, since it was to be shipped the next day. I waited patiently, and at last my waiting was rewarded. I was getting cold, but forgot that when I saw a man approaching the tent. He listened carefully, then crawled under the tent. Everything was done so silently, that if I had been a light sleeper, and still sleeping, I would not have heard a sound. In a few minutes the man emerged from the tent with the strongbox under his arm. He had not taken more than a few steps before a gun was poked in his ribs. "Stick 'em up, or I shoot!" I took the man's gun and knife away.

"For God's sake, don't shoot!" he cried.

"All right, get going,"

"I'll do anything for you, if you don't take me to the barracks."

"Afraid of your friends, eh? You've been pretty chummy with the police. Why afraid? You damned snake!"

"Please don't take me to the police."

"All right, to the right, down to the wharf. If you don't want to go to the police, stop at the edge. The water is deep enough. Step right there. Here's your gun. I'll count three, then protect yourself. "One . . ."

No sooner had the word been spoken than the prisoner raised his gun and fired. "Just as I thought, you dirty coward!" I cried. "I pulled the cartridges on the way down to the wharf! Now, off to the barracks, or by God, I'll shoot you and toss you into the lake."

Once again there was the cowardly cry, "For God's sake, don't!"

"All right, I'll give you three alternatives: go to the barracks, jump into the lake with a shot, or hit the trail at once. If you hit the trail, I'll give you an hour's start before putting anyone on your trail."

"Oh! You would, would you?" I ducked just in time to avoid the gun that was flung at my head.

"No, I won't shoot, damn you. Get, before I do!"

The man went and was never seen again. Knowing full well that if the Mounties got on his track he would be incarcerated, he hid behind the skirts of a woman. This man had thought he could get away with anything. He had planned on casting the blame for the robbery onto me. The battle of wits was over.

Dr. Wann, who had drifted into Bennett some time prior to this event and obtained a job with the BL&KN company, told me about his experience on the Teslin Trail.

"We left Chicago with an outfit we thought would take us through to Dawson. When we left Edmonton our troubles commenced. By the time we got into the Peace River country our mules had succumbed. In fact, we left them all along the line from Edmonton to Peace River.

Some were left in muskeg, others with broken legs. This was in ninety-seven. Our outfits were cached all along the route. Many other outfits were in the same predicament. Everything had to be abandoned but what we packed on our backs. We went back to Edmonton, and then on to the coast where we again got an outfit and booked passage for Wrangell and the Teslin Trail. The people who recommended this trail to us should have been dragged on to the muskeg and left there. After our Peace River experience, we were hardened and seasoned, but the Stikine proved to be just as bad as the Peace River. The poor greenhorns had a hell of a time. We met with disaster after disaster and again lost everything. The rest of the crowd went back to Chicago, and now here I am, busted, but I'm going to see it through."

Dr. Wann was a great help in straightening out the BL&KN company's business at the close of the season. The morning after the attempted robbery of the strongbox, I told him about the thief. Dr. Wann had heard the shot in the night, but had paid no attention to it. He said it was the best thing that could have happened to the man, whom he had known previously. The ungrateful wretch was always creating dissension, he said. Expressing it nicely, he said, "Ingratitude more base than traitors' arms." I hushed the matter up for the sake of the fellow's family. Only I and the doc knew the details of the attempted robbery.

Is it any wonder murder is committed? People who are fond of saying that you shouldn't take the law into your own hands have obviously never been confronted by rotten, despicable villains who have no sense of right or wrong. Things would have been far worse in the Far North than they were if it had not been for the handful of Mounties who were there. Their presence restrained many a rascal from doing what he would have liked to do. They knew that the Mounties, once on the track of a murderer, would never let up until the man had been traced and caught.

For instance, two men, O'Brien and Graves by name, lay in wait for and murdered three Skagway merchants named Clayson, Rolfe, and Ohlson, who were on their way out from the Yukon over the ice. O'Brien dug a hole in the ice and flung the bodies into the raging waters, hoping that the swift waters would carry the bodies away in the spring and make identification impossible. Later the three bodies were found, miles away from one another. One turned up five hundred miles from the scene of the tragedy. O'Brien never confessed, but his dog finally pinned the crime on his master. Graves was never found. Some believed he was also murdered. A policeman, sent down from Bennett to investigate, discovered a tent and an axe near where Minto now is. Where a fire had been, odd buttons, and metal from clothing believed to be the murdered men's, were unearthed. The dog belonging to O'Brien was sent for, and when he arrived, the constable started with him up the trail away from the tent. Suddenly, he stopped, and in an incisive manner told the dog to go home. The dog looked at the constable as though to say, "This is funny, I thought this man was my friend, now he tells me to scoot." However, the dog did not hesitate, but ran off toward the unseen tent. The constable took a shortcut to the tent and, opening the flap. he saw the dog contentedly curled up, thoroughly at home. It took a great deal of coaxing before he would accompany the constable back.

The axe, when traced, was proven to have been bought by O'Brien. The trial was delayed for some time in the hope that Graves would be found. At last the search was given up, and O'Brien was tried, found guilty, and hanged. O'Brien never confessed. In fact, up to the last he professed his innocence of the deed. Chained in his cell, O'Brien tried to kill the parson who sought to give him spiritual aid, and later he tried to strangle his guard. Had Clayton and the others carried rifles, perhaps O'Brien's job would not have been so easy. But he had his good points. A lady who conducted a road house said that O'Brien stopped there, and that she thought him such a nice man. He had been so fond of his dog, buying the best in the road house for him.

Small bodies of water at this time of the year were frozen. Stampeders from Atlin were coming in overland to Bennett, having travelled by water where it was open, and over the ice the rest of the way. Some of them had never before had such experiences. They brought with them beautiful samples of gold taken from the different creeks where they had staked. Every arrival claimed that Atlin district would become a permanent camp. Great preparations were made throughout the winter. Freight was hauled in for the working claims. It was no small rush in 1899, when thousands went into the Atlin country in the hope of coming across another Klondyke.

~

Everyone was waiting for the day when Burnett was to be tried for the murder of Jim Cowie. The day came. Burnett had the sympathy of the majority of stampeders, many of whom had been misused on the boats, and been short of grub. The witnesses, who had been loud in their talk about seeing Burnett hang, were less confident and scared at the eleventh hour. They were afraid of having justice meted out to them for the rotten practice of purloining the boat's provisions. When the case came up, Burnett's stand was that he shot in self-defence. Burnett was proven not guilty, and there was great rejoicing amongst the staff of the BL&KN company.

The three Indians who had been accused of killing Fox's partner on the M'Clintock River were found guilty. Two of them were hanged, the youngest let off because of his youth—a good lesson for the Yukon Indians scattered throughout the country.

A case of wages was brought before Judge Dugas. The plaintiff was a Swede, the defendant a French Canadian. After hearing the case, the judge was in a dilemma. The French Canadian denied owing the Swede anything. The Swede was emphatic in his claim. The judge, in summing up, said that the French Canadian seemed to be a man of character. The Swede, he said, did not seem to have a good character. So the case was dismissed.

Outside the court house, the French Canadian taunted Ole (the Swede), saying, "You know, I bet you I would win! Didn't you know the judge was a Frenchman?"

Ole said, "Yeh. I knows. You owes me the money. The judge he not right to give you the case because you Frenchman."

"I won the case, Ole, so we be good friends again."

"I show you who straight man is when we go out of town! I take you and snap you across my legs, like that. You Frenchman, aye! Me Swede, aye! Judge, Frenchman, aye! Judge no Swede, aye! I show you now who is best man." And he did, to the French Canadian's discomfort.

How often do we feel that there is no such thing as an unbiased mind? The Swede was in the right. The French Canadian, a volatile and excitable man, in the wrong. Many are suffering today from biased judgement, not only in courts, but in personal affairs. Yes, Judge Dugas was a good man. After the Swede had given the French Canadian a good thrashing, he said, "Now we are square." He was perfectly satisfied and said he got his money's worth.

CHAPTER THIRTY-SEVEN

December in Bennett

The month of December 1898, brought many to Bennett. They braved the storm and the blizzard. The White Pass Railroad was handling freight to the summit, and gradually the great hardships were disappearing for those who could afford to have their freight hauled by rail. Still, a great number used the old trail from Skagway and experienced the misery that so many had before them. Men were arriving from Dawson. The ice was not good. Many had to make part of the journey overland. Those who did were seasoned and hardened. How they made these trips was the main topic of conversation at Bennett. There they were, with their dust and dogs.

How exceedingly interesting to hear what they had accomplished in their six-hundred-mile trek. Often they had to pay one dollar a pound for fish for the dogs. At the stopping houses, the price of get-away from pork and beans. It was good to see these old-timers relax after having arrived at Bennett from Dawson, in weather that was often sixty degrees below zero. The first words you would hear after they had pealed their parkas or mackinaws off, would be, "Come on, boys, have a glass on me!" and then, "By Gad, that touched the right spot! I've been looking forward to this ever since we left Five Fingers. Well, here's another one."

Many of those men had only a trip of thirty miles to make from post to post. Some were coming out for the first time since 1896. They thought it was heaven compared to the trip going in. Then they had to make their own camps and cook their own meals. At night they would feel their lungs rattling and shaking inside, wondering if they would live to see the morn. How happy these boys were now. No one knew, but those who had undergone the same experiences. It mattered now not how hard-won their riches, it was a pleasure to be able to spend.

A young fellow timidly approached one of the boys. "Say Mister, can I talk with you for a minute?"

"Sure, son." They edged away from the crowd. "Well, son, what's the matter?"

"It's hard for me to ask a favour, but you looked so happy. I thought perhaps you could help me. I lost my wad. It wasn't much, but I lost it. No! I never gamble, Mister."

"You want me to lend you some money?"

"Yes, Mister, I'll pay you back in Dawson when you get back."

"I know you will son, how much do you want?"

"Twenty dollars."

"Aw, shucks," said the old-timer.

"Honestly, Mister, I'll pay you back." Out came the old-timer's pocket-book. Fifty, seventy, ninety, one hundred. "Gee, Mister, I only asked you for twenty."

"Twenty won't last you long up in this country, boy. You'll need the hundred."

"Give me your address in Dawson, Mister, I'll be there waiting for you with the money to pay you back."

"Aw, shucks, boy, forget it! I may want to borrow from you some day. Next summer, if you are broke again, ask anyone where you can find Moosehide Jack."

Which of the two was the happier, it would be hard to say. Moosehide went to have another drink. The youngster was asked to have one, but he politely refused. "Stay with it kid! But remember, don't be mean. Make everyone happy and you'll be happy yourself.—Now boys," he went on, "there's a good kid. I like that boy."

"Here's your drink. How much did the kid do you for?" asked one.

"Aw, shucks, that's a good investment!" Thus, the boys spent their money, putting it into circulation, making rich the merchants, gamblers, and girls, and making themselves poor again.

Some of the men came out over the ice by dog team, hired for twenty-five dollars a day. If conditions were good, the trip took from fifteen to

Above: (PLATE 18) *Boat builders at Lindemann, 1897.*

Below: (PLATE 19) *Klondykers on shore and sailing down Bennett Lake, 1898.*

Above: (PLATE 20) *Men relaxing at Taku Landing, 1900.*
Below: (PLATE 21) *Boats and scows at Bennett Lake, 1900.*

Above: (PLATE 22) *Prospectors at Bennett Lake bound for the Klondyke, 1898.*
Below: (PLATE 23) *One Mile River between Lindemann and Bennett, 1898.*

(PLATE 24) *Crew building a sternwheeler at Bennett Lake, April 20, 1899.*

(PLATE 25) *The S.S.* Clifford Sifton *entering rapids in Miles Canyon, 1900.*

(*PLATE 26*) *The S.S. Flora, first to arrive in Dawson from up the river, May 23, 1899.*

Above: (PLATE 27) *Passengers posing on the Bennett Lake & Klondyke Navigation Co. steamboat* Nora, *1898.*
Below: (PLATE 28) *Staff and customers in front of the Yukon Hotel at Bennett Lake, 1900.*

(PLATE 29) B.N.L.K.& Co.'s S.S. Ora, entering Miles Canyon, 1899.

twenty days, but if it was stormy, it took the whole month. One man hired a dog team and driver to get out simply because he could not stand the intense cold. He had come from warmer climes, and meant to get back to them as soon as he could. He came into Dawson from his claim one day when it was perishing cold. He swung open the saloon doors. He was more dead than alive. The men in the saloon gave him a drink, and thawed him out by the fire.

When warm once more, he said, "Boys, oh boys! Talk about hell. I want to get there damn quick and get good and warm. For a month I've lain in a damn old cabin, shivering and shaking. Is it worth it? No! I'm skinning out. Any of you fellows want a claim? Go to it. Stake. All the gold in the Klondyke wouldn't keep me here." Several hit off to restake the claim in a wild scramble. The weather was sixty degrees below zero. The best man would win. Our friend went to the bank, drew all his money out, and said, "What's the best way of making the outside?" The banker told him the name of a good musher. The man hunted him up, and struck a bargain with him. He was to be taken to Skagway for one thousand dollars.

They started next morning. Before many days had passed on the trail, he longed to be back by the pot-bellied, red-hot stove. Blizzard after blizzard struck them. It was hard travelling over the hummocky ice where the water had overflowed. Where the snow drifted they had to travel for miles on snowshoes. After weeks of hardship, weary and exhausted, he was landed in Skagway, a sadder and wiser man. Really, there are a lot of men in the interior today who feel the same way, and yet they stick to the country year after year, hoping against hope that some day they will strike it lucky. There are men in the Far North who have not seen tidal water for thirty or forty years. Some of them make money and spend it as they make it, where they made it. This circulation makes it easy for a parasite to live and grow fat on the miners' excesses.

Often Bennett was the recuperating place for men on their way to the outside. The mushers pushed on and did not stop to revel, they were eager to be on the comfortable steamboat at Skagway. These men were hard as rock. They did not require any ease up at Bennett. They had blazed the trails for the cheechakos. Perhaps the difference between the cheechakos and the sourdoughs is best described by the following lines:

If you've lived up in Alaska where the Arctic breezes blow,
Till you've seen the autumn ice come and you've seen the spring ice go—
And you've lived through the dark winter when the mercury ran low,
You can drop the name Cheechako and become a Sourdough.

If you've planted in your garden by swift and dextrous throw
Many demijohns and bottles in the deep drifts of white snow—
And in May you are not speechless when you find this soil can grow
Mammoth crops of "Lemps" and "Lacy," you're a seasoned Sourdough.

If you have no tender feelings, and with pride you do not glow,
When you take out last year's headgear with its feather quill or bow—
If you've felt the tragic moment when the first boat deals the blow,
Then, you are a Sourdough.

If you listen to the wailing of the malamutes who throw
In their voices, all the wildness of a wolf in pain or woe—
And it soothes you into slumber like a sweet song, soft and low,
And you feel that you belong here, and you are a Sourdough.

If you say "Mush" and "Peluk," just as if you want to show
That your tongue can twist the language like a native Eskimo—
And you say, "The air is balmy, only thirty-five below,"
Everyone will surely tell you you've become a Sourdough.

If you chat in careless accents of a thaw or overflow
And you can show why luck's against you and your fortune did not grow—
If you talk of dumps and ditches, say a lay pays well or no,
Have a lawsuit over boundaries, then you are a Sourdough.

Many evenings and nights were spent talking of the early adventures. There was always someone to tell a yarn about different individuals they had met. When blizzards raged it was a favourite way of passing the time. One man told the story of Gowan. He said, "Talk about prospectors. Old Gowan told us in Dawson that he was in the valley of the Yukon in 1892, and had rocked bar after bar. He drifted into the little-known country of the Peel River. I want you to know that getting into the Peel country is no easy task. The Peel enters into the delta of the Mackenzie close to the Arctic. The old man describes it as wonderful country.

"When some Indians came across him in 1896–97, they told him of the great number of people on the River Klondyke. Knowing what that meant, he and his partner pulled up their stakes from the Peel and trekked across to the Klondyke. They had not struck enough gold to write home about. They had to pass over the Ogilvie range, which divides the two watersheds, the Peel flowing east and north, the great Yukon flowing north and west. This is the kind of man we must take our hats off to, boys!"

Another man told about another old pioneer. "He was a grizzly headed old bloke, and came into the country the same time as Jack McQuesten. He found gold on the Fortymile. He told us how he lost his partner in the canyon. Left by himself, he moved out, and to his surprise, found his partner alive and kicking at the mouth of the Fortymile on the Yukon. He could never get his buddy to relate his experience after he was washed downstream. If he would speak out, he would have made your hair raise. But all he would say was, 'Forget it!' He tried hard to forget the past."

Some fellows are like that. They know more about the creeks and rivers from the Arctic down through Alaska and the Yukon than anyone in the country. They can give good tips about the great country to the north and east, but steer shy of their own experiences. And so the conversation would continue into the small hours of the morning, with drinks in between. Nearly all of them would stay awake and keep the fires going as long as possible, rather that shiver in a cold bed, especially if that bed were in a tent.

Sometimes a newcomer would break in upon the scene, and start telling of bad luck and harrowing experiences. His description of them would be most entrancing. Generally, those who had not the gift of speech had far greater thrill of the trail than many who were so flowery in their utterances.

One party came in from downriver enquiring, "How long is it since Sixty Mile Jim passed through?"

When told, "Yesterday," they said he must have had some trip, for every roadhouse told them to look out for him. They all had to thaw him out: hands, face, and feet.

"We followed him as the weather cleared. Came through flying, thanks to Jim, who broke the trail for us. He is some man! And travelling all by his lonesome."

Cheechakos could hardly credit some of the stories told, but the pioneers never doubted the truth of them, for had they not all been through like experiences? Some trips were without mishap. But when hit by a northern blizzard, whether it be on lake, river, or in open country, and you want to make the next stopping place, and find darkness upon you, there is nothing left to do but curl up in your blankets night after night in the raging storm. The result is that you take four or five days to make a trip that should be accomplished in one. Can anyone describe these trips? Many have tried. Only those who have gone through it know; they are the ones who can truly sympathize with tough luck on the trail.

Some paths through life are strewn with roses. Others have their path strewn with obstacles, hard to surmount. Picture the case of the man travelling on the northern wastes who was unfortunate enough to have his dogs' feet freeze. He might have to turn them loose, but then he would be no longer able to keep up with the others. At times he would be short of grub for himself as well as for his dogs. Often it would be everyone for himself. What was all this punishment for? Was it for glory? Can it be explained why men went through all the bitter experiences of the North? Service again sums it up:

The nameless men who nameless rivers travel,
And in strange valleys greet strange death alone;
The grim, intrepid ones who would unravel
The mysteries that shroud the Polar Zone.

The month of December was well advanced. The White Pass Railroad would be held up for days by the drifting snow when blizzards raged. At the summit of the pass, it was a Herculean task in December and January trying to build a railroad. Yet, like other enterprises, they wanted to be in on a share of the vast amount of money spent on shipping freight to Bennett and Dawson. Gradually the people came to appreciate the effort made by the railroad on their behalf. It was not only on behalf of the public, but to fill their own coffers as well. Traffic was practically nil with the railroad now. Men and women bound for the Atlin field braved the storms, going as far as Log Cabin, where they branched off and went overland to the south Taku arm of Tagish Lake, opposite the Golden Gate that led to the portage to Lake Atlin. Breaking the trail over this route was no easy task. It came near to breaking the hearts of a good many cheechakos. Still, some considered the Dyea trail was the best to take.

Lindemann was now almost deserted, but in January camps were being erected on the shore that was now denuded of trees. Mute evidence of the busy scenes of the spring before was now the funeral scenes and silence over everything. Frames of old sawpits and frames of poles stood like sentinels watching the dead post. Silence would occasionally be broken by the ring of an axe, as some virile voyageur felled another tree which had been too far away for the stampeders of 1898 to bother with.

A repetition of what took place in 1898 happened again in January of 1899, the worst month of the year. Unexpectedly, someone would arrive, generally looking like a man from another world, having been buffeted about in the blizzards, cheeks and nose frozen, icicles hanging from his moustache or beard, and cursing the day that gold was discovered in the Klondyke. Cursing too, the man who had opened up such a trail as the

White Pass. They were artists and poets when it came to describing, in language unprintable, what had taken place on their trips.

"Forget it, boys," an old sourdough would tell them. "You'll thrive on it after a few trips. Wait until you get thawed out! And wait until you get a full belly. You'll be eager and champing to hit her again—I mean the trail."

There would be the cheechakos, standing around the stove thawing out their faces, with the drip, drip, from the icicles falling on the hot iron as they carefully tried to pry away the ice. After getting warmed through, some would subside into perfect peacefulness till the call for supper came, when they would become normal again. The old sourdoughs, after hearing them boast of how they got through drifts, and of the prowess of their dogs, would encourage the cheechakos, saying, "That's the spirit, boys, I knew you would be itching to hit the trail again!"

One would laud the good qualities of the leader dog. That dog would have a place by his side. "Old boy! You brought me through. I trusted you. At times I doubted, until we struck Log Cabin. You went right ahead when everything else was a blur. Nothing but drifting, blinding snow, and I didn't know where in hell I was. Good dog!—Cook, give him the best you've got. I hope, Cook, the blow will be over by morning. They are expecting me in Skagway tomorrow night.—Give me your paw, doggie. That's it. They aren't frozen, you're good for the trip back." After supper he would boil the rice and tallow for the other dogs, or perhaps it was bought from the cook, already prepared. Then he would fall into that blessed sleep—the sleep only sourdoughs of the trail experienced, after being exposed to the fury of the elements all day, and thoroughly weary and exhausted. Oblivious to the noisy chatter and the whoops of the inebriated. Ah, what peace!

Constable Dixon was at Bennett, where he had procured a furlough after his arduous labours at White Horse, piloting boats, scows, and steamboats through the white waters. Hearing of his furlough, I thought it might be wise to have him protect a shipment of gold. A Mountie guarding the shipment would then comply with insurance arrangements and regulations. We were to start in the early morning; the pack mule was made ready to take along the gold.

Morning came, and with it a change of weather. Stars were shining and the cold intense. The tops of the mountains were tinged with a faint glow, hinting of the coming dawn. It was a great contrast to the darkness of the lake. The mule known to be the most reliable (having once belonged to Feero), was brought out, and loaded with the pokes of gold. We finished our flapjacks and coffee. In the still hush of the early morn, we wended our way up the trail toward Skagway. We were making good time. The mule ahead of us broke trail. How beautiful to look back toward Bennett! The scene of many busy occasions, dangers, fights, and rescues. The variegated colours playing around the mountains, as the sun rose, struck a note of joy into our beings. Who, having travelled the mountain trail in the dark, hasn't experienced the thrill of sunrise, giving new hope, new life, and an impetus for the day's task?

We went on, between the rocks that hemmed the narrow trail, until we reached the stunted spruce, whereon hung the hanging veils of moss. Suddenly, without warning, the mule broke off into a gallop, leaving the old trail, for no apparent reason. There was no sign of wolf, or of any kind of life, but away he plunged with our precious freight of gold, away from the regular course of travel, Dixon and I striving to catch him. The faster Dixon went, the faster the mule travelled. Where he was bound to, no-one knew. Dixon's agility often brought him near the mule, and then he would fall back where the snow was deeper. The safety of the gold was uppermost in our minds. The mule was slowing down again. All at once he went nearly out of sight, in a pothole covered with snow.

We had emerged into a meadow, where here and there the heads of grasses showed above the snow. Afterwards, we learned that the meadow was a favourite pasture for horses and mules, when turned out to rest and recover from galls and sores caused by the rubbing of the packs tied on with the diamond hitch. No time was lost in tramping down the snow around the mule, and then in piling in more snow and tramping it down, until gradually he rose in the pit. After manoeuvring for some time, one held the halter, the other gave the mule a whack on the rump, and out he jumped. The gold was saved.

Before reaching the regular trail we, and the mule, were fagged out. We went to Log Cabin and refreshed ourselves. After leaving Log Cabin and passing over the moraine the snow was deeper. The trustworthy mule was now led. Dixon would often miss the hard trail underneath, and the mule would stop dead in his tracks, but as soon as he hit the right one again the mule would go ahead. He was a regular pathfinder, for he had travelled the trail for the past year during the rush as leader of the train, and the mule knew exactly where to place his feet.

We were making good progress and were only a few miles from the summit when a mighty wind sprang up. The trail was soon obliterated by a powderlike snow. We debated whether to give the mule the lead and trust to his finding the trail, and decided that his sense of direction was probably better than ours. We plugged along after him, the gale increasing. Holding on to the tail of the mule, merely a blur just in front, we trudged on. The old mule brayed and turned sharply to the left, floundering in a drift. We had to follow and a fierce gust of wind blew away our fur caps. It was thirty degrees below zero. We stumbled up against the mule and found he had stuck his head in a tent, which turned on our examination to be the mule's old barn. After much scraping and tramping we got the mule inside and fed him.

We knew the stopping house was just across the trail, but nothing could be seen. We made a run for it and found we were tramping on the roof of a tent. The proprietor shouted at us to hold on, that he would dig out for us, which he did. He enquired how we had found the place in such a blizzard, and we replied that we had not found it, the mule had.

"Ah," said the proprietor, " it must have been old Satan, he's saved a good many from blizzards such as this." Our ears were puffed, our cheeks and noses frozen. We greatly appreciated the warmth and food. The wind was still howling and roaring and we thought we must stay all night. There was a stir outside, the flap was opened and another traveller was hauled to safety.

"Well, I'll be damned! I've just come from Skagway. Two hundred yards from here the sun is shining and the sky is bright. You can see away down the valley. I've just met with a wall of snow and a gale which is a ring-tailed snorter."

After this we determined to push on. The mule had helped himself to a bale of hay and it was hard to get him to face the blizzard, but with coaxing he faced toward Skagway. Dixon and I borrowed caps and after going two hundred yards, emerged into another climate. Proving the truth of the traveller's words, eventually we reached Skagway.

We made for Clancy's saloon, expecting there to find sourdoughs while waiting for a steamboat to go south. Lined up along the bar were many from the interior. Their good intentions gone to the winds, they had missed several boats. Their pokes of dust as well as their pocket-books had dwindled considerably. Although Soapy was out of the picture, Skagway still had many working for the saloon business who made themselves good fellows, coaxing and cajoling, luring on many to games of poker. Their only object was to divert the riches of the victims to themselves. Those rascals were responsible for the fact that many a miner coming out to the civilization he had dreamed of in his toil got no farther than Skagway. He returned over the ice, his gold gone, and nothing before him but a repetition of all the hardships he had endured to get the riches that were so easily stolen from him.

Dixon and I were greeted as we entered with invitations: "Fill 'em up." We were both well known and wanted to get the boys away from the saloon. The boat was leaving for ports south the next morning. Telling the boys we would like to travel down all together, we received a promise they would be ready. The barkeepers barely concealed their surly looks and displeasure that anyone should try to lead away those who had been drinking steadily at the bar and playing cards. It was unwarranted interference with their business. The next day the boys went aboard. It was not long before they realized their folly of the past few days and became sadder and wiser men.

CHAPTER THIRTY-EIGHT

Sourdough Roll Call

The boat started on her return journey with what was as fine a lot of true comrades as might be found. Time passed rapidly as one after another told his little story of Tom, Dick, or Harry, or his own experiences. Some of the finest yarns were spun on this trip, for there were master hands aboard. At times a whole crowd would be held spellbound. Some of these fellows have now passed over the Great Divide, but some of them are still in the evening of life, and love to live over and dwell upon blessed friendships formed in strange predicaments. There is no greater pleasure for the old sourdoughs that meet annually even now, than to recall, with those who travelled the same trail, the wonderful experiences of those days.

Among the passengers were some bound for Africa and Australia who had made good, sold out, and were returning to their homes. After the first night on the boat, and having a good sleep and rest, the crowd had congregated in the smoking room. Some settled down to cards. Among those were professional card sharpers posing as casual passengers and merchants, yet on the lookout for victims to fleece their hard-won riches. There were conspicuous placards announcing NO GAMBLING ALLOWED, but no attention was paid to any of these. Occasionally a lucky cleanup would be made by the professionals from a carefree miner who had the money and enjoyed spending. Sometimes their tactics would give rise to quarrels, in which the victim's friends had to join to extricate him from his difficulties. No one dared show any gun violence. The card sharpers knew the miners were "one big happy family" who were loyal to each other.

Although it was not until the spring of 1899 that the Arctic Brotherhood was organized, the question had been long mooted and was actually put into effect on this trip by the mutual help and protection assured to every miner by his fellows.

Conversation was animated during the whole trip. The name of Swiftwater Bill was mentioned, and the story was told how he derived this sobriquet by portaging around the swift waters and not taking any chance of losing his outfit. Many names were similarly mentioned. They are still remembered with affection as belonging to heroes of that Northland. Yet, there were others spoken of with loathing. Thank God, these were only a small minority. Hark, someone is talking.

"Talk about Swiftwater Bill, let me tell you about Swiftwater Johnnie. He was a good scout. He had run the swift whitewater of the Fraser and Thompson and navigated the Liard. He claimed to be an expert canoe man. Our crowd was a little concerned about the White Horse Rapids. Quite a few had been wrecked going through with their unwieldy scows. Therefore, Johnnie was elected to put the craft through Miles Canyon, the Squaw Rapids, the White Horse and all the other rapids. We made a landing (where Macauley's was later located) and ate supper. In the meantime Johnnie had gone down the banks to look at Miles Canyon and the waters further on.

"After some considerable time Johnnie came back and said, 'Boys, you must get someone else to run the waters. I've lost my nerve. Something has come over me. I can't describe it, but I just can't take responsibility of having your lives on my hands. If it was just myself I wouldn't hesitate.'

"One of the number replied, 'You yellow-livered skunk, and you bragging about running the Fraser and Thompson!' Johnnie made one jump at the fellow. Talk about a mix-up. Johnnie had the best of it. The other fellow cried enough and Johnnie made him apologize.

"'I don't allow anyone to call me yellow,' he said. 'Anyone else craving for it? Now's your chance if you think I'm yellow.' The way Johnnie handled himself, we came to the conclusion he was best left alone when it came to a scrap. 'Boys,' Johnnie said, 'one of you can put her through. Me, I'm going to take my pack and walk around the waters. If you won't pick me up at the foot of White Horse, that's up to you.'

"'Chuck it,' we all said, 'come aboard, we'll put her through.' Would he come? Not him. Away he went with his pack.

"'He's a conundrum,' said one fellow.

"'By gad, he's got a wallop,' said the one who had the licking. However, we eventually made our start, and shot through the canyon, the Squaw, and White Horse safely. There was Johnnie walking down past White Horse and not deigning to look our way.

"'What shall we do?' said one, 'Shall we pick him up?'

"'Let the damn fool walk,' said another.

"'Forget it all, and take him aboard,' said a third. 'Hi, Johnnie, catch the rope and snub it to a pine.' He dropped the pack and we were soon snubbed to shore. Johnnie jumped aboard, shook hands all round and said we were all gentlemen. We shoved off, and Johnnie told his story.

"'It was this way,' he went on, 'My pal and I were running the Fraser. We were advised against it but we never knew what fear was. We struck a submerged rock. I got through, but my pal was never found. Recovering from the shock, I later joined a party bound for the Liard. It was a hard trip overland portaging the canoe. We had not travelled far by canoe when we struck a snag and the canoe upset. I saved two of the party, the third was drowned. That was my second wreck. I couldn't afford to run the chance with you fellows a third time. With myself it would be different. Now, boys, I hope you understand.'

"We slapped him on the back and said he was a fine fellow, and he was. Say! We were going down the Thirtymile when nothing seemed to be able to keep us off that darned rock in the middle of the river. You should have seen him grab the sweep and handle it. It seemed as if the old scow would do anything for him. We grazed the rock and on we went. Johnnie was an artist with the sweep. We called him "Swiftwater" after that, and he didn't mind. He was always called to take charge when we were in a tight place and he always brought us through."

⁓

Arriving at Juneau, we were reminded of the early days of 1882 and onward. Bill McPhee's name was mentioned as one of the hardy pioneers of that time who made Juneau a starting point for the then unknown and little-prospected interior, especially the Yukon Valley, running for thousands of miles to the Bering Sea. It was not surprising these men in and around Juneau and those of Douglas Island should have a hankering to find out what lay beyond the adjacent mountain ranges. True, many had climbed the high hills and gazed on the panorama of valleys, islands and inland seas opened up to view, but up until the 1890s few had been inspired to break through the barrier and prospect the vast hinterland.

One of the men who had been working on Douglas Island was McPhee. The Treadwell Mine, at one time, employed most of the intrepid men who started out to find greater riches than the neighbourhood afforded. First, one of these men would hit out for the interior, then another, and so on, each having first made a grubstake by working at the Treadwell Mine on Douglas Island. To these adventurers we must take off our hats. They blazed the trail, which for others reached its climax during the Great Rush of 1898 to the Klondyke.

Although many came back after covering hundreds—thousands—of miles without success, broken in health, they never lost faith in the wonderful country. Some stayed on Cassiar Bar, earning a grubstake by the simple method of rocking and then proceeded down the river by raft to the earlier settlements established by Jack McQuesten and others on the lower reaches of the Yukon. It became no surprise now to see men rafting down from the upper to the lower reaches.

McPhee was an old Bluenose from Nova Scotia. Like all Bluenoses he was fond of moving around, travelling from place to place. He had been in many mining camps throughout the United States and the tales of placer gold found on the other side of the Continental Divide caused him to make the venture. After getting over the Chilcoot Pass and exploring the creeks and rivers during the summer, as winter approached he came out without having found anything worthwhile in the way of a strike of gold. It was about this time that he interested himself in building and establishing what he called an "Opera House."

The old building was pointed out to us old sourdoughs who had a few hours on our hands before the boat left again. We were told of the wild jamborees that took place there, which sometimes resulted in loss of life through jealous squabbles over some of Bill's imported bits of femininity. He eventually sold out his interest in the Opera House, and tried his luck again, staying in the country until he heard of the Klondyke strike.

At Dawson he joined with others and did well. Taking the boat out for Seattle and Vancouver in the late summer of 1898, he bought a winter supply of liquor and merchandise. Returning from his trip, a great strike was reported from Nome and he set out, anxious to be in on the ground floor. Arriving there, he was one of the first to bring about something like law and order in that cosmopolitan country. Tex Rickard, who afterwards became famous as the fight promoter at Madison Square Gardens, was one of McPhee's right hand men. McPhee was always on the lookout for other fields of promise.

From Nome he went to Fairbanks, and then to the new field of Tanana, which had been favourably looked upon as a placer field before the Klondyke was discovered. Here disaster overtook McPhee. His saloon burned down, but he was soon building again. The story is told, how on the opening night of his new saloon, a tub was placed at the bar instead of a cash register, and pokes of gold were thrown in, with no change given. That night Bill was again set on his feet financially, but Tanana was his last stand.

There were rumours of Prohibition then, and he gathered in all business possible. He had known poverty and affluence, and when Prohibition came he decided to retire to California and enjoy the remaining years of his life. He always enjoyed meeting anyone from the Northland, and old comrades, after having made good, would hunt up old Grizzly Bill (as he was often called), and enjoy going over the rollicking and hazardous happenings of those days once more.

McPhee was a great sourdough, and an ardent supporter of the Arctic Brotherhood in the North. He enjoyed the yearly stampede gatherings of the sourdoughs. His last greetings to the sourdough convention were sent in writing when he was eighty-four years of age. When read to the assembly it brought tears to the eyes of those who were present. He passed the Great Divide in 1934.

Billy Owens was intimately connected with many of McPhee's undertakings. His jolly disposition while employed as barkeeper in McPhee's saloon endeared him to all who enjoyed his special concoctions. He had interests with Jim Dougherty, and many wild times were experienced in the old town with Jim. He would spend a fortune in a night. The next day he would go to his claim and dig out another fortune. Owens went in over the Chilcoot Pass in '98. It was amusing to hear his humourous accounts of obstacles overcome on the trail. Jim Dougherty was one of the 1896 men. What he made was spent where he made it. Many were the lady gold diggers who made fortunes out of Jim's squanderings. They hung around him until there was no more to be had. After leaving Dawson he went to Fairbanks and died there.

Another well known figure was Pantages. Afterwards, he was the head of the Pantages vaudeville shows. He was Grecian-born and from boyhood had experienced many rough knocks. He had travelled in many countries and at different times worked as labourer, waiter, sailor, and a host of other things, until the gold rush. He went to Dawson over the trail of '98, made good, went out, started his vaudeville and motion picture shows, and died in California a millionaire.

The old steamboats *Ora* and *Nora*, in the fall of 1898, brought out many interesting characters. Their faces still linger in memory, though names are forgotten. Some never were known by their real names. There were many who allowed themselves, through disappointment, to slip to the lowest depths of despair and degradation. Others rose above their despondency and hopelessness to higher planes through their hardship, ultimately gaining affluence and influence. In many instances, virtues which had lain dormant for years were awakened, capabilities were born of rough encounters and hopeless plights, and foundations were laid for lasting friendships.

One would frequently hear a man admitting that his success was due to luck rather than any shrewdness or brilliancy of his own. A word may be said for those luckless ones. There was no work for thousands. Mining was foreign to them. They were unsuitable for prospecting. Some moved down the river leaving the overcrowded Dawson. Others stepped in an old boat and kept on drifting, perhaps stopping at the Fortymile River or Circle City. A lot drifted out of life altogether.

Dr. Grant, the officers of the Salvation Army, Father Judge and others had their hands full looking after the trail-weary ones. There were a noble lot of men who rose to the occasion and donated poke after poke of gold dust to keep the good work of these men going. And later, after the fire that was so disastrous to Dawson, large donations were forthcoming to erect the edifices which became a pride to their builders. In the first year or two of Dawson's existence its buildings were largely old packing boxes, planks of old boats and scows, tarpaper and canvas. In fact, anything that would keep out the intense cold of the winter months was building material. True, there were a few frame buildings where comfortable accommodation was well paid for.

Captain Constantine and his wife were in Dawson in the summer of 1897. He soon realized that there would probably be a shortage of grub during the coming winter, as articles of consumption were getting rather low owing to the continuous influx of adventurers from the outside. While there was a shortage, no great privation existed, although Captain Constantine put the force of the NWMP on short rations for a period. Sergeant Jim Wilson was stationed at Dawson at this time. After retiring from the force he settled down in Calgary, where he carried on business under the name of Buffalo Real Estate Office. In the year that he was elected president of the sourdoughs, he met with an accident at the bridge at High River while driving in an automobile with a friend. Both he and his friend were killed. It was mainly through his efforts that the sourdoughs' stampede became successfully and permanently established. May it continue to flourish so that the pioneers in the mad rush for gold in the North may be remembered.

Another name which should be mentioned is Jack McQuesten, the father of all the mining population. Although located in Alaska, on the Yukon River, he helped as much as anyone in developing the Yukon valley by establishing posts from the mouth of the Yukon up to Selkirk on the Yukon River. He was the owner of steamboats operating from St. Michael to Circle City and the Fortymile River. He grubstaked the early pioneers who came in by way of St. Michael and prospected as far as the upper waters of the Yukon and the great tract of land watered by the Stewart, Pelly, White, and other rivers. The aim of the old prospectors was to find rich placer ground. Thousands of miles were covered. During McQuesten's time, miners' meetings were held in his stores and matters of vital importance decided. Problems such as the stealing of grub, jumping claims, murder, and so on, had to be solved in those days, as now. These were the days before the advent of the Mounties, so aptly described by Tom Wiedman, the poet of the Yukon in 1898. He was inspired to write the following poem, *The Laws of Ninety-Eight*, at the time of the San Quentin jailbreak in California.

Each year they're making lots of laws which tell ya "how" and "when"
Smart lawyers quickly find the flaws which save ya from the Pen.

It isn't all the laws they make keeps us on the straight course.
Nor trouble to explain they take. It's how laws they enforce.

Now take way back in ninety-eight among us Sourdoughs,
Ya found the most of us went straight, as history to ya shows.

We wasn't loaded down with laws, leastwise the fancy sort,
We had no lawyers to find flaws an' often had no court.

We had our laws—though very few, the kind that makes one pause,
Before dishonest things he do. We called 'em miner's laws.

No "whereas," "therefore," all that stuff, where lawyers could appeal,
But tha' straight warning, without bluff, "Yer done for if yer steal!"

The latch string on our humble shack, o' hearty welcome told,
An' we would find when we go back no one had swiped our gold.

So it's not the amount of laws that marks the honest course,
It's rules ya make without no flaws, and then strictly enforce.

If we had laws o' ninety-eight instead of thirty-five,
We wouldn't need no prison gate an' gangsters wouldn't thrive.

Tanana, Circle City, and Fortymile were looked upon as promising ground, and in fact a great amount of gold was taken from the rivers and creeks in these areas. Little did they dream of the fabulous wealth stored within a few miles of their operations. Time and again they passed over the Klondyke region, casually panning here and there, but finding only a few colours. It remained for that hardy man, Robert Henderson, who persistently stayed with the country, to expose the riches of the Klondyke. Yet, as in so many cases, he never enjoyed the great riches he was instrumental in discovering for others.

Bob Henderson will always have a place in our memories as the one individual who, in spite of accidents and hardships, stayed with his task only to have others reap the benefits of his labour.

CHAPTER THIRTY-NINE

Remember the Trail

Our journey south, at the end of the year, continued. Many were bound for 'Home, sweet home' and were looking forward to a good old time. Others had no home. How nice it would be to give the names of all on this trip out from the Klondyke. We enjoyed many a laugh over the telling of predicaments experienced during the mad scramble over the Chilcoot Pass. It took a skookum man to mount the Scales in the summer when the snow was off the Chilcoot. Often it was a case of one boosting the other and then the boosted one pulling up the booster. With a pack on your back it was no easy task. What a sigh of relief when the last pack was at the top, and what a compassionate feeling arose in one's breast as he looked down on the toiling crowd struggling like ants with their burdens below.

"Soft? I was soft! The calves of my legs hurt. Gad! How they hurt. I was not accustomed to hardship, and there I stood looking up, a fifty-pound sack of flour strapped to my back. I felt it would be impossible for me when I saw great hardy fellows puffing and blowing. One after another passed me, remarking, 'Come along!' or 'Cold feet, partner?' or 'What's the matter, boy?' or 'Come on now, let's try it!'

"At the first scale, about two feet up, I was stuck. 'Now, just hold on, boy! I'll be there. Take this rope and fasten it under your armpits. Now, climb.' I felt the rope tighten, and found myself being lifted, and soon was sitting by my newfound friend.

"Others had not thought of helping me, no doubt thinking I was the right build to help myself, and probably doubting their own capacity. My freight had been brought to the base by pack train. Therefore, there was no occasion for any strenuous effort on my part to that point. How I envied those who had packed all their freight themselves from Dyea.

They had gradually hardened themselves so that they seemingly could do anything, and here I was, a man in stature, about to give up the undertaking of climbing the mountain before me. What a surprise it was to find myself sitting on this scale beside a man grinning with good humour. 'Who are you?' I asked. 'Scores have passed me, but you have put yourself out to help me. I have no money to pay you mister, if that is what you expect.'

"'Ready, come on, you're doing fine,' was all he replied. I thought he would be insulted at what I said. Had he heard it, I wondered.

"There he was on the next scale, his pack on his back, looking down at me with his rope dangling, saying again, 'Under the armpits, lad, and help as much as you can.' This good Samaritan stayed with me until I reached the top. My back was aching and I was sore all over. While we rested I wondered about my next move. The man answered my unspoken question by saying, 'That's my last climb. You had better come along to Bennett. It will be a change and a rest for you. You can take it easy and then you will be better prepared to tackle the balance of your freight over the pass.'

"I acquiesced, not wanting to part company with such a man. It had snowed the day before. The snow apparently stopped at the summit. It seemed strange to be in a white world. We went to his cache, where I found he had a sled. Taking off my sack of flour, and starting a cache of my own near his, I sank down on it. Then I really knew how thankful I was and what a real rest could be. Methodically this new acquaintance packed his sled, fastened on what he called a gee pole to steer the sled with, lashed his freight (at least a part of it), and threw the rope that was fastened on the sled over one shoulder. Then taking the gee pole in hand as a lever and with a pull on the rope, the sled started. 'Ready, come on, we'll take it slowly at first,' said my friend. Stiff and sore, I followed behind, thinking to myself, 'If he calls this slowly, what must his gait be when normal?'

"I never knew there were such men. Before this my experience had been every man for himself and the Devil take the hindmost. This man acted like a big brother. We passed over the remnant of what in ages past had been a great glacier. This we descended into level going. He made me lie on the sled. It was snowing again and the sled went easily. He pulled me for quite a spell.

"'Now then, out you jump and stretch your legs before they get stiff,' he said. Out I got. 'You go on, friend,' I said. 'I'll take my time.' 'Oh, no you don't,' said he. 'Come on.' Pain! Gad, it made me squirm. But he made me walk, saying, 'You're doing fine,' but in a short time, I fell exhausted. 'Now then, don't let your legs get stiff, come on.' I begged to be let alone, but no, he kept me moving. When coming to a decline I was to fall on the sleigh, which, thank God, was often. At long last, Lake Lindemann, and the man's tent. 'You lie there,' he said pointing to a bed of spruce feathers. I fell on them, watching this superhuman bustling around. With the thought of all my freight at the foot of the Chilcoot Pass and my condition, I felt myself a weakling, seeing so many cheerfully carrying on. I cried, 'Oh, God, can I make it?'

"I awoke to his, 'Come on, breakfast is ready!' 'Breakfast?' said I, 'Have I been sleeping?' 'You bet you have, and screaming with cramps.' Lord, was I stiff and sore. 'While I make the coffee, you run along and limber up your limbs. Take a short run.'

"Darned if I didn't try to run, and it certainly limbered me up. Never was a breakfast more enjoyed. 'Think you can make the Chilcoot?' 'I don't think so.' 'Well, come on, try it.' The Chilcoot was made with much of the weariness gone.

"'You'll do,' this newfound friend said. 'The first time I tried it I was as soft as you. I came near giving up when on came a man, whom I'll never forget. He took compassion on me and made a man out of me. My thanks to him, like yours to me, seemed to fall on dull ears. All he said was, 'Pass it on. You'll make the next trip by yourself or I miss my guess.'

"And so we parted. It took me some time to scale the summit again that day, but I made it. Thank God for men like that. Now, boys, I am looking forward to the time when again I will climb old Chilcoot and enjoy it."

Still on, and the vessel held her way, bound for Victoria, Vancouver, and Seattle, and everyone enjoying the trip. After meals we assembled and someone would be asked for a yarn. It generally took a bit of coaxing to get a response. "Come on, Ruperty, you went in ninety-six, how about it?" So Rupert starts in a very indifferent way:

"You've heard all about the Chilcoot Pass and our troubles there. Eventually we got our stuff to Lindemann. We built our boat and skidded down to the rapids. There we got wrecked, lost a lot of stuff, and were held up where Bennett is now. Luckily we saved our axes, and went up a draw where Mike King later started his sawmill. He was the guy we met when he had the jamboree at Bennett, the fellow they called the Lovely Dove. We shaped a lot of dry logs and made a raft, little knowing whether we would be able to make six hundred miles with it or not. We already had made a bad start. The raft was completed, but it wasn't long before a wind came up, which increased to a hurricane, and away went our sail. Andy and his partner thought the raft would go to pieces. Our provisions and bedding were soaked and we were as wet as drowned rats. The combers rolled over us up to our waists. All the rope we could find was used to lash what little we had left. There was no time for commiseration, as it required all we had to keep from going overboard.

"When we were about to lose heart completely we came to the narrow stretch of water formed by the spit that ran out from the west, and the island near the opposite shore. After going through the narrow channel, we swerved to the right, and got into a calm bit of water that was sheltered by the island.

"There on the shore was a silvertip bear looking at us with those darned little eyes. A rifle was packed up in our bedding, but it would take too long to get it; Mr. Bear was swimming toward us, in a hurry. He was a beaut. Before we could say 'Jack Robinson,' the bear was close to the raft. Andy said, 'My God, boys, I'm so cold and stiff he'll get us!' He grabbed a spar and brought it down on the bear's shoulder. It was like water falling on a duck's back. One paw of the bear was on the raft. Andy's partner had an axe, and with a mighty stroke he chopped off the paw. Talk about growls, and blood flying! I caught hold of a spar that had been sharpened to a point at the end, and with a great lunge, thrust it through him, behind the shoulder. That was the end of Mr. Bear. In a very short time he expired.

"We tied his body to the raft and made for the shore in calm water. We could hear the wind roaring and whistling over the island. Mike dragged the carcass to shore and started to skin it. We made a fire, and soon were enjoying the best meal of our lives. It was about time we had fresh meat, for we were all approaching the stage of scurvy. We stayed in camp for a few days. Mike, Andy's partner, smoked the bear meat for future use. Once we were refreshed, we felt like giants, equal, we thought, to any emergency that might arise.

"We repaired our raft. The wind dropped, but then arose 'the terror that flieth by day'—mosquitoes. They darkened the sky. Once again we erected a mast, and Mike made a square sail out of the bear skin. We sailed, catching a faint wind when off shore. 'Glory be!' said Mike, when out of the clouds of mosquitoes, 'I would sooner tackle a bear any day than those dirty little critters.'

"It was very shallow at Cariboo Crossing, and so we poled much of the distance over Lake Nares. Nice bluffs of trees grew on its shores. As we emerged into Little Windy, we scarcely knew what struck us, and again we came very near disaster. However, we managed to cross over to Big Windy, and with the aid of Mike's bearskin square sail, defeated the raging elements. We were near shipwreck when suddenly, an exclamation from Andy: 'Calm water ahead! Hurrah! The Six Mile! Mike, you old son of a gun, I was just beginning to think you were a hoodoo, but I guess it's all right. Good going from now on, boys!'

"What a pleasure, drifting down the Six Mile after the buffeting we had received from Lindemann down to this point. Then came Wind (or Marsh) Lake, where we disturbed millions of ducks. Thank God, our guns and ammunition were dry and in order. How we revelled in bringing down food enough to last us for days! Our little battered telescope stove was a godsend. We cooked a lot of mulligatawny (bear meat and duck). Mike was an artist at this. Our flour was caked about half an inch in and the rest was in good condition. Mike made dough into little round balls, and put these into the mulligatawny, calling them sinkers. These sinkers stayed with us, all right. It took days to digest them.

"It was a lazy life, drifting down the Six Mile, until we came to Miles Canyon, and spun round and round. There we were, going backward into that inferno, the whirlpools keeping us ever turning round. Once we thought we were out of the trap, but we were disappointed, rotating until old Mike was nearly crazy. He was beginning to think that he was Jonah. We made a determined effort by taking down the mast and using it as a pole. Now had come our opportunity. We were near the current, and with a mighty effort we managed to put the raft's nose into it, and away we went at once, bouncing into the Squaw Rapids.

"Then, in front of us, we saw the mane of the White Horse. No one said a word. Our faces depicted what each was feeling. Everything was lashed tight. We took the final plunge into the mad, raging waters, hanging on for dear life. Our craft was not buoyant. She seemed to sink under us. We were all three tossed and torn from our faithful old raft and swept into the turmoil, fighting for our very lives to gain the shore. We landed, far apart. Andy was the first to espy our raft going downstream. It was comical to see him running after it in his waterlogged garments. 'He's gaining on her!' shouted Mike. 'Holy Mother, he's ahead!' Andy went into the water, us scrambling after him. 'Yes, he's aboard!' He had found a rope dangling, and in some manner had snubbed our old faithful to the shore.

"'Good old Andy, a Swede for luck,' quoted Mike. 'He's a good pal, but I don't think our luck will last.' 'Don't worry, Mike,' I said, 'remember, the Irish are noted for their luck!' 'Yes,' said Mike, 'but I've known a lot of Irish who didn't have any luck. Take my old father, but that's a long story, I'll tell you some time.'

"We again dried our clothes. We had lost a lot of valuable stuff in our last encounter, yet we were in good spirits—all except Mike, which was strange. Being an Irishman, he burst out, 'Ya know we can't go on

like this. Yer tempting the gods with a craft like this for a makeshift.'
However, we still had our ducks, and our bear meat, and the thought of
some more mulligatawny made us lighthearted. Our guns were safe,
our flour gone, but we were thankful that the old stewpot was safe.
Lightheartedly we resumed our journey. How we enjoyed the night,
gliding down the last of the Six Mile. Andy said, 'Enjoy it boys, you'll
soon be in Laberge.'

"Lo, we beheld before us a beautiful expanse of water. We thought
things were easy, with a light breeze offshore and the square sail rigged.
But the wind gradually increased, and we were dangerously close to
one of the islands. There was no time or way to avoid it. Crash! And
there we were onshore. We pulled our frail raft up out of the way of the
pounding surf, and enjoyed a well-earned rest. Once more the wind
died down to a mere breeze, and we made the Thirtymile. Everything
had been made shipshape once more. The current took us downriver at
a good clip. It kept the three of us busy, keeping our unwieldy raft in
midstream.

"Mike shouted, 'Look out, we'll pile ourselves on that rock in the
middle of the river!' By dint of strength we managed to miss hitting the
rock, but grazed its side. When we thought everything was safe, the current swerved the raft. The end received a thud. Mike lost his balance,
and in falling, his head struck the rock. Before we could reach him, poor
old Mike was overboard and was swept away unconscious. Andy made
preparations to dive over board and get him, but Mike was nowhere in
sight. There we were, going downriver at a mighty rate, but no Mike in
sight. He was evidently caught in an eddy. We steered for a bit of beach,
and after a struggle effected a landing and rushed upstream. Still there
was no sign of Mike.

"Regretfully, we went on our way, coming to the conclusion that
perhaps, he was ahead of us. We snubbed up at the confluence of the
Hootalinka, and watched the waters for several days. At last we were
rewarded; Mike's body was washed ashore. We found that he had
received a nasty gash in the head, and believed that he never regained

his senses. Andy and I were not ashamed when moisture came to our eyes. We buried him away from high water. First, though, we searched him for any mark of identification. All we could find was one hundred dollars, in bills, inside his belt. Andy, in his rough way, spoke a few words eulogizing Mike's sterling qualities, and ended with an impromptu prayer that came from the heart of a grief-stricken man. To that I added, 'Amen.' We felt very lonely without Mike. He had come into our lives as many others had, ready to cast in his lot with men bound for the unknown, for the sake of company.

"We reached Fortymile without mishap. We did fairly well on the Fortymile, and when dividing up the gold we religiously put Mike's share in a separate sack, to be used for some cause which we thought Mike would have liked. We had not heard of the Klondyke strike that was taking place. When we did hear, no time was lost in making for it from Fortymile.

"On Eldorado, we were sold a claim, supposed to be worthless—at least, the parties who sold it believed that it was worthless, and smiled at our efforts when we spent most of our pile in sinking a shaft. They told us that we would have to 'go to kingdom come' before we would strike bedrock. Not downhearted, we kept on, and eventually were rewarded by a layer of gold. Our fortunes were made.

"Later we talked of Mike's share of the Fortymile gold. Having heard of the good work of Father Judge, we donated it to that good man last summer. He needed money badly to enable him to carry on his great work as physician, nurse, undertaker, and man of all work."

Thus ended another story told by an old sourdough.

〜

In casual talk, the name of Swiftwater Bill was mentioned again. One said, "Oh, I've met him in and around Dawson, this Bill Gates. The girls made a fool out of him. He was spending his money, trying to make people think that he was somebody. He cornered the egg market for a time, but in the long run, he was a loser. We looked upon him as a joke. He was fond of having his name and picture in the papers. Always in a tangle with the girls at Dawson. No one seemed to have any use for his particular kind."

Bill Gates was found in Peru years later. Many of the old sourdoughs thought Bill was all right. They said that he was still young when in the North, and only letting off steam, as all young men will. The last news this writer had of him was that he was holding some valuable placer ground one hundred and fifty miles south of Cuzco, Peru. He had lost one eye in a brush with some Indians while acting as guide for a company down the headwaters of the Amazon. The story that one of the sourdoughs told of him "walking around swift waters" must have been a travesty, however. In Peru, Bill is looked upon as one of the best guides and swift water men in that country. He is always sought for by parties wishing to travel by water. His experience in the North stands him in good stead. He has directed the building of many boats of whipsawn lumber during his long sojourn. His fondness for eggs is as keen as ever. Rather than have the canned variety, he prefers parrot's eggs, and is adept at making omelettes with them. Everyone gathers in the evenings to hear Bill tell his tales of the North. In Peru he is looked upon as a "hale fellow, well met." If you have never tried baked monkey, write Swift (as he is called in Peru), and he will gladly send you the recipe.

One of his favourite stories is about a contract he made with a young doctor while living on Quartz Creek with his wife. The stork was expected in about a month. The doctor was to spend his time on the creek until it arrived. When everything was over, 'boy or child' (to use Bill's expression), the doctor was to receive twenty-five hundred dollars. The end of the month came, but instead of the doctor receiving twenty-five hundred, he owed Bill twenty-five hundred. One can easily form a conclusion as to how that happened.

~

The history of the finding of gold on Cheechako Hill was given by one who was there. A cheechako asked a man where he could stake a claim. Satirically the man pointed to the top of the hill, and said, "Boy, you see the top up there? It isn't staked, and it's lousy with gold. Go up and stake." The young man went up, believing what the man had said. As the boy turned his back on them, and made for the hill, carrying over his shoulder a sack to carry the dirt in, the man cocked his eye to his partner, and both of them chuckled.

In about an hour, the boy came down and started washing the dirt in a pan, also borrowed. Noticing that the boy was taking a long time to wash the dirt, the men went over to him. He had already lined his pockets with nuggets. In looking over the boy's shoulder into his pan, they were amazed to find a lining of gold. Imagine their chagrin! The boy lost no time recording his claim. He took out nearly one thousand dollars the first day, and the next morning he filled his poke with nearly fifteen hundred. Then he was taken ill with scurvy and went to the hospital.

He rented his ground to two men who made good. These men also bought a thirty-five-foot piece of ground from a Swede who believed it to be no good. The cheechako offered to buy it from them, but they refused to sell, and started to work it. The summer's work netted them twenty-two thousand dollars apiece.

The cheechako, coming back to his claim again after his recovery, took out, during the rest of the summer, more than twenty thousand dollars. Then he sold out to a man named Doig (of the Bank of Commerce) and Senator Lynch (of California), who opened up the property on a big scale, and took out between half a million and a million dollars. It was some task packing the dirt to water—or the water to the dirt—for the dirt was taken from the top of the hill, and the water was at the bottom.

~

In concluding these memoirs, I must allude to a beautiful bit of verse, written years ago on Saint Valentine's Day by Mort Craig. Craig has reached the end of the trail long since, but the Klondyke valentine remains with us. It was written whilst sitting in his log cabin, as many others have done. Craig put his thoughts into words, as he reflected, while the smoke from his pipe cast fantastic shapes around him.

Sleeping under the canopy of the heavens, listening to the wonderful song of the aurora borealis or the discordant screeches of the northern blizzard, no wonder Craig wrote his Valentine.

Tonight, as I sit in the Klondyke Vale,
My fancy takes flight over river and vale,
To where, in those halcyon days gone by,
We were together, you and I,
And I find myself wishing to God that you
Often think of the boy who so longs for the sight
Of your beautiful eyes—and your kisses tonight.

I light my tobacco, its powers invoke,
And presto! your astral shines out of the smoke,
A face of sweet beauty, a form of rare grace,
Half-hidden by billows of shadowy lace.
You hover above me, O vision of mine,
And your dear dreamy soul passes quickly to mine.
So I sit here and silently long for the sight
Of your beautiful eyes—and your kisses tonight.

A rich mellow perfume, while memories roll,
Brings the flavour of age to the wine of my soul,
You fill up the glass, dainty sweetheart of mine,
Your soft, gentle voice pulses down through the air,
And I thrill to the thought that it murmurs a prayer,
A prayer for the boy who so longs for the sight
Of your beautiful eyes—and your kisses tonight.

On the breast of your astral, O lady of mine,
Let me pin with a nugget my heart's Valentine,
That the gold in the Klondyke in naught can compare,
With the velvety masses of gold in your hair.

The wine of your breath and the touch of your hand,
  Seal my senses in sleep in this shadowy land.
I slumber, and sleeping, long for the sight
  Of your beautiful eyes—and your kisses tonight.

The Arctic Brotherhood

How many beautiful dreams and thoughts have gone up in smoke! The thoughts and dreams of others who also sat in solitude in those wonderful hills and vales. How many found their real selves when, with only their malamutes as companions, they were going over the vast tundra to (as they termed it), "God knows not where!" Many, through their loneliness, have turned from wasted lives to lives of usefulness, lives with a nobler purpose. Having had time to meditate on misspent, selfish, and greedy lives, out of the vast spaces men have returned, reformed and ennobled. They had witnessed Nature's wonderful works and ways.

Stories told by sourdoughs have no doubt often been heard before by many who may happen to read these memoirs. I would like to mention the names of some of the old pioneers who have not been mentioned yet. Some of them formed the jolly crowd I found on the steamboat, going south to spend Christmas, only to return again at the beginning of the year. They departed at their different destinations, and bid each other good-bye and good luck. They all hoped to meet again in the new year to have another jolly time together when returning to the North on the steamboat.

The little company knew that the return trip this year would be comparatively easy. There would be no more roughing it as on their first trip into Dawson, for they had now earned a competency, and could well afford to pay for accommodation in winter or summer. Passage could be booked in 1899 from Portland, Seattle, Vancouver, Victoria, or other ports to Dawson. Thanks to the enterprise of those who saw the possibilities of making fortunes by catering to the public and to those who could afford to pay high prices for accommodation, there were good roadhouses.

The little party had earned a long rest, and they were bent on having it. They were eager to enjoy the comfort and good things that they had been deprived of for so long. Many were eager to get to their destinations in Toronto, Montreal, New York, the southern states, or in the fast-growing cities of Portland, Seattle, Vancouver, or Victoria. These new places were making rapid strides in growth due to the gold rush and the business it brought with it.

No curiosity seemed to be aroused when the little groups disembarked with their wirebound satchels and other receptacles that strained the wrist to carry. Their packs of gold, in many cases, were to be taken home to their loved ones to exhibit proudly before selling. Many were going home with drafts for a few thousand to three hundred thousand dollars. One man called a hack to take him to his home on the outskirts of the city. It was midnight when he arrived, and he handed poke after poke of gold to the hackman, who laid them outside the gate of the house. The pokes were gathered up, and taken in the house, where they lay for several days before being taken to the bank. In these days of gangsters those pokes would not have remained in the house for long!

The year 1899 saw the return of many who had enjoyed a really good holiday. Some were returning sadder and wiser, having been lavish in spending their riches. Others, who had invested in sound enterprises, were able to lay the foundation for a durable fortune.

In February a goodly number of sourdoughs returned to the goldfields, as well as a few newcomers, on the SS *City of Seattle*. On this trip, the Arctic Brotherhood was organized, which was really the foundation of what is today known as the Alaskan Yukon Pioneers.

The original members of the Arctic Brotherhood were Alexander Berlenberg, William J. Blackwell, J. H. Escolme, Thos. W. Farnworth, George de Goldenheindt, John C. Hunter, J. Keller, Augustus H. Miller, Ernest F. Miller, C. J. Reilly, J. Stowell, C. S. Strickland, Lord William Tell, and G. F. Williams. The honorary members were: John Green Brady, A. Melville Carpenter, W. C. Coulson, E. A. Henderson, Captain John Irving, Ezra T. Pope, G. O. Rincarson, and William Smart.

The order of the Arctic Brotherhood grew by leaps and bounds. It was decided that a clubhouse should be built at Skagway. Captain Johnson donated a large lot in Skagway for this purpose. Frank M. Woodruff donated the next lot, so the building could be more commodious than had been first planned. Captain John Irving, the member for that great district of Canada in the British Columbia legislature, donated the lumber for the building, showing his interest in developing the northern country. He still believed that someday this northern country would astonish the world. His faith has been rewarded. He lived to see the time when the inlets and branches of the great inland waters were dotted with mining and fishing villages. Captain John was a man of few words, especially when seeking election to the British Columbia legislature.

In the early 1890s, once in Victoria, when he was seeking election, he was introduced as the prospective member for Cassiar. He was called upon to make a speech. The applause greeting him was great. He stood up. The man who had braved tempest and storm, quelled disturbances among longshoremen and crews, rescued people in distress on land and sea, was stage-struck. Not a word came from his lips. The audience, wishing to encourage him, applauded once more. At last he said, "Ladies and gentlemen, you ought to know the great country in the North."

A great silence ensued. Someone said, "Go on, Captain John."

Encouraged, he shouted, "Fish, by heavens, the fish!"

Another silence. "Go on, Captain."

"Fish, you should see them. By heavens, the fish!" Silence. Then Captain John took his seat, amidst great applause. The chairman came to the rescue, eulogizing the captain as the only man who could represent the constituency of Cassiar, for he knew of its requirements. He was known by a vast number of pioneers, who loved his gruff ways. He was a man whose word was his bond and who was always a genial host or guest. And he had seen rough days. He had sailed the southern seas before turning his attention to his father's fleet of several boats on the inland waters and large rivers such as the Fraser and the Stikine. When his father died, he became owner and manager of the fleet of boats. Among them were the SS *Premier*, the SS *Charmer*, and later, the SS *Islander*. This last was lost on a voyage from Skagway to Vancouver, when she struck an iceberg. Several prominent men perished with her, among them, Mr. Douglas of the firm of Kelly Douglas of Vancouver.

At another time, when Captain John was again a candidate to represent the Far North in the legislature, it was impossible for him to be on hand in the Atlin district, then a mining camp. Professor Barnes, knowing that it was impossible for Captain John to leave the south, even to do any electioneering, took it upon himself. He approached a man he knew, to advance the money for soliciting votes for Captain John. Not understanding why there was no communication from him, he took it upon himself to act as his agent. The money was advanced, the country canvassed. The electors were scattered over a vast expanse of country. The captain was defeated, for it was rumoured that he was not running. During the summer the captain appeared at Atlin, hunted up the man who had advanced the money to the professor and wrote him out a cheque. Acts like this endeared Captain John Irving to all as a man absolutely to be relied on. He took a great interest in the sour-dough organization up to the last. I believe the greatest blow in his life was the death of his only boy, killed in Flanders during the Great War. He passed away recently, a notable figure in steamboat life and in all progressive movements in building up a wonderful province. "Cast off!" will be heard no more from that well-known voice. He has gone on his last long voyage.

The Arctic Brotherhood grew in leaps and bounds. Its object was to inculcate in all members the great necessity of helping the fortunate as well as the unfortunate, especially in always having the latchstring out for the needy one. To start no stampedes, false stampedes. To boom no mine above its value and to be a brother at all times to the next man seeking fortune in the great Arctic spaces. To be a trailblazer in developing the great potentialities of the vast wilderness of the interior, and to be brothers in weal or woe to those met on unmapped creeks and rivers. Thus, initiation in the order would be a protection from the unscrupulous, from the men who came into the country with no principles, ready to prey on those fortunate enough to have found a rich claim.

The organization recognized that many characters were slipping into the country who would stop at nothing to gain their ends. Who shall say what crimes have been averted by this banding together of the early Arctic brothers?

Several respected brothers were commissioned to establish Arctic Brotherhood camps in their spheres of influence. Captain Cartwright of the NWMP started a camp at Bennett. He was a son of Sir Richard Cartwright, a member of the Dominion cabinet. He was killed in the war. J. E. Hennessy was given a commission to organize Log Cabin. J. D. Thagard was to look after the growing mining camp of Atlin. Chief Farnsworth organized a camp at Tagish. J. H. Escolme was appointed to look after Dawson. Sam Dunham was to carry the good work on toward the Arctic.

It was good to hear the password mentioned in lonely places when meeting someone. Often, though, the password was not mentioned, showing that the individual had not joined the order. Many good deeds have been done in the Yukon by and for people using the password.

Today, in the year 1937, the same spirit pervades the Alaska Yukon pioneers. Homes for the old pioneers have been provided in Alaska, and interest is taken in those still struggling under less fortunate circumstances.

Many of the old pioneers have crossed the Great Divide, from which there is no return. A goodly number, still living, love to keep alive the spirit and memories of the old days. Mention must be made of Jim Wilson, or Sergeant Wilson, late of the NWMP, who was instrumental in starting the movement of reunion, and the former international president, Mr. Eckelman, who assisted him. Also, we must not forget Lulu M. Fairbanks, the indefatigable secretary of the Alaska Yukon Pioneers, and the late Bruce E. Slater, loved by all. Numerous other names could be mentioned, some of which have already appeared in these pages.

Some of the old pioneers, through lack of sufficient finances, were unable to enjoy the reunion that was held in Toronto. The beaming face of Dr. J. N. E. Brown, as the old sourdoughs came in, one after another, and registered at the King Edward Hotel was a picture to see. What a happy meeting, when the addresses of welcome were given by the Honourable Herbert Bruce and Mayor Robbins! The names of the real old pioneers were read out, as follows: Honourable T. D. Pattullo, Honorable W. L. Walsh, Honourable Joe Clark, Mr. and Mrs. George Black, Lieutenant Colonel G. V. Howard, Harry Ewart (of the mint in Ottawa), Dr. J. B Tyrell and Dr. J. N. E. Edwards. All understood the rough-and-tumble in the scramble to arrive at the goldfields. Surmounting obstacles and difficulties was good training for these men, fitting them to become factors in public life, and thereby contributing to the Canadian and United States progress commercially, as well as politically.

You can imagine the remarks made about: Galleger "Spuller" Kelly, who mined on Dominion Millet of Cheechako Hill. Paul Dinhard, one of the founders of the original Yukon Order of Pioneers in 1897, who after leaving Dawson, struck it rich at Nome, Alaska. Murdock and Angus, who made good at Cheechako Hill. Charlie Anderson of Eldorado. The Berry brothers. Mike Mahoney, president elect of the Alaska Yukon Pioneers from 1937 to 1938. Old "Itchfoot" Swanson, who struck it very rich—approximately three hundred thousand per month for the season, and died in poverty. King, Little, and the Grants, who published the first paper in the Yukon valley, while waiting for the ice to go out at Cariboo Crossing, so that they could pursue their journey to Dawson. Graff, the old pioneer merchant, John Lemon, who rode horseback all the way to Dawson, but whose luck was always against him. Helshier, who shipped steers to Dawson by scow and who was wrecked at Laberge. Ericson, John Lee, Apple Jimmy, and Sloan of Nanaimo.

Many interesting characters whose names are forgotten but whose faces are indelibly photographed in the minds of those who met them, are remembered by the heroic deeds they performed on rough and perilous journeys through mountain and vale. The Smiths (of this memoir), who used that name as an alias, made good. Their experiences were duplicated a number of times by others. Frank, Percy, and Gwen, after accumulating a generous proportion of the precious metal, to use an oft-quoted expression, left the country "well-heeled." Frank and Gwen were married, and settled down in the West. Knowing the freedom of the West, they found it more congenial than the formalities of the old countries of Europe.

Ed Ironsider was a pioneer who was a victim of the SS *Sophia* disaster, when all hands were swallowed by the sea. I think it fitting to end my memoirs by quoting a few lines which he wrote.

> To the North, where the Goddess of Fortune
>   Spilled her golden tears long ago,
> Where some of her paystreaks lie hidden
>   In frost-shackled gravels below.

> To all these I mention, I drink not
>   Though strong is the lure of their call,
> But I pledge in this toast that I give thee
>   The finest, the best of it all.

> To the friends we made, in the Northland,
>   Ah! Where can the equal you find?
> So, I pledge to you this token,
>   Their memories are dear to my mind.

> So long as the sun shines in summer,
>   Or Northern lights dance in their glee,
> You're dearer than gold in the Klondyke—
>   Old friends of the North, 'Here's to thee!'

THE END

Photography Credits

Front cover: Klondyke Outfitters, 1989. B.C. Archives
Frontispiece and Memoirs of My Grandfather: Photos courtesy of Evelyn Johnson

Photos in text

Plates 1, 2 and 3 courtesy of Evelyn Johnson
The following plates from the B.C. Archives:

PHOTOGRAPH	REF NO.	PLATE NO.	PHOTOGRAPHER
Francis Mawson Rattenbury	#F-02163	4	H.U. Knight, *circa* 1924
Leaving Nanaimo for Klondyke	#E-02637	5	Unidentified, 1898
Members of the VON	#G-01132	6	Sinclair, 1898
Prospectors scaling Chilcoot	#B-01320	7	Larrs & Ducos, 1898
Summit of Chilcoot Pass	#D-06283	8	Hirschfeld, 1898
Boundary at Chilcoot Pass	#B-06743	9	Larrs & Ducos, 1898
Summit of Chilcoot Pass	#D-04550	10	J.M. Bond, 1898
Chilcoot after snow slide	#C-05166	11	E.A. Hegg, 1898
Exhuming bodies	#C-05172	12	E.A. Hegg, 1898
Prospector and short-haired dogs	#G-03085	13	Unidentified, 1898
Victoria Hotel at Log Cabin	#D-01522	14	Unidentified, 1898
Klondyke Outfitters	#A-00515	15	Unidentified, 1898
Soapy Smith	#A-06673	16	Unidentified, 1898
Boat building at Lindemann	#A-07415	17	La Roche, 1897
Klondykers at Bennett Lake	#D-04553	18	E.A. Hegg, May 30, 1898
Taku Landing	#D-01519	19	Hirschfeld, 1900
Boats and scows, Bennett Lake	#A-05138	20	Unidentified, 1898
Prospectors at Bennett Lake	#D-04555	21	Unidentified, 1900
Boats on One Mile River	#D-04552	22	E.A. Hegg, 1898
Crew building a sternwheeler	#G-01975	23	Unidentified, April 20, 1899
The SS *Clifford Sifton*	#B-00056	24	Unidentified, 1900
The SS *Flora*	#-39722	25	Larrs & Ducos, 1898
The SS *Nora*	#-71552	26	Unidentified
Yukon Hotel, Bennett Lake	#A-07527	27	Unidentified, 1898
The SS *Ora*	#-45714	28	Unidentified, 1899

Personal Notes

Tim Lawson
THE RIGHT WAY ON CD
Global themes layer Tim's second album. The Gold Rush, poet Robert Elliott, Brazilian Rainforest, Berlin Wall, Love, Life.

Tim Lawson
THE QUIET CANADIAN CD
Dedicated to Sir William Stephenson. Includes She Can't Be Blamed, Wartime Letters, Falling Water, Spirit Song.

LIGHTLY WEAVE:
The Poems of Robert Elliott
Century-old poetry inspired by nature, friendships, courage, patience and the graces of humanity. A rediscovered work of art, limited to 1500 copies, signed by Tim Lawson.
HC 112 pages

THE TRUE INTREPID:
Sir William Stephenson
and the Unknown Agents
The National Bestseller
The amazing story of Sir William, the "Man Called Intrepid".Newly uncovered secrets about a life well-lived.
HC 432 pages, 41 b/w photos

Name

Address

City   **Prov/State**

Postal/Zip Code

○ *I have included a cheque / money order*

○ *Charge my Visa*

Card #

Exp. Date

Signature

Please photocopy or detach this page and mail or fax to:

Timberholme, 159–19567 Fraser Hwy, Surrey, BC V3S 6K7
Phone (604) 532-8464 Fax (604) 533-6578
Toll Free 1-877-789-2966
          1-877-(rt way on)

Postage and handling $5.00 per item, $2.00 for each additional item.

Order 3 or more items and get a FREE videotape, which includes 6 Tim Lawson music videos.

Please make cheque or money order payable to Timberholme.

Music		Quantity	Cost
The Right Way On	$19.99		
The Quiet Canadian	$19.99		
Books			
The Right Way On	$29.95		
The True Intrepid	$34.95		
Lightly Weave	$47.95		
Audio Books			
The Right Way On	$29.95		
SUBTOTAL			
DIRECT ORDER DISCOUNT 35%			
GST (if applicable) 7%			
PST (BC residents, CDs only) 7%			
Postage			
TOTAL			

We are developing new projects all the time.
*Please visit our web site **www.timberholme.com** for more details or to place your order by e-mail.*